OUR SACRED MAÍZ IS

Our Sacred Maíz Is Our Mother
Nin Tonantzin Non Centeotl

INDIGENEITY AND BELONGING IN THE AMERICAS

*

Roberto Cintli Rodríguez

with
Verónica Castillo Hernández, Maestra Angelbertha Cobb,
Luz María de la Torre, Paula Domingo Olivares,
Tata Cuaxtle Félix Evodio, María Molina Vai Sevoi,
Francisco Pos, Alicia Seyler, and Irma Tzirin Socop

THE UNIVERSITY OF
ARIZONA PRESS

TUCSON

The University of Arizona Press
www.uapress.arizona.edu

Printed in the United States of America
21 20 19 18 17 16   9 8 7 6 5 4

Cover design by Leigh McDonald
Cover art: *Sacred Maize* by Laura Vazquez Rodriguez. Acrylic on canvas, 30" x 24".
© 2014.

Library of Congress Cataloging-in-Publication Data
Rodríguez, Roberto Cintli, 1954–
    Our sacred maíz is our mother : indigeneity and belonging in the Americas / Roberto
Cintli Rodríguez ; with Verónica Castillo Hernández, Maestra Angelbertha Cobb, Luz
María de la Torre, Paula Domingo Olivares, Tata Cuaxtle Félix Evodio, María Molina
Vai Sevoi, Francisco Pos, Alicia Seyler, and Irma Tzirin Socop.
        pages cm
    Includes bibliographical references and index.
    ISBN 978-0-8165-3061-8 (paperback)
    1. Indians of North America—Food—Four Corners Region. 2. Indians of North
America—Agriculture—Four Corners Region. 3. Corn—Social aspects—Four Corners
Region. 4. Mexican Americans—Ethnic identity. 5. Mexicans—Ethnic identity. I. Title.
    E98.F7R64 2014
    306.4—dc23
                                    2014007750

♾ This paper meets the requirements of ANSI/NISO Z39.48-1992 (Permanence of Paper).

This book is dedicated to my parents and first teachers
Ricardo Rodríguez, April 3, 1923–January 10, 2011
Juanita Rodríguez, May 15, 1928–June 14, 2014

Contents

Illustrations

Figures

Color Plates

Acknowledgments

To my father, who raised me on stories of our ancestors—stories which form the basis of this book. To my mother, who has always supported me spiritually and who gave me a Nahuatl nickname as a child: Cincuate (Cincoatl), serpent that drinks milk. To my family, for their lifelong support, including, and especially, Laura V. Rodriguez for the most special front cover here. To UCLA professors Reynaldo Macías and Juan Gómez-Quiñones, for inspiring and guiding me since my undergraduate days. To my former University of Wisconsin PhD advisor, Professor Patty Loew, who recruited and mentored me throughout graduate school, plus Carol "Dr. Corn" Cornelius, Rosemary Christianson, Arnoldo Vento, and Greg Cajete, for introducing me to the concept/practice of elder epistemology and the importance of story. To Andrea Romero, who has mentored me since I arrived at the University of Arizona. To my lifelong friend Carmen Paul for assistance in translations, and Andrea Holm, who edited several versions of this manuscript. Thanks also to Kristen A. Buckles, Amanda Krause, and David Hill at the University of Arizona Press, for believing in and editing my book. Thanks also to research assistant Connie Yelitza Lira-Saavedra. A special thanks to Patrisia Tzicatl Gonzales, who collaborated and lived with me through much of this amazing journey. To every elder who is mentioned here, for trusting me with their stories—including Thomas Banyacya, Maestro Andres Segura, Florencio Yescas, Tlakaelel, Don Felipe Alvarado Peralta, Mariano Leyva, Steve Casanova, Corbin Harney, Luis Leal, Jack Forbes, Cecilio Orozco, Frank Gutierrez, Gustavo Gutierrez, and Jose Montoya, all of them now in the spirit world. To Grandma Emma Ortega, for recognizing me as a storyteller, and Maestra Angelbertha Cobb, Maestra Paula Domingo Olivares, Don Aurelio Cazarez, María Molina Vai Sevoi, Francisco Pos and Irma Tzirin Socop, Luz María de la Torre, Alicia Seyler, and Tata Cuaxtle, for trusting me with their knowledge and with their stories of a ceremonial discourse that teaches that for many of us on this continent, the *maíz* tree is the center of the universe: *non kuahuitl cintli in tlalnepantla*. Also a special thanks to Tupac Enrique Acosta, Jerry Tello, Rocky Rodriguez, Celia Perez, Raquel Salinas, Irma Cuicui Rangel, Nancy Martinez, and Susana Sandoval, for their lifelong support, friendship, and guidances. And thanks to Calpolli Teoxicalli in Tlamanalco (Tucson) and Kalpulli Izkalli in Albuquerque . . . and their sacred fires, drums, and staffs that accompanied me throughout this entire journey. Thanks also to the youth and elders of Arizona, especially the DREAMers, who have taught me the meaning of creation/resistance and of what it means to be human, this while battling fearlessly for our humanity, in the very dehumanizing state we live in. And lastly, a special thanks to Vivian G. Lopez, for her lifelong intellectual and spiritual support always, and to all those who have left their footprints along this most sacred journey, especially the ants of Quetzalcoatl: without them, this "story of the continent" would not have been possible.

A Note on Translation

The narrative pieces placed between the chapters are in multiple languages. Only the English translations are by me.

All quotations from Spanish-language sources listed in the references are given in English translation. These translations are by me.

Figure 1. Humans emerging from maíz. Untitled painting by Tanya Alvarez, based on a thousand-year-old mural in Cacaxtla, Mexico. Courtesy of the artist.

Cente Tlakatl Ke Cente Cintli

Paula Domingo Olivares
CUENTEPEC, TEMIXCO, MORELOS, MEXICO

Tlayolli ke cente tlakatl. Cente tlayolli amo hueya tla amo kimokuitlahuiya cente tlakatl uan cente tlakatl amo hueya tla amo kikua nin tlayolli. Kion kinemilia cente masehualle. Tujuan tichiktikate ka tlayolli. Non okua-huitl ke nin Ometeotl, tlakatl-cihuatl, tajtle-nantle. Nin Imiahuayo kampa hualehua nin iyechio uan huetze ipan non olotl. Ijkion ixhuaz oksekin tlayolli. Inin ijtek nin totomachtle ke cente chichile kuak paka ijtek nin inana. Ompa nin yelotl nin kuak lak celik, huelik, tzopelik uan kuakualli nin tlatlatolli. Ke cente piltontli uan telpochtli. Ompa mokuepa Cintli kuak tepitzahue nin tlayolli kuak ikualika mokopehuaz itech nin ikuajyo. Ke cente tlakatl yochichijka kuak ikualika moxeloz uan kichihuaz nin tlenon oayiko nikan panin tlalli. Satepan nin Cintli moojoya kuak ikualli tetlakualtiz uan motokaz okuetl ijkion kinoma oyes nin tlayolli. Sikion ke cente tlakatl nin yomoxelo uan ikualli tetlakualtiz uan ikualli moxinachos, ijkion oyez oksekin tlaka. Kion nin inemiliz cente tlakatl uan cente tlayolli.

El Ser Humano Es Como un Grano de Maíz

El maíz es como el ser humano, no crece sin el cuidado de los seres humanos y los seres humanos no crecemos sin el alimento del maíz, es la creencia indígena. "Somos hombres y mujeres de maíz." El tronco del maíz es la dualidad de Ometéotl, es mujer y hombre, es padre y madre. La espiga es el polen que cae en centro del olote para darles vida a los granos que están envueltos en las hojas de maíz. Es como un bebé envuelto dentro del útero de su madre. Después el elote es la etapa más rica y hermosa del maíz porque es dulce y tierno, igual que un niño o joven. Luego se convierte en mazorca, es cuando los granos se ponen duros, y están listos para separar del tronco. La representación de una persona madura que ya está lista para ser independizada y así emprender su función aquí en la tierra. Finalmente, los granos de maíz es cuando ya está desgranado, que ya está listo para alimentar o nuevamente ser sembrado y así continuar con su especie. Al igual que una persona independiente que está lista para alimentar y procrear, para mantener la raza humana. Es la vida del maíz y el ser humano.

Human Beings Are Like Kernels of Corn

Maíz (corn) is like a human being; it cannot grow without human care and human beings cannot grow without maíz. It is our Indigenous belief. "We are men and women of maíz." The trunk of the maíz is the dual spiritual force of *ometeotl*. It is female and male. It is father and mother. The ear is the pollen that falls into the cob to give life to the kernels that are wrapped in the leaves of the maíz the way a baby is protected in her mother's womb. At this stage, the corn is rich and beautiful because it is sweet and tender, akin to a child. It later converts into a cob; it is when the kernels become hard and are ready to separate from the trunk. It is the representation of a mature human being, ready to become independent and to understand his/her role on earth. Finally when the kernels are removed from the cob, they are ready to eat or to once again be planted and thus continue the species. It is similar to the human being becoming independent, who can provide for him- or herself, ready to procreate, to continue the human race. That is the life of the maíz and the life of a human being.

$\mathscr{P}rologue$

The Ants of Quetzalcoatl

Atop the hills of the Nahuatl-speaking[1] village of Ocotepec, Morelos, Mexico, a student calls to my attention a colony of red ants carrying maíz kernels on their backs. It is a crisp early morning on the grounds of Nahuatl University. I rush to my room and return with a camera. As I film the ants carrying the maíz into their place of emergence, an elder, Mariano Leyva,[2] explains from behind me: "These are the ants of Quetzalcoatl."[3]

The sight and sensation is magical, and as I shoot, instinctively, I know this is the story I have been looking for. It is the beginning and end of a ceremonial discourse, a discourse of memory inscribed in the *Legend of the Suns* that arguably goes back to "the mists of time."[4] It will also become the beginning and end to a documentary on origins and migrations that I have been working on for several years (*Amoxtli San Ce Tojuan*, R. Rodríguez and P. Gonzales 2005). The story that the ants are acting out is a historic and cosmic drama that has been performed in Mexico since time immemorial. It is the story, recorded in many of the ancient Mexican *amoxtlis* (codices), murals, and architecture, of how maíz or *cintli* came to the people and how it became sacred. It is also recorded in the many songs and dances and in the psyche and collective memory of Indigenous Mexico. It is a drama that takes place in Tamoanchan. Most maíz-based cultures of Mexico and Central America—the Americas, for that matter—tell similar stories of how maíz came to them. For example, the ancient *Popol Vuh*, the Maya book of creation, teaches that human beings are made from maíz. This Maya drama also takes place in Tamuanchan.[5] And here, before me, I am witnessing the story of *centeotzintli* or *teotl cintli* (sacred maíz)—of how it came to the people. For some, the *Legend of the Suns* is the story of the

Fifth Sun, or the time of maíz. In Nahuatl cultures, the earlier four suns have been destroyed. It is the ants of Quetzalcoatl and this sacred maíz that bring coherence to the living story I have been searching for.[6]

The Ants of Quetzalcoatl

In the nearby ancient Nahuatl-speaking village of Amatlán—reputedly the birthplace of tenth-century Toltec leader Ce Topiltzin–Quetzalcoatl—the elder Don Felipe Alvarado Peralta related from memory[7] the following story:

> At the dawn of the Fifth Sun, after Creator couple, Quilaztli and Quetzalcoatl, created humans, many thousands of years ago, they soon realized that the humans needed to eat.
>
> So, Quetzalcoatl—bringer of civilization—is put in charge of bringing food to the people. Walking along, Quetzalcoatl notices red ants carrying kernels of corn. Quetzalcoatl asks one of them: "What is that on your back?"
>
> "Cintli," one replies. "Maíz. It is our sustenance."
>
> "Where did you get it?"
>
> The ant hesitates. At that, Quetzalcoatl tells the ant that the newly created humans need food. The ant still refuses. "The people will die without food," Quetzalcoatl pleads. Reluctantly, the ant points toward Tonalcatepetl—a nearby mountain—also called the Mountain of Sustenance.
>
> "Follow me."
>
> When they arrive, the ant informs Quetzalcoatl that the only way into the mountain is through a small opening. At that, Quetzalcoatl transforms into a small black ant. Once inside the mountain, Quetzalcoatl sees the maíz and takes it,[8] proceeding to bring it to the "Lords" in Tamoanchan.
>
> There, they approve of it as food for the people.

*

Shortly after relating this story, Don Felipe passed away in 2004. This ancient story is one often repeated by elders throughout the Nahuatl-speaking regions of Mexico. It was told to me several times by Don Felipe, who I first met in Amatlán in 1992. There, he was recognized as the keeper of the stories of Ce Topiltzin–Quetzalcoatl. One of the stories was about the association between Nahuatl-speaking Mexican revolutionary Emiliano Zapata and Ce Topiltzin–Quetzalcoatl; Don Felipe said that during the Revolution, Zapata hid in the caves above Amatlán, caves associated with Ce Topiltzin.[9]

After Ce Topiltzin's schooling in the nearby city of Xochicalco, he left his impressive civilizational mark throughout Mesoamerica, including the ancient cities of Cholula, Tula, Cacaxtla, and Chichén Itzá. He was known as a peacemaker and took his name from the much older and original Quetzalcoatl—the plumed or beautiful serpent—whose presence in sculpture form is recorded in the ancient city of Tollan/Teotihuacan (just north of present-day Mexico City). The original Quetzalcoatl's or Kukulkan's[10] presence is also memorialized in the oral traditions of many of the peoples of Cemanahuak/Abya-yala/Pacha Mama, also known as Turtle Island or the Americas. Per the ancient Mexican codices, it is Quetzalcoatl who is reputed to have brought civilization, writing, time, and the arts to these same peoples.[11]

I recall this story because in 1992, Don Felipe spoke about a nearby sacred site called Cinteopa, where a yearly ceremony to Quetzalcoatl and maíz are held. A decade later, I trekked by foot up some hills to Cinteopa with another local elder, Don Aurelio Cazarez. He explained that it was not simply a temple to maíz but that it was the birthplace of maíz itself. The surrounding area is also the sacred ground where Ce Topiltzin–Quetzalcoatl's parents, Mixcoatl and Chimalma, were purportedly buried 1,200 years ago. On the climb up, he noted that every time he came to Cinteopa, he saw Quetzalcoatl in the form of an eagle. Only moments later, I filmed the flight of an eagle overhead.

I start with these stories, ancient, though not frozen in time. They explain the creation of the cosmos and the creation of human beings and maíz, but more importantly, they create a cultural coherence stretching from mythic-ancient times into historical times and into the present and future. They are alive, relevant and dynamic, and they explain how "we" got here. As Mexican scholar Enrique Florescano (1999) notes, while there are plenty of variations, Mesoamerican narratives appear to have sprung from a common root and that root is maíz. It is that sacred sustenance that permitted human beings on this continent to arrive at the concept of time by observing the cyclical nature of the universe, which enabled them to produce advanced, astronomically and mathematically based calendars.

When I first set out to do research on origins and migrations, it had nothing to do with stories of creation, maíz, ants, or Quetzalcoatl. Instead, it had to do with an old map that was passed on to me (in my capacity as a columnist) by an elder, Frank Gutierrez, in Los Angeles in the mid-1990s. The map noted several features, one of them being the Antigua Residencia de los Aztecas (Ancient Dwelling of the Aztecs). That note was cited as proof by Gutierrez that Mexican peoples are not alien to this region. As intriguing as this revelation was, my research trail can actually be traced back to that first trip to Amatlán in 1992, and perhaps to a visit twenty years before that in the 1970s to the ancient city of Teotihuacan, a monumental city some forty-five minutes north of Mexico City that now appears to be the mythical or "legendary" Tollan of the ancient Toltecs (Florescano 1999, 2006). All of these experiences no doubt contributed to shaping my research interest.

The very act of writing this causes my mind to drift to Tollan/Teotihuacan:

As I stand atop the temple of the sun, I am compelled to climb back down and walk towards the surrounding undisturbed area below. There, as I walk away from the crowds, far ahead of me is an object protruding from the earth. I walk toward it and pick it up. It is an ancient arrowhead.

Ten years later, in 1986, that same arrowhead is in my suit pocket when I go to trial, as a journalist, for supposedly trying to kill several sheriff's deputies in Los Angeles in 1979, with a deadly weapon: my camera. Of course, I win . . .

Almost seven years later, on October 11, 1992, as half a million people gather at the pyramids of Teotihuacan to commemorate the last day of freedom on this continent five hundred years earlier, I find myself there with arrowhead in hand when runners from the first Peace and Dignity Journeys arrive.

Over the years, I have been inexplicably drawn there repeatedly. And as the years pass, indeed, I learn that many peoples believe this is Tollan, a place of sacred caves and sacred maíz—where peoples came from afar for legitimation, for their sacred bundles.

Perhaps it is the legitimation that I feel I lost when I was five years old, when my family crossed the border from Mexico into the United States. That was when I first heard the word *wetback*—a pejorative term that was constantly hurled at me by seemingly everyone, including people who looked just like me—within the context of "Go back to where you came from." At that age, my parents reassured me that "we didn't swim across an ocean to get here."

Thus, my book project can be traced to a lifelong attempt to understand societal notions of belonging and not belonging. It is an attempt to

understand how and why peoples who are clearly red or brown and unde-
niably Indigenous to this continent have allowed ourselves, historically, to
be framed by bureaucrats and the courts, by politicians, scholars, and the
media, as alien, illegal, and less than human.

Several thousands of hours of research into the possible geographical
origins of Mexican Indigenous peoples in what is today the United States
finally evolved into work that centers on understanding the much larger
story of maíz and its relationship to the culture and identity of peoples of
Mexican and Central American origin who live in the United States, and
on understanding their relationship to Indigeneity (which in this country
often goes unrecognized or is denied).[12] As I have come to comprehend
some of these narratives, I have also come to understand the centrality
of maíz—and the centrality of the feathered serpent (with its varied
names)—for many if not most Indigenous peoples of this continent. For
example, in Ysidro Macias's "Feathered Serpent: A Journey Through Chicano Serpentine Philosophy" (2007: 77), Nahuatl scholar Andrés Segura
explained Quetzalcoatl or the feathered serpent to Macias as the balance
between the material and the spiritual: "The feathered serpent represents
the Unknowable, Unthinkable, Consciousness of the Giver of Life, The
Giver of Time and Space, Ometeotl/Omecihuatl, God. Es conciencia de
Dios—He/She is the Consciousness of God." Ideas regarding Quetzalcoatl
and maíz, I believe, continue to be central also for de-Indigenized peoples
of this continent, even if only at a subconscious level.[13]

My work here examines the resilience of maíz culture and how it continues to inform the lives of peoples of Mexican and Central American origin,
particularly in the United States. It also examines how that culture is kept
alive and how it is communicated through stories, song, *danza*, theater, art,
oral traditions, ceremonies, rituals, celebrations, and diet. If some come to
regard my work as an attempt to rearticulate the reality of these peoples,
that is partially correct. More correct is that it is an effort to understand the
relationship of these peoples to the seven-thousand-year-old ceremonial
discourse of centeotzintli.

The old map I referred to earlier, which is justifiably a research project
unto itself, was key in pointing me in the direction of this ancient living story.
As part of this research process, I read many codices and colonial chronicles
and also visited many archives and many ancient sacred sites. What I found
in my initial research was fascinating: sixteenth–nineteenth-century cartographical documentation of a thousand-year-old origins-and-migrations
story, telling of a migration from what is today the United States into
what is now Mexico. On their face, these maps appear to confirm the

Aztlan–Tenochtitlan-migration story of the Aztec/Mexica, emblazoned on Mexico's flag (the accuracy of the story merits its own separate treatment).[14] Yet even more exciting is that these maps pointed me toward much older stories. By then, I had come to realize that where I was being guided was not to a point on a map, but toward maíz, toward that much older story involving and connecting virtually all the peoples of the continent. "If you want to know who you are, follow the maíz," I was told. "Maíz is who you are, who we are." "We not only eat sacred maíz, we are maíz." Many of the statements were consistent with the *Popol Vuh*—about how humans were created from maíz. It was also consistent with the "*escrituras-pinturas*" (painted books or codices) and ancient murals scattered throughout the continent that depict the creation story of humans and maíz.

On the same trip I took to Ocotepec, a visiting elder at Nahuatl University, Julieta Villegas, told some Mexican American educators who were there to learn the Nahuatl language, "I know most of you have lost your original [Indigenous] language, culture, and ways, but do not for one second doubt that you are Indigenous. If you ever do, eat a tortilla."

When I first heard this, like everyone else, I thought it was funny. It also conjured up the idea of "we are what we eat." As profound as her statement was, it took a while for me to understand the depth of her observation about peoples who had seemingly lost most of their connection to their Indigenous cultures, traditions, and ceremonies. The observation was very simple: that the connection of de-Indigenized peoples to Indigenous America, while seemingly distant, was actually being reinforced and nourished daily, through diet/sustenance.[15]

It was an accumulation of these and similar thoughts that set me off on my maíz-research journey. Later, this journey actually involved the creation of, and the enactment of, maíz narratives. This, in turn, revealed the importance and sacredness of maíz to Indigenous peoples, including those who have been de-Indigenized.[16]

Years ago, an Apache elder, Grandma Emma Ortega of San Antonio, told me that to do this work on origins and migrations, I needed to become a storyteller; this while recruiting me into her native storytelling circle. The primary thing that storytellers do is share stories. And in return, people share their own stories with them. Becoming a storyteller requires first and foremost respect: respect for the story, for other storytellers, and most of all, for those who listen to one's stories. It entails understanding the power of words and its relationship to memory. This process, which began, in effect, outside of the academic world, nevertheless informs my work. It also taught me something else; in order to understand the stories I began to receive,

I had to unlearn some of the (colonial) Western ideas and knowledge imparted to me regarding Mexican and Indigenous cultures. The world of storytelling taught me a new vocabulary, including the language of maíz, which is at once a scientific language, a ceremonial language, and a deep and metaphorical language that is spoken throughout the continent. Like tobacco, whenever maíz is presented it is recognized as a gift by Indigenous peoples most everywhere on the continent. This understanding taught me a different worldview or cosmovision and different ways of learning—from elders, teachers, scholars, storytellers, and even plants and animals, purportedly our most ancient *temixtianis* or teachers. In all this, I never developed a traditionally Western research relationship with anyone. Instead, I developed "collaborative research relationships," built partly on the idea of exchanging stories about origins and migrations and stories that explore maíz culture. In my work, there is no such thing as an "object of study" or a passive "informant." Traditionally, informants are thanked, but are rarely credited with intellectual authorship.

After returning to the academy to pursue my PhD on this topic, after being gone a generation, I realized that much of the Western thinking and the Western academic language that I had unlearned, I had to relearn. It was yet again a shock to the psyche. The notion of getting myself to "study" the very people who had shared stories with me, including a way of life, often in ceremony, was out of the question. And to this day, I refuse. With good reason, peoples from non-Western cultures have an aversion to being "studied," as it still connotes a colonial relationship. It also conjures up research abuse from the mid-twentieth century when researchers still openly spoke of the need to civilize savages. In an even earlier era—which actually never ended—European friars, living in the dark ages, felt the need to Christianize Indians and save them from the hell that surely awaited them. Such books live on as standard texts and assigned readings, and in many cases, the same basic relationship remains: Westerners purportedly have history and knowledge and the ability to critically analyze and interpret, while Indigenous peoples simply have the ability to recall and spin myths/fables, legends, and folktales (another definition of an informant).

In doing my maíz research, then, concerns about exploitation emerged. The question of who owns the knowledge became central. I also grappled with another question: What is knowledge and who makes this determination? These are the questions I had to contend with as I began my studies. Initially, I saw few written models for conducting my research (Linda Tuhiwai Smith's *Decolonizing Methodologies* [1999] was one exception). So, I ended up creating my own research protocols, devised to ensure that I conducted research in an ethical and transparent manner, stressing, above all, respectful relationships.[17]

These protocols that I developed continue to guide my research. They help ensure that I remain cognizant that stories cannot be claimed as personal intellectual property, and they are a reminder that elders should always be recognized for contributing their cultural and intellectual knowledge.

Reliance on elder knowledge did not and does not mean giving up critical thinking; quite the contrary. In my work, I attempt to reconcile scientific knowledge about maíz with elder stories about maíz, helped by guidance from Indigenous scholars. For example, it is now a generally held scientific belief that maíz is Indigenous to the Americas, and more specifically, that it developed somewhere in the region of southern Mexico and Central America. It was not always so. For many years, scientific debate raged regarding maíz's possible origin from Asia. The settling of this debate generally coincides with oral traditions throughout the continent that have always insisted that maíz is an AmerIndigenous[18] gift to humanity. Once maíz was created, it, along with its culture and technology, spread throughout the continent. To this day, maíz cannot grow without human care or intervention. Virtually all maíz-based peoples of the Americas have stories of how maíz came to them. None of the stories point to an "Old World" origin. It is my expectation that by collecting maíz stories, one day a fuller narrative of maíz culture on this continent will emerge and be revealed, including ancient migration patterns. Many of these instructive stories, some of which appear here, have long been in circulation, but Western scholars have traditionally paid no attention to them, labeling them as simplistic fables or legends.[19]

My research already indicates that the stories do not contradict the scientific story of maíz, as the path of maíz's spread from southern Mexico to the rest of the continent can generally be mapped. Additionally, what I have found is that contrary to Western scholarship, many Indigenous peoples believe that all peoples with maíz-based cultures are related, regardless of whether stories match in every detail or coincide with the Western scientific story of corn.

A Personal Note Regarding Ceremonial Discourse

My work here examines the resilience of maíz culture and how it continues to inform the lives of Mexican and Central and South American peoples, despite centuries of efforts to eradicate it. It explores the relationship and dialogue they/we have with maíz in a society that is also now permitting the radical alteration and destruction of this relationship, even more so through the worldwide introduction of genetically modified corn.

That is the core of my work. The following is the personal. A few years ago, while visiting my parents in southern California, I had a conversation with my then eighty-four-year-old father, who had Alzheimer's.[20] We spoke about my research. I had spoken to him in the past about how his stories, from when I was a child, motivated me to do my work—stories that are not only in my memory but became an integral part of my dissertation, and now this book. These stories tell not only of our own family migration but of ancient migrations as well. At that point he said: "The Aztecas migrated from somewhere in the north." Pausing, he continued. "I think they left from somewhere in the United States. They then went south until they founded Tenochtitlan—Mexico City."

"Those are the stories you told me when I was a child," I told him. "That's what triggered my research on origins and migrations. Now, I study how our peoples migrated in earlier times. I do this by studying maíz."[21] I related how it is possible to know human migration patterns on this continent by tracking the migration of corn. This is possible, I told him, because corn cannot grow by itself, nor can it migrate on its own. That is how we know that maíz traveled from southern Mexico into what is today the U.S. Southwest thousands of years ago, and later migrated east and then to Canada. People took maíz into the Andes also, I told my father.

At this, he said: "As children, you didn't know the maíz or the bean. Well, you ate it, but you did not work the fields. It is hard work. That's why I brought our family to this country, so that you and your brothers wouldn't have to do that backbreaking work."

I had learned the Aztec/Mexica migration story that he told me on this visit from both my parents when I was a child. While growing up, my father told me many stories about ancient Mexico—and he continued to do so even to his last days in 2011. My father, with but a third-grade education, passed down to me stories with clear pre-Cuauhtemoc[22] roots, but he also created a spark of desire within me to learn more of these stories.

When I was speaking to my father on this morning, the most intriguing thing about his talk was that he zeroed in on the crux of my argument. I, like most Mexicans living in the United States, no longer "know the maíz or the bean." So how do I, how do Mexicans and Chicanos/Chicanas and Central and South Americans, connect with our maíz-based culture, if we no longer know it? My own father gave me the answer: no matter where I have lived throughout my life, I have been nourished daily by the maíz/

tortilla and the frijol (bean), by the squash, nopal, and chile. In that sense, my story is not unique. Mexicans are nourished daily by what we eat and by the culture and the stories that we share. And similar to Quetzalcoatl's search for food, Mexicans who migrate north do not come searching for mythical origins, they come looking for a better place to live, looking for that elusive Tonalcatepetl or Sustenance Mountain. That is part of what this book tackles: is sustenance enough to maintain the culture? If people are not part of tribes or clans and if they no longer grow, harvest, and partake in ceremonial activities, can they still have a connection to their ancient maíz cultures? If so, what is that connection and how is it maintained and communicated? Is knowledge of maíz narratives, is knowledge of the philosophy of Quetzalcoatl—of creation stories—enough to maintain that connection? Are new stories needed? Is eating a tortilla, as Julieta Villegas suggested, enough to connect one to one's Indigenous culture or to the maíz cultures of this continent? Perhaps it is a starting point.

OUR SACRED MAÍZ IS OUR MOTHER

Figure 2. Ce Topiltzin by Paz Zamora (Mapitzmitl). This is a depiction of Ce Topiltzin–Quetzalcoatl, a bringer of civilization to the continent. The original Quetzalcoatl is often represented as a feathered serpent. Courtesy of the artist.

Introduction

Okichike ka Centeotzintli

They came together in darkness to think and reflect. This is how they came to decide on the right material for the creation of humans. . . . Then our Makers Tepew and Q'uk'umatz began discussing the creation of our first mother and father. Their flesh was made of white and yellow corn. The arms and legs of the four humans were made of corn meal.

—POPOL VUH

The *Popol Vuh* is the most sacred book of the Maya.[1] It is both a creation story and a cosmic drama. It is a thousands-of-years-old narrative regarding the creation of the universe, human beings, and maíz, and a recipe by which to live in peace and harmony.[2] Mexican anthropologist Enrique Florescano (1999) argues that this ancient story of the Quiché nation of Guatemala is part of a larger narrative that is similar to the narratives of virtually all Indigenous peoples from central and southern Mexico and Central America. They are the sacred maíz narratives of the continent or what I refer to as the centeotzintli narratives.

The term *centeotzintli*, or *teotl cintli*, translates from the Nahuatl language of central Mexico as "sacred maíz." The concept *okichike ka centeotzintli*, which was developed in collaboration with Nahuatl educator Paula Domingo Olivares of Cuentepec, Mexico, means "made from sacred maíz." The centeotzintli narratives encapsulate the idea "We are the people of sacred maíz," "Somos gente de maíz sagrado." The narratives also encompass a related idea: that one's identity is derived not from one's

3

nation-state citizenship but from one's relationship or "dialogue with maíz" (Esteva and Marielle 2003: 26). It is an identity that binds many peoples of this continent, without nation-state borders, an identity that speaks to a millennia-old relationship to maíz, the continent, and the universe.[3]

The maíz narratives are linked by similar creation stories: stories of creator couples and of hero twins who battle lords of the underworld in a cosmic or celestial ball game; stories of a plumed or beautiful serpent (Kukulkan/Quetzalcoatl); and stories of the attempts of various spiritual forces to create humans, first out of mud, then wood, amber (in some versions), and finally maíz. It includes maíz-based methods of counting time (calendars) and similar cosmovisions, including the belief in the sacredness of maíz. As Mexican anthropologist Guillermo Bonfil Batalla (1996) argued, maíz itself is the civilizational impulse or seed (*xinachtli*) that triggered the development of what is today known as Mesoamerica. Traces of that impulse can be seen beyond Mesoamerica, throughout virtually all the maíz-based cultures of Turtle Island or the Americas.[4]

The very concept "Mesoamerica" leads us in the direction of cultural similarities that in turn suggest broadening its definition. It is not a native concept; archaeologist Paul Kirchhoff first coined the term in 1943. The word conventionally refers to the geographic area of central and southern Mexico and Central America. As such, it encompasses cultures with various common characteristics, chief among them that they are politically, socially, culturally, and ceremonially organized around maíz. Kirchhoff expected his term to be redefined (López Austin 1993). Indeed, Mesoamerica could easily be defined in cultural terms instead, to include maíz-based cultures beyond that geographic area—including in what is today the U.S. Southwest and actually anywhere maíz was grown. This is not to suggest that all maíz-based cultures are the same but that they generally do exhibit traces of that civilizational impulse.

Maya linguist Domingo Martínez Parédez explains the centrality of maíz to Indigenous peoples and Indigenous cultures. In *Un Continente y Una Cultura* (*One Continent and One Culture*, 1960), he wrote that in prehistory, Indigenous peoples of Mesoamerica "developed the capacity to create the most stupendous feat in the form of a cereal: corn" (23). Continuing, he wrote that as a direct result of having maíz, the peoples were able to studiously observe the various phenomena caused by the sun, moon, and universe, which allowed them to arrive at a concept of time and formulate an advanced calendar. It also allowed them to discover the concept of zero: "All this was possible with the help of a language that was able to express thoughts of a disciplined manner and organize them as a philosophy, science and religion . . . at the same time that it facilitated the spread of their culture and civilization" (23–24). For him, these ideas regarding the centrality of maíz spread throughout the Americas, creating a symbolic unity for the continent.[5]

Hugh Iltis (2000), a botanist at the University of Wisconsin and one of the world's leading authorities on maíz, argued that teosinte, the "mother of maíz," was at least initially "not grown for its grains [kernels], but for other culinary virtues" (30), namely for sugar. Teosinte itself, he argued, was not eaten, mainly because it was inedible. Another virtue was the fungus *huitlacoche* or *cuitlacoche* (corn smut), a delicacy even to this day. Iltis wrote: "There can be little doubt that the use of *huitlacoche* is a very ancient one, and for the sake of argument, may well predate the domestication of teosinte" (34). He posited that the transformation of teosinte into corn most likely occurred as a result of a "maizoid Eve"—a founder plant—and that it occurred but once. Iltis places the evolution of maíz at eight thousand years ago (9), though other botanists' estimates range from seven to nine thousand years. Iltis and other botanists have charted maíz's domestication in southern Mexico. Once it was mutated and edible, humans carefully selected the seeds and caused it to grow in abundance. But Iltis also notes that maíz functioned more as a snack than a staple for centuries (36).

Synopsis: The Resilience of Maíz Cultures

The above centeotzintli narratives, the ancient maíz stories of the continent, are the backdrop for this work. My work here (1) examines the resilience of maíz cultures and maíz narratives among Mexicans and Central Americans (some of whom are, in effect, modern-day Mesoamerican peoples) who live in the United States; (2) explores how these narratives and cultures continue to inform their identity; (3) examines how they continue to be transmitted and maintained despite centuries of efforts to eradicate them; and finally (4) demonstrates how new stories—based on ancient stories— continue to be created and adapted to modern society, some of which are included here.

This work also examines how maíz culture has been transmitted over the millennia. One method is an examination of maíz narratives that trace back (in content) at least seven thousand years—to the birth of maíz—along with codices, artwork, songs, dance, theater, and recorded stories that can be traced back at least two thousand years. The *Popol Vuh*, murals, and sculpture can be traced back 2,200 years. These are the ways and the tools by which the ancient Mesoamericans transmitted their cultures and worldviews and engaged in ceremonial discourse.

I also view the four areas of inquiry listed above through a communications and historical prism within the context of colonialism. I do this by examining the spiritual and cultural metaframe that was superimposed or transplanted to this continent by Spanish friars—that of a millennial struggle pitting the forces of good against those of evil.[6] While colonialism is not unique to the Americas, it does help to contextualize my approach here. This imposed view of the world, as elucidated most poignantly by Jack Forbes in *Columbus and Other Cannibals* (2011) and Steven Newcomb in *Pagans in the Promised Land* (2008), maintained that European missionaries and the conquistadores had been sent by God to spread Christianity and civilization to Indigenous peoples, who were under the sway of the devil. From this perspective, Indigenous beliefs and cultures needed to be stamped out because they were demonic. Mexican scholar Alfredo López Austin (1993: 97) wrote:

> What had originally been an opposition of reason to myths became for many Christians an opposition between revealed truth and belief in false gods. Once the source of the fallacious narrations was identified, the myths, attributed to the devil's inspiration, were literally satanized. This idea lasted for centuries. . . . The Spaniards believed they had found the devil on this continent.

In this analysis, I examine not simply the origin of that imposed metaframe and master narrative but the means, methods, and tools that were utilized to accomplish this assault on the ancient cultures of the continent. It was part and parcel of the violent era of colonialism, but it has its own name: *la Otra Conquista* (the Other Conquest), as memorialized by the Spanish-language movie of the same name (S. Carrasco 1999). This Other Conquest is the spiritual conquest of the Americas.[7] The first Conquest refers to the military campaigns, led by Hernán Cortés.[8] La Otra Conquista included religiously motivated crusades to destroy all the temples,[9] "idols," and books of Indigenous peoples. It took place during an incredibly violent era, one that saw millions of Indigenous people devastated by war, mass killings, rape, enslavement, land theft, starvation, famine, and disease. Force and the threat of force facilitated this Other Conquest during the sixteenth–nineteenth-century Spanish-colonial era. Its primary objective was the destruction of the maíz-based beliefs and cultures of Indigenous peoples, ushering in a radical shift in the *axis mundi* or center of the universe from maíz to the Christian cross. Failure to accept the imposed frames or world-view of good versus evil, God versus the devil, was to risk death or torture and eternal damnation (Gruzinski 1993). While force is no longer associated with Christianity in the Americas, a 2007 papal address in Brazil, in which the Pope admonished Indigenous people to abandon their pre-Columbian spirituality or face eternal damnation, reminds us that such threats have not yet been remanded to history. He stated that the church did not impose itself on Indigenous peoples; that, if anything, the church helped to purify their souls; and that a return to their pre-Columbian religions would be a step backward (Colitt 2007).

Despite an unprecedented three-hundred-year colonial mass-conversion project (known as *reducciones*), plus another two hundred years of non-Indigenous cultural domination, maíz cultures and narratives were in fact not eradicated; they continue to be a resilient part of the culture of many AmerIndigenous peoples, including those that live in the United States. Despite attempts at complete erasure, maíz culture can be seen everywhere in Mexican and Central American and Andean culture. The reason for that persistence may be due to the simple fact that maíz-based cultures hold this ancient crop to be sacred. Another reason for the persistence of maíz cultures and narratives, as will be examined shortly, is the strategy of syncretism, the fusion of at least two belief systems—employed by both European priests and Indigenous peoples. On the priests' part, the strategy was to utilize Indigenous culture to promote Christianity. For example, in pre-Columbian times, the day that honored Chicomecoatl (as mother of maíz) was celebrated on Huenitl de Mayo (Third of May). In the colonial era, Spanish priests substituted that day with a celebration of Santa Cruz (Nash 1997: 351). They utilized syncretic strategies for their "civilizing" purposes; Indigenous peoples, on the other hand, accepted Christianity into their cosmovision for purposes of cultural survival, though some did accept Christianity willingly. Both used the same cultural devices, but the friars were aided by force, or threats of force, to accomplish their goals.

This book also contextualizes my work on maíz by examining contemporary U.S. narratives about whether Mexicans and Central and South Americans belong in the United States. In this clash, these peoples find themselves struggling to assert a sense of belonging and even, more importantly, their full humanity. The context for this is the phenomenon of peoples Indigenous to this continent being alienized and dehumanized, not simply five hundred years ago but even to this day.

To examine the imposition of the good-versus-evil/God-versus-the-devil paradigm, it is first necessary to have a basic understanding of the major maíz narratives associated with Mesoamerica. The decision to relay these narratives first is a conscious attempt to decenter the hegemonic Western narrative of history. In a similar vein, the prologue explained my positionality, my relationship to this research and these narratives. The key feature of my work is that it does not involve the studying of others but rather collaborating with storytellers, elders, and knowledge keepers. In my work, there are no "others."

In the examination of the metanarratives and countermetanarratives found in Mesoamerican culture, I include Chicana/Chicano culture. Many of the people from these cultures are classified as mestizos or mixed-race peoples, but are perhaps more accurately what Bonfil Batalla (1996) characterizes as "de-Indianized" (or de-Indigenized) Indigenous people.[10] I offer no strict definition at this time of the term *Indigenous* because the entire book examines the very dynamic of Indigeneity and de-Indigenization, particularly as it relates to maíz-based peoples. At the same time, one of the primary objectives of my work is not to establish whether de-Indigenized peoples are Indigenous but rather whether they are connected or affiliated to maíz cultures.[11] That said, here is a useful observation from Virginia Tilley in *Seeing Indians* (2005: 13): "Most basically, Latin American thought today generally understands the term Indian not as a racial identity, but as an ethnic one, signaled by behavior, rather than physical criteria." This also applies to the term *Indigenous*. For instance, in Mexico, phenotype is not considered the determining factor; historically, language, residency, dress, and education have been the determining factors. Additionally, most definitions of *Indigenous*, particularly in the United States, include a continuing relationship to the land; yet such a definition is problematic as a result of the massive and historic and continual forced removals and uprooting due to colonialism and modern-day globalization and U.S. imperialism. This dynamic regarding the definition is the subject of Reissner's *El Indio en los Diccionarios* (*The Indian in the Dictionaries*, 1983), in which he posits that *Indio* (Indian) is an ideological construction. More than an erroneous name for the occupants of the Americas, it was the ideological justification for colonization. As defined during colonial times, an Indian was less than human, backward and under the sway of the devil. Reissner argues that it was the dictionaries of the Spanish-colonial era that assisted in the construction of Indian stereotypes. In fact, the entire notion of the Indian is itself a European construction. It is akin to the European construction of the Americas.[12]

My research examined the systematic method by which Europeans (friars) managed to turn the Indigenous world upside down and the tools that made this hegemonic feat possible—a feat that in many cases continues to go unchallenged. I explored literature, insurgent reframing literature—Linda Tuhiwai Smith (1999), Otto Santa Ana (2002), and George Lakoff (2004)—that presents strategies to counter hegemonic framing. Similarly, I examined visual theories that help to explain the use of imagery to inculcate European and Christian ideas in Indigenous peoples (Gruzinski 1993, 1994). These same theories may help to explain the survival and resilience of ancient Indigenous images, iconography, and cultures.

In my work, the centeotzintli narratives decenter colonization by restoring the centrality of maíz and of Indigenous history, language, culture, and cosmovision to this continent, including voice. The placing of these narratives under the rubric "centeotzintli" may be thought of as what Rudolfo Anaya (1989: 230) calls a ceremony of naming: "the ceremony of naming or of self-definition is one of the most important acts a community performs." Beyond naming, in this work, I take part in the construction of new maíz stories and narratives. This is key in demonstrating that story making is not simply the art of repetition but rather an act of creation. As someone who grew up de-Indigenized, the fact that I am able to partake in the writing of (creation) stories by itself also demonstrates that peoples who are de-Indigenized can be reconnected to ancient knowledge.

Centeotzintli: Before the Continent Was Framed

My work argues that the seven-thousand-year-old story of centeotzintli frames the history of this continent, a history that is later reframed by European friars and other subsequent Western writers and scholars. Don Aurelio of Amatlán, Morelos, marks the age of maíz at ten thousand years. Another Mexican elder says that maíz was created in the original homeland of the Tamoanchanes/Toltecs, which is reputed to be a land to the East, nowadays submerged in waters, and that it was brought from there many thousands of years ago.[13] This elder requested anonymity for fear of being ridiculed. However, this story is not entirely unknown. A similar story appears at the opening of the 1500s-era Codex Anónimo Mexicano in which the Toltecs arrived in Mexico with dried maíz, cotton, and other seeds.

Maíz stories must be told within the context of decolonization,[14] yet, at the same time, it must be understood that the centeotzintli narratives begin long before Spanish-Christian colonization with arguably the most important event in the history of the continent: the creation of maíz, an event that radically altered the continent's landscape. The narratives continue with efforts to not only preserve the memory of that event but also to preserve and protect maíz as "sacred sustenance." These efforts continue to inform the identity of many peoples on this continent, and this is one meaning of ceremonial discourse: an explanation not only of that historical memory but also of one's living relationship to maíz. For de-Indigenized and deceremonialized, often dehumanized, peoples, this ceremonial discourse represents more than a reconnection to story and place, it represents a reconnection to humanity itself. In Spanish, I use the term *historias profundas* (deep stories) to refer to many of these same narratives. This term refers to the foundational stories of peoples and cultures, including those with roots prior to maíz.

This examination of competing narratives also necessarily involves being aware of a different historiography or periodization for the continent, marked not by Western calendars or markers but by the introduction of maíz and the methods of measuring time that developed as a result. In Mesoamerica, beginning with the Olmecs, peoples have continually developed calendars and writing based on maíz. Perhaps the most well known is the misnamed "Aztec Calendar"[15] or the Tonalamatl, which is actually composed of two calendars: the *xiuhpohualli* or solar calendar, which consists of 365 days, and the *tonalpohualli* or ritual calendar, which consists of 260 days.[16] Miguel León-Portilla (2003a) argues that this system was known to most of Mesoamerica, going back to at least 1000 BC. Connecting Mexicans and Central Americans to this seminal moment helps to contextualize their history as part of the ancient maíz cultures of this continent.

Many scholars within Raza studies see the clash over whether Mexicans and Chicanas/Chicanos belong as a battle that has been waged since 1848, when the United States, through war, took half of Mexico's territory (Santa Ana 2002). However, in examining the cultural attributes that are associated with these peoples, including media stereotypes, we find that this dynamic has actually been going on for some five hundred years, from day one.[17] Actually, day one has little to do with 1492; day one, for maíz-based peoples, is symbolically the day of the creation or "gift of maíz."[18] Understanding these competing histories helps contextualize the narratives I have examined. I provide this context through a methodology I created, which includes a reliance on elder epistemology or elder knowledge, as well as collaborative research.[19] Developing this methodology also involved creating research protocols.

Maíz Methodology: Research Protocols

*Kenin itech tikitaske kenika tik zaloske nin tlalnamikitliztli kanin to
koltsiuaan.*
Una guía para saber cómo aprender los conocimientos de nuestros abuelos.
A guide to learning from the knowledge and wisdom of our ancestors.

The protocols that guided my research as a scholar are and have been
virtually the most important aspect of this work because they involve transparency and relationships. It is only proper that they be at the heart of this
book, though for reasons of space I will give but a synopsis. They were
developed for the purpose of conducting my own research on maíz. Carrying on Indigenous research—in my case maíz research—is decolonization
work. Such research is fraught with many dangers, primarily to do with
violation of privacy and exploitation of knowledge, intentional or otherwise,
and misapplication of Western ideas, theories, language, and vocabulary to
an Indigenous universe. All of these things can lead to misinterpretation.
The idea of creating research principles is to avoid these traps, but it is also
about being clear that my work is not neutral. In the tradition of Indigenous
scholars—and many scholars of color—my work is intended to solve a problem, not simply analyze it. The overarching problem I decided to tackle
is that phenomenon of how peoples that are Indigenous to this continent
became alien in the United States.

The protocols for this maíz research were developed in three phases.
Phase 1 involved developing questions about my own work. This phase
occupied several years during which I examined my work and the nature
of my work. The questions were generally about my research, my research
process, and my relationship with all those I came across as a result of this
research. Phase 2 involved answering the questions, with an emphasis on
my own clarity and transparency. Phase 3 involved taking the answers and
creating the research principles or protocols from them.[20]

I created the following principles: (1) reasons for research, (2) the receiving of knowledge, (3) full disclosure (what is my relationship to this topic
and from what community do I come?), (4) the nature of the research,
(5) dissemination of the research, (6) compensation and acknowledgments,
and (7) respectful relationships with elders and other storytellers and knowledge keepers.

This explanation of my methodology here is necessary because much
of my work on Indigenous maíz narratives rejects the privileging of European sources, which traditionally devalue the views of Indigenous America.

My methodological approach, which relies heavily on elder epistemology and oral traditions, also affects the literature I surveyed for this work. For instance, literature reviews tend to privilege the written word of conquerors over the words of the so-called conquered, which often take the form of nonwritten traditions, and are generally branded as less credible by Western scholars.[21]

The Nahua cultures of Mesoamerica had schools for oral teaching and memorialization, which brought a coherence to their knowledge: "In Mesoamerica, both calendar and writing had been the indispensable complement of oral tradition since at least the beginning of the first millennium B.C." (León-Portilla 1980: 31). It is in these schools, or *calmecacs*, as the later Mexica called them, where writing and memorialization of historical events were also taught through poetry known also as *in xochitl, in cuicatl*. Florescano argued in *Memoria Indígena* (1999) that the oral tradition was also inscribed in the landscape, in the architecture of pyramids, and that cities such as Tollan/Teotihuacan and Tenochtitlan/Mexico City were oriented and aligned not only astronomically but also according to their peoples' belief system with respect to creation and origins. Doris Heyden commented on the oral tradition: "In short, myth and its close companions, ritual and symbol, cannot be divorced from historical fact in pre-Hispanic Mexico" (2000: 166). In this sense, it is clear that there was a discipline and relationship between orality, writing, and memory.

American Indian scholar Greg Cajete explains why and how Indigenous cultures survive: "What is the plot of the story? All peoples have to answer this . . . have to create their own stories . . . and create the plot—the meta-narrative" (2005: 66).[22] In one example of this, at least 1,500 years before the arrival of Europeans, many of the peoples of Mesoamerica plotted out their story (or stories) through the peoples of Tollan/Teotihuacan. They preserved their story—knowledge and traditions—through the *Teoamoxtli* or *Tulan Zuyua* book, a sacred book that was distributed to rulers throughout Mesoamerica who sought legitimation from the peoples of Tollan/Teotihuacan. Only three things were required of those who received it: (1) honor their ancestors, (2) visit Tollan/Teotihuacan, and (3) honor their sacred bundles (Florescano 1999: 184). In regards to legitimation, Saburo Sugiyama wrote: "The feathered serpent seems to have been established, since his very inception, as a mythical entity legitimizing rulers' political authority before society" (2000: 138). Teotihuacan was not the "City of Gods," but rather where Lords were legitimated. In the *Popol Vuh*, the elders similarly speak of the importance of their bundles (Goetz and Morley 2003: 155).

Today's oral traditions are interrelated with much older written and non-written traditions. In addressing the validity of the Maya oral narratives, Rafael Girard, in *Los Mayas* (1966), noted that there are several layers of evidence for their authenticity, starting with the ancient stories and living traditions, all of which revolve around maíz.[23] Another layer is the living spiritual traditions, as enacted by ritual and ceremony. These rituals and ceremonies utilize the same personages as those from the ancient Mayan stories: Gucumatz/Quetzalcoatl, Hunahpú and Xbalanqué (the cosmic twins), and so on. The stories are also recorded in the ancient codices, including the *Popol Vuh*, the *Anales de los Cakchiqueles* (*Annals of the Kakchikels*), and the Dresden Codex, which constitute a third layer of evidence. The recent unearthing of *Popol Vuh* stories in mural form by archaeologist William Saturno in San Bartolo, Guatemala (dated at 200 BC), along with more recent sculpture finds at nearby Nakbe and El Mirador, constitute a fourth layer. The same stories are also found on ancient pottery, stelae, and monuments, comprising a fifth layer. The Maya Calendar, which continues to govern the life of many Maya, is the sixth piece of evidence because those same personages are part of its core. Maíz itself is the most important proof. Girard wrote: "The Maya continue to plant maíz in the same manner as their ancestors, which goes back to the origins of agriculture many thousands of years ago" (vii). Amid change, this evidence demonstrates consistency and continuity.

Generally, the same layers of evidence are applicable to other Mesoamerican peoples in that they have similar narratives and similar methods of recording them. During colonization, maíz, rather than being destroyed, was more heavily relied upon to feed the exploited masses, hence the continuation of the culture.

Thus, while I do not reject the written word—quite the contrary, since Mesoamerican peoples have at least a three-thousand-year writing tradition—the importance of, and my reliance on, the oral tradition is paramount. It cannot be sufficiently reflected in a review of the relevant oral literature, but such a review is a necessary task nonetheless.

Three Sets of Narratives

My work examines three basic sets of narratives, which I break down into narratives and counternarratives. One set of narratives that I examine is used by Mexican and Central American peoples, including Chicanos/Chicanas, to assert a sense of belonging to this continent. These are the centeotzintli narratives, the "Somos gente de maíz" or "We are people of maíz" narratives. They are several thousands of years old and are clearly documented in Maya-Nahua cultures. This includes the culture of Tollan/Teotihuacan, a Toltec city (built atop a sacred cave where corn was grown) that influenced the cultures of virtually all of Mesoamerica. While maíz culture is much older, it is expressed there, at least two thousand years ago, painted/written in stone (Florescano 2006). The Mexica[24] believed that Teotihuacan was where the events related to the Fifth Sun took place, at which time maíz was gifted to the people. These narratives are recounted in various ancient texts, including the Palenque texts (recorded in AD 692), and the *Leyenda de los Soles* (*Legend of the Suns*, Codex Chimalpopoca [1558] 1945), the *Historia de los Mexicanos por Sus Pinturas* (*History of the Mexicans Through Their Paintings*, [1531] 1965), the Boturini Codex ([1530–1541] 2000), the Sigüenza map, and the "Aztec Calendar" (Florescano 2006: 57). These maíz/creation narratives serve as the basis for the understanding that Mexicans and Central Americans are firmly rooted to this continent, regardless of where they live, even if many are de-Indigenized. While no consensus exists as to the definition of *de-Indigenized*, it generally centers on language, culture, and religion, though it is quite arbitrary. Generally speaking, most de-Indigenized peoples do not consciously partake in ceremonies or regularly practice Indigenous spiritual ways. Many are no longer aware of these practices, or if they are, they have a Christian-inspired fear of being denounced as pagan or demonic.

The second of these sets of narratives is what I term Aztlan resistance narratives, which argue that Mexican people are not simply Indigenous to the continent, they are also Indigenous to what is today the U.S. Southwest. *Aztlan* is a Nahuatl word that refers to a thousand-year-old story of Nahuatl-speaking peoples migrating from an ancestral homeland, somewhere in the north, until reaching and founding Mexico City/Tenochtitlan.

This narrative that locates Aztlan in the current U.S. Southwest is prominent in the Mexican American– or Chicano-studies canon of the late 1960s and 1970s. It is also found in colonial chronicles from the 1500s–1600s. Many if not most of the colonial chronicles are actually based on pre-Columbian narratives that allude to a southward migration from Aztlan/Chicomoztoc.

Utilizing these narratives, Chicanos began to politically assert in the 1960s, particularly through poetry and the arts, not simply that the U.S. Southwest was Aztlan, the reputed homeland of the Aztecs/Mexica, but that it was also the (future) homeland of Chicanos (Anaya and Lomelí 1989).

While the maíz narratives are also important to peoples of Mesoamerican descent in the United States, due to the context of the political upheaval of the 1960s–1970s, the resistance narratives or Aztlan narratives were more significant during that era. This is so because within the Chicana/Chicano community, these "belonging" narratives have been useful for responding to hostile anti-Mexican attitudes in the United States. It is worth nothing that the story of Aztlan was/is used differently in the United States than in Mexico. In Mexico, the Aztlan-to-Tenochtitlan-migration story informs part of Mexico's psyche, as it is emblazoned on the nation's flag. In the United States, for many Chicanos/Chicanas of the 1960s–1970s era, Aztlan is where the Aztecs came from but it is also where they live today.[25]

To understand these two sets of narratives, the maíz narratives and the Aztlan narratives, one must see them in relationship to a third, more familiar and dominant "master narrative" of U.S. history. This master narrative—or one strand of it—generally locates or frames Mexicans and Central Americans within U.S. society as an alien, suspect, illegitimate, and nowadays inferior and subservient population. This narrative also views them as descended from peoples and cultures that are but generations removed from barbarism and savagery. UCLA scholar Otto Santa Ana, in *Brown Tide Rising* (2002), argues that these same peoples continue to be treated today as both alien and less than human and asserts that the ideology from which these attitudes emerge can be traced to the U.S.-Mexico conflicts of the nineteenth century. My research shows that de-Indigenized Mexicans and Central Americans are often perceived today not as Indigenous peoples but as mongrels, and these views can actually be traced to the 1500s.[26]

In this work, I also examine how the ancient maíz narratives of the continent continue to be communicated, albeit below the radar or "hidden in plain sight" (Esteva 2003b). This exploration involves an examination of the imagery of maíz in the pre-Columbian and colonial eras, but also in the modern era, and particularly in the United States, including contemporary culture of Mesoamerican communities.

Master Narratives and Master Languages

In examining these three seemingly disparate sets of narratives, I challenge the standard notion of what constitutes a narrative and what constitutes a counternarrative, particularly, the notion of a master narrative. I also challenge the language of the dominant used in analyses of such narratives, primarily because language itself has a long history of being implicated in colonial pursuits (Johnson, Louis, and Pramono 2006).

For this reason, I give priority to Indigenous names in my work. As Charles Cutler points out in O Brave New Words! (1994), many thousands of native words are embedded in the English and Spanish languages as loanwords, especially in the realm of food vocabulary and place-names—important signifiers of culture. These words provide a linkage to thousands of years of knowledge of the continent, from Alaska to Tierra del Fuego, and help preserve Indigenous memory. Many of the place-names are simply descriptive, but some also allude to relationships, connote ideas, and describe historical events.

The challenge in doing this work, examining several cultures across a large expanse of time, is not simply dealing with issues of translation among languages (primarily Nahuatl, Maya, Spanish, and English) but with different frames, stories, and narratives, and even more importantly, different timelines and worldviews. The Indigenous worldviews included here are derived primarily from the maíz cultures of Mesoamerica; the European worldview or worldviews were brought primarily by Spanish priests of the fifteenth to sixteenth centuries and spread unevenly over time throughout the Americas. Ojibwe scholar Rosemary Christensen (2004) notes that peoples operating from different worldviews are bound to interpret the same language differently, with negative consequences. This is particularly true when one of the parties is hostile, and especially when one is speaking the language of maíz, which, in effect, is to speak of many different Indigenous cultures, including Mexican cultures.

This includes the food, language, dress, customs, traditions, ceremonies, rituals, family and social structure, economics and politics. All revolve around maíz. Despite the seeming unity in time and space of Mesoamerican cultures, there have always been and continue to be, as with any society or societies, multiple cosmovisions among the many maíz-based cultures of this continent. Multiple cosmovisions existed on both sides of the Atlantic, among peoples of all cultures. Not all appear to be consistent, some sound contradictory, some are a fusion of two or more cosmovisions, and yet they continue to serve a purpose.

Given the five-hundred-year European presence in the Americas, few cultures can claim to be free of European influences, particularly considering the tools that were utilized for the purposes of mass conversion. To cleanly divide society into an Indigenous-European/Western binary, to pit it against itself in that manner, is not possible. As will be made clear in the conclusion, the conflicting narratives do not necessarily have to be in competition, or at least do not have to be oppositional or mutually exclusive. That is precisely why there is no reason to act as though Indigenous peoples and their/our ancient and thriving cultures have disappeared. Neither can the issue of narratives and counternarratives on this continent be examined outside of their colonial context, nor can they be divorced from today's aforementioned reality. For many Indigenous researchers, embracing that reality means recognizing that there is no postcolonial (L. Smith 1999) and that the pursuit of social justice cannot take a back seat to things ancient. Being blinded by pyramids has plagued Mexican and Central American societies since independence from Spain. This can often be noticed in museums throughout the Americas where the past is celebrated and highlighted at the expense of the present.

In addition to those sources mentioned already, my research methodology was also influenced by scholars Devon Abbott Mihesuah and Angela Cavender Wilson's *Indigenizing the Academy* (2004), and a collection edited by Wilson and Michael Yellow Bird, *For Indigenous Eyes Only: A Decolonization Handbook* (2005). Virtually all the teams of research collaborators stress the need for utilizing the scholarship of Indigenous researchers, particularly when the topic is Indigenous research. Also, going to the heart of my question regarding the alienization of Mexicans and Central Americans, Cornell Pewewardy, in "Ideology, Power, and the Miseducation of Indigenous Peoples in the United States" (2005), posited that the number-one objective of the U.S. colonizers was ethnic cleansing and the second was mind control. He wrote: "The only education allowable was education for pacification, servitude and inferiorization" (148). While the above-named American Indian scholars are critical of hegemonic Western research practices, they have more importantly also been instrumental in putting to paper Indigenous methodologies and knowledge systems, which include the use of critical thinking and variations of elder epistemology (Yellow Bird 2005).

Part of the reason for seeking out the work of these scholars was to be able to locate even de-Indigenized Mexicans and Central Americans within a seven-thousand-year discourse, as opposed to viewing them as recent immigrants. Most academic disciplines, particularly in the United States, generally discourage research across such an expanse of time (Billig 1995).

"Reducing" the Peoples and "Reducing" Their Narratives

The same tools that were utilized for communicating Indigenous ideas in public before the arrival of Europeans, including ancient *amoxtlis* (codices),[27] stories, song, *danza* (traditional dance), theater, art, oral traditions, ceremonies, rituals and celebrations, became the mediums or tools that the Spanish friars utilized to convey syncretized messages and carry on their mass-conversion project.[28] This illustrates how Indigeneity, romanticized history aside, was and has been suppressed or manipulated for five centuries, through the use of signs, symbols, and imagery. Much of the exploited imagery is associated with maíz and the Mexican nation, such as the eagle and serpent and Guadalupe/Tonantzin. They are all related. These iconic symbols and imagery are emblematic of the epic struggle by Spain to attempt to culturally and spiritually colonize Indigenous peoples. They also are reminders that Indigenous and de-Indigenized peoples resisted that colonization.

Yet the backdrop to colonization and de-Indigenization was extermination and genocide begun by Europeans in the 1400s–1500s. It also included the establishment of *congregaciones* (the congregation of peoples) and the project of *reducciones* (spiritual "reductions").[29] In effect, the objective of these two de-Indigenization projects was to corral Indians into missions or pueblos for the purpose of reducing or eliminating or "killing" the souls of the Indians, creating Christians in their place (Craib 2004). The idea behind reducciones was similar to the ideological basis for the boarding-school policies in the United States in the nineteenth to twentieth centuries, shaped by Captain Richard C. Pratt's dictum: "Kill the Indian—save the man." However, this method of spiritually reducing Indians also served to facilitate land theft. This began in 1546, by order of King Charles V, who "resolved that the Indians would be reduced to pueblos and that they not be divided or separated by the sierras and mountains, so as to be able to benefit spiritually." This order was apparently reaffirmed numerous times, including in 1681 as part of the Laws of the Indies. It continued the reduction of Indians (their instruction in the Holy Faith) "so that they can forget the errors of their ancient rites and ceremonies" (Sarmiento Donate 1988: 178). The reducciones included the systematic demonization by Spanish friars of virtually all things Indigenous, particularly the people themselves, unless saved or baptized (Olmos [1547] 1992). Once the reducción was accomplished, the process of constructing a Christian could commence. This totalizing process did not apply only to the people but also to their knowledge, spirituality, and worldviews. This is what I refer to as "narrative reducción," an extension of the church's reducciones of the people themselves. Such practices resulted in the imposition of a single "master narrative" upon an entire continent.

Under this theory and practice of reducción, all things Indigenous were reduced by Spanish friars to being evil and Satanic, including Indigenous narrative histories and cosmovision. The codices, murals, and architecture were burned, destroyed, discredited, or badly misinterpreted throughout the entire three-hundred-year colonial era—though actually the misinterpretations continue. However, the stories that were useful, for the purposes of imposing Christian narratives, were kept. For example, the Mesoamerican "God" Quetzalcoatl is generally given Christian attributes by Europeans in contradistinction to virtually all other Mesoamerican "gods." The friars attempted to Christianize native peoples by asserting that Quetzalcoatl, who had brought maíz and civilization to this continent and who the friars claimed was white, was either Christ himself or one of his apostles.[30] This precipitated an Indigenous backlash, and new narratives were created in response to the imposed European narratives. Due to the repressive colonial infrastructure, with the accompanying strict censorship of the Catholic Church, these new resistance or opposition narratives—those that went against the conversion project—generally were not published, though many have survived through the oral tradition. As an example of these resistance narratives, in Ysidro Macias's "Feathered Serpent: A Journey Through Chicano Serpentine Philosophy" (2007), scholar Andrés Segura explains that the notion that Quetzalcoatl was a bearded white man reflects unfamiliarity with Aztec/Mexica writing and the meaning of the attributes "bearded" and "white" in Mexica cosmology. White represents the east and a beard represents the rays of "our Padre Sol"—our father, the sun (79).

Today, the dynamic of reducción continues, and its primary or underlying question continues to be, Are they human? With Mexican and Central American peoples in the United States, that question is further complicated: they are not viewed as Indigenous, nor as Americans, and many question whether they/we belong. As in the original reducciones, the subtext is not restricted to the theological question of who has a soul but who is entitled to full human rights. Also caught up in this civilizational clash is a corollary battle over whose metanarratives are valid: the continent's historias profundas or stories about Columbus and Plymouth Rock.[31] For my work, all of these questions are predicated on that of why Mexicans and Central Americans are viewed as the alien, enemy, and inferior "other." A consideration of media stereotypes may provide some illumination. Scholars such as Santa Ana (2002) argue that the basic stereotype of Mexicans in the United States emerged after the 1840s U.S. war against Mexico; this was basically the same time frame in which media stereotypes of American Indians and

Blacks emerged. Mexicans were stereotyped as backward, less intelligent, and associated with the past. Their culture too, particularly their foods—maíz, beans, and chile—were also associated with "conquered, inferior, or lower-class working peoples" (De León 2002). These are generally the stereotypes of Indigenous peoples, going back to the 1500s (Steele 1996).[32]

All the while, my broader research for this book includes an exploration of media from those earlier times: codices, colonial chronicles, and oral traditions. It involves ancient and living knowledge, of which the oral tradition is considered living memory; hidden knowledge—hidden texts and hidden transcripts; and suppressed knowledge, including syncretized rituals/ceremonies.[33] Some of this knowledge is not accessible, even to Mesoamericanists, because to this day much Indigenous knowledge continues to be fiercely guarded; many of those that hold it are unwilling to share it with Western academia.[34] My research also looks at debates in the academy itself over whose narratives, history, and memory are valid.

Regarding syncretism, Bonfil Batalla argued that throughout the post-Columbian history of the Americas, "Diverse Indian societies have taken the signs, symbols and practices of the imposed religion and made them their own by reorganizing and reinterpreting them within the core of their own religious beliefs." These imposed beliefs, however, "have been subordinated within a framework that is not Christian and that has its origins in Mesoamerican religion" (1996: 136). During the colonial era, syncretism appears to have been a two-way street. Fray Andrés de Olmos in the recording of the *huehuetlahtolli* or sayings of the ancients (Silva Galeana 1991)[35] and Fray Motolinía in his early writings believed that by associating the Aztec/Mexica deities with Christian ones—or by superimposing Christian feasts upon the ceremonial days of the Aztec/Mexica Calendar—conversion would be easier (Broda 2000). Fray Bernardino de Sahagún and Fray Diego Durán, on the other hand, were opposed to syncretism, believing that it would permit Indigenous peoples to continue to pray to their former deities, particularly to Guadalupe/Tonantzin, in place of the Virgin Mary.

This work is also about how peoples' beliefs are perceived. As López Austin (1993) has argued, all peoples have histories and all peoples have foundational stories/myths (historias profundas), and the two are intertwined and difficult to separate. He defines myth as "a text that relates the emergence of the other time into human time" (32). This definition affirms that all peoples have myths, not simply non-Westerners.

This work entailed examining the language of poetry (*in xochitl, in cuicatl*, "flower and song") and comprehending the metaphoric language of pre-Cuauhtemoc peoples, known as *in tlili, in tlapilli,* "the red and the black" (ink). This expression signifies not just knowledge of a writing or communications system but also knowledge of a way of life (Boone 2000). It also includes understanding the language of ritual and ceremony—including danza and music—which are places of communication and sites and repositories of memory (Boone and Mignolo 1994, Mignolo 2006).

This analysis has to be done cognizant of another great challenge; many of the recognized primary sources from the 1600s were written in an era of extreme censorship shortly after Indigenous codices and other historical records were destroyed en masse. That is why the post-Cuauhtemoc codices and colonial chronicles—guided and/or written by Spanish priests—can be viewed with suspicion. In effect, these priests, at the same time as they were "documenting" Indigenous reality, were the frontline soldiers of the colonization of Indigenous peoples. While these sources have thus always been suspect, only very recently have modern scholars begun to question their validity and accuracy publicly (Galarza 1992, Mignolo 2006, Florescano 2006). For years, many scholars have taken the words of European chroniclers at face value, even though they were cognizant that many sixteenth–nineteenth-century priests facilitated executions and practiced torture, brutality, and extreme censorship during the colonial era as part of de-Indigenization and mass-conversion projects.[36] Until recently, it was thought that Indigenous peoples, including the Aztec/Mexica, the Zapotec-Mixtec, and the Maya, did not know how to write phonetically or in a precise manner. It was thought that they simply painted pictures and that those who read or interpreted these painted pictures relied on (faulty) memory to tell the stories. In the past generation, because the Maya writing system has been generally deciphered, historians are now actually beginning to reconstruct Mesoamerican history. Similarly, through the work of the late Mexican scholar Joaquín Galarza and his colleagues, we now also know that the Aztec/Mexica utilized a complex system of *escrituras-pinturas* (writings-paintings), developed over several thousand years, originating with the pre-Olmec period. This was a very advanced form of writing, including a precise phonetic component. Galarza (1992) also informs us that the Nahua codices are generally also written in multiple layers of meaning, integrating the linguistic and the visual. He argues that scholars are now reading what Mesoamerican peoples actually wrote, as opposed to interpreting or misinterpreting it.[37] This dynamic is deprivileging the early European friars who have long been credited with interpreting the history, language, knowledge, and maíz-based culture of Indigenous peoples. This process, Galarza argues, will require unlearning much of what has been written, and it will take perhaps two generations for scholars to complete this work. The success of this process will also require understanding that there is a direct relationship between the codices and the lives of people and that this link remains unbroken.

Conclusion

While some will see this work as interdisciplinary, I see it as a meditation, as learning about and actively participating in the continuation of a ceremonial discourse, this in the process of coming to understand how, despite hundreds of years of attempts at erasure, maíz cultures remain resilient.

My research methodology includes my research protocols, collaborative relationships, and elder epistemology; that is, listening to elders and acknowledging, rather than seeking to validate, their knowledge.[38] Elder epistemology includes respect for stories and oral traditions and respect for the elders who pass on their knowledge. My particular work and research is guided by a series of elder interviews (dialogues, actually) and a collaborative research relationship with elders.[39]

It also involves keeping in mind that many scientists consider the creation of maíz one of humanity's greatest feats. Maíz-based peoples have always known and understood this. They all generally tell a variant of how they received maíz, beans, and squash, or the Three Sisters, and how they incorporated them into their cultures. In Mexico, the Three Sisters are known as Las Tres Hermanas. For some, the food complex is corn, beans, and chile, also known as Los Tres Amigos del Pobre, "the three friends of the poor." There, *poor* is synonymous with *campesino*, and campesinos are predominantly Indigenous (Esteva and Marielle 2003). Chile is purportedly the oldest domesticated crop in the Americas, going back possibly nine thousand years (Long-Solís 1998).

Scientists marvel at the horticultural interrelation of corn, beans, and squash. Together, these crops combine to provide a sufficient diet—one that has sustained peoples for several thousands of years on this continent. Dr. Carol Cornelius, in *Iroquois Corn in a Culture-Based Curriculum* (1999), refutes the notions put forth by American and European scholars such as Henry Wallace and William L. Brown (1956) who assert that American Indians had no scientific knowledge of corn, merely a religious understanding of it. As cited in Cornelius 1999, Wallace and Brown posited that while Indians did not know the white man's science, over the millennia, by patience and prayer, they changed the plant more radically than any other plant in the history of humanity. Dr. Cornelius responded: "This paragraph both acknowledges the genetic engineering of Indians, yet determines that improved varieties were an accident tied to religious beliefs" (1999: 160). This attitude, she added, is common to all books on corn in which Indigenous contributions to corn are dispensed with in but several pages.

It is within this context that I have examined the corresponding narratives in regards to whether Mexicans, Mexican Americans, and Central Americans living far from home—most of them urban—remain connected to those ancient maíz narratives.[40]

Figure 3. Temple of the Foliated Cross, Palenque, Chiapas. Courtesy of Foundation for the Advancement of Mesoamerican Studies.

Maíz Sagrado

Francisco Pos and Irma Tzirin Socop

TECPÁN, GUATEMALA—CUNA DE KAQCHIKELES

Eterno maíz, elemento infaltable en la alimentación de los abuelos ancestrales, después de la creación del universo, las aguas, la tierra, los animales, las plantas y el hombre. Al maíz se le denomina con mucho respeto como Madre Maíz, *Qanan Ixim* en el idioma y cultura K'iche', porque de ella mamamos la leche de la vida, porque de ella dependemos para nuestra alimentación, porque su existencia es motivo de alegría y esperanza de una vida. He aquí unas de las razones del porqué se llama Qanan Ixim.

Qanan Ixim, porque cuando se siembra el grano de maíz, se realiza un ritual que comienza desde la alimentación de las personas que participan en la siembra; las personas comen hasta saciarse, para que el grano de maíz sepa que no se está siendo egoísta con los que realizan el trabajo de siembra durante la jornada de trabajo.

Qanan Ixim, porque es seleccionado con mucho cuidado para que la mazorca tenga trece hileras de maíz, para que la siguiente cosecha tenga la misma consistencia y fuerza del maíz a sembrar.

Porque las primeras hojas de milpa que serán utilizadas para envolver el tamal para las comidas, estas serán amarradas al cabo del azadón como muestra de agradecimiento porque este fue un material que participó para que el mismo volviera a nacer y dar vida, por eso se le llama Qanan Ixim.

Qanan Ixim, porque las personas no pueden pisotear el maíz, porque es como faltarle al respeto a la madre que nos ha dado vida; por eso se compara con ella y no se puede pisotearla, porque entonces se está quitando la vida a ella misma.

Sagrado Maíz, porque cuando el maíz es cosechado, la luna debe estar en su fase de luna llena para que el maíz tenga consistencia y perdure durante un año para volver a ser sembrado de nuevo.

Sagrado Maíz, se le denomina porque debe ser secado a la luz del sol por un tiempo de cuarenta días, lo que matemáticamente conlleva el sistema vigesimal que han utilizado nuestros abuelos desde tiempos ancestrales.

Es el Sagrado Maíz porque los abuelos afirman que el maíz tiene oídos y puede escuchar cuando se le trata con respeto, cuando es bien tratado, cuando es recibido con el pom en el momento de llegar a casa cuando es cosechado.

Es Sagrado porque no se puede abrir la troja con mazorca después de las seis de la tarde, porque con esto se está ahuyentando su corazón, su *k'u'x*, por eso se respeta y se deja reposar cuando el sol ha caído.

Por eso, eres Sagrado Maíz.

Sacred Maíz

The eternal corn, indispensable sustenance of our ancestors, after the creation of the universe: the waters, the earth, the animals, the plants, and human beings. With much respect, the corn is viewed as Mother Maíz, *Qanan Ixim*, in the K'iche' language and culture, because our sustenance depends on her, because her existence is the reason to be happy and to have hope in life. Here are some reasons we call her Qanan Ixim.

Qanan Ixim, because when the grains of corn are planted, a ritual takes place that begins with the nourishment of the people that plant the seeds; the people eat until satisfied, so that the grains of corn know that they are not being selfish with those that work the harvest during the growing season.
 Qanan Ixim, because they are selected very carefully so that the ears of corn will have thirteen rows, so that the next harvest has the same consistency and strength starting from when it is planted.

Because the first leaves from the cornfield that are used to wrap tamales for meals will be tied to the *azadón*, the tilling stick, as an example of our appreciation, because it is from this substance that the maíz comes back to life again; that is why we call it Qanan Ixim.

Qanan Ixim, because the people cannot step on our maíz because it would be the same as disrespecting our mother, who has given us life. That's why we compare the maíz with our mother, and that's why we can't step on the maíz because that would be to take the life out of it.

Sacred Maíz, because when the corn is harvested, it must be a full moon so that the corn has consistency and will last during the entire year, so that it can be planted the following year.

Sacred Maíz, because it must be dried by sunlight for forty days, which mathematically contains within it the base-twenty number system that our ancestors have used since ancient times.

It is Sacred Maíz because our ancestors affirm that it has ears and it can hear when it is being treated with respect, when it is well treated, when it is received with incense at the moment it is brought into the home from the harvest.

It is sacred because one can not open a granary that has corncobs in it after six p.m. because it is at this time that the heart of the corn, its *k'u'x*, is being protected. That's why it is respected and allowed to rest at sunset.

That is why you are Sacred Maíz.

CHAPTER ONE

Spiritual Colonization

A Totalizing Reframing Project

The Hopi believe that if you want to teach a person the history or the song that is deeply connected to our history you feed them corn. You're planting this history into the person. That way that history will grow inside him.

—HOPI ARTIST MICHAEL KABOTIE[1]

The peoples of Mesoamerica were no strangers to writing, nor to remembering their histories, particularly in regard to maíz. Despite this, the view widely persists that they were illiterate and unable to record, like the peoples of Europe, their stories, beliefs, and histories.[2] Thus, much of what we know about Indigenous peoples before 1492 and the colonial period is determined, even to this day, by the writings of Spanish friars.

Maíz, the First Books, and the First Recorders of History

Many of the pre-Columbian amoxtlis (codices or books) represented mathematical, astronomical, calendrical, and ceremonial knowledge based on maíz. Boone, in "Maps of Territory, History, and Community in Aztec Mexico" (1998), noted that while there are fifteen surviving pre-Columbian amoxtlis, there are perhaps another 160 colonial-era pictorial codices, often written by priests in collaboration with Indigenous scholars. The amoxtli was a communications technology that ritually governed peoples' daily lives — from birth to death. Unlike Western books, amoxtlis were read from back to front. The Maya, the Mixtecs, and the Mexica wrote the ones that survive.[3] While it was the *tlamatinis* or *Amoxhuaque* (wise elders) who could read the codices, and the *tlacuilo* who painted them, the average person also had a dialogue with amoxtlis via the calendars, which were linked to birthing and naming ceremonies. Indigenous scholar Patrisia Gonzales wrote: "The *amoxtli* was opened ceremoniously; the knowledge contained therein was performed with song, dance and oratory. . . . They are a communication system that combines the spoken, heard (tonality) and felt" (2007: 31–32).

History is also recorded on less known maíz-based calendars with start dates more than five thousand years ago. These calendars, primarily associated with Mesoamerica, speak not only to this history but also to a different worldview, corresponding to ideas about the creation of the cosmos, maíz, and human beings. Citing petroglyph evidence, Cecilio Orozco posited in *The Book of the Sun, Tonatiuh* (1992) that the Aztec Calendar was neither Aztec nor a calendar but actually a living book that developed on different parts of the continent, including what is now the United States, over the course of several thousand years.

Inscriptions at the Maya city of Palenque, Mexico, dated to AD 692, reveal the calendrical systems used by the Maya and other Mesoamerican peoples. June 16, 3122 BC, or *Hun Nal Ye*, marks the "First Seed of Maíz" or the birth of the First Father. November 16, 3121 BC, marks the birth of the First Mother. The date August 13, 3114 BC, corresponds to the end of a world or cosmic era and the beginning of a new one. This new era is what the Aztecs/Mexica referred to as the Fifth Sun (Florescano 1999).

Florescano observed that while Mesoamerican history is dynamic, it is also uniform for some three thousand years in regard to the culture that flowed from the development of maíz (1999: 226). León-Portilla, in *Native Mesoamerican Spirituality* (1980), noted that while a record of writing first appears in 600 BC in Monte Albán, Mexico, the subsequent writing and calendrical systems throughout Mesoamerica show continuity through the sixteenth century.

After the arrival of Europeans in Mesoamerica, two new kinds of writers emerged: Spanish chroniclers (primarily priests) and, later, Christianized Indigenous or "mestizo" writers. There is little evidence that non-Christian Indigenous or mestizo writers publicly wrote opposition literature during the three-hundred-year colonial era, which featured tight censorship. During that era, mostly the friars and other Europeans wrote the "official history" of the colonies. During the Mexican War of Independence (1810–1821), there was an accompanying explosion of literature, fueled by what Victor Turner (1974) refers to as a "primary process." This volcanic eruption, in response to three hundred years of repression, saw Mexican writers "return" to the Aztec/ Mexica for "lost knowledges" and inspiration. Florescano (2002) describes this process as *principio* (first things), a purported return to authenticity. This return was led by *criollos*, or descendants of Spaniards, and not generally by Indigenous peoples.[4] The same process of turning to the Mexica occurred during and after the Mexican Revolution of 1910. It may have also fueled what Carlos Vélez-Ibáñez in *Border Visions* (1996) terms the Chicano Convulsive Transitional Movement of the 1960s and 1970s, in which all looked to their "ancestors" for authenticity. During this era, the ancestral affiliation was generally limited to Aztecs and Mayans. Many Mexican and Chicana/ Chicano writers of the next generation viewed identification with these forebears as "romanticization" and began to de-emphasize Indigeneity. It has taken yet another generation of scholars to move beyond seeing Mexicans and Chicanas/Chicanos as "descendants" of Indigenous peoples and start to see them as Indigenous peoples, and/or as part of the same historical process that produced "gente de maíz."[5] Influencing this discussion are Indigenous scholars from throughout the continent who emphasize the oral tradition and who have written about the narratives of this continent.

The Nondebate of 1524

In 1524, three years after the official military defeat of the Mexica by Spaniards in Mexico, twelve Franciscan friars entered Mexico, commencing an unprecedented project of mass conversion of Indigenous peoples. Shortly after their initial arrival, they conducted a "dialogue" with Mexica elders. A record of the proceedings was kept (Sahagún [1564] 1944), and it clearly shows the inability of the priests to understand Indigenous worldviews and their dismissal of the beliefs and understandings of the Mexica—which were actually based on the much older Maya-Nahua and Teotihuacan-Toltec traditions. The proceedings were temporarily lost, then rescued and edited by the famed Sahagún in 1564. They were censored by the Holy Office of the Inquisition and ensconced in the secret archives of the Vatican for nearly four hundred years before being published.

In this exchange, the Mexica representatives were conscious that they had inherited their ancient knowledge from Tula, Huapalcalco, Huchatlapan, Tlamohuanchan, Yohuallichan, and Teotihuacan. On the other hand, the following is an example of the attitude of the Spanish friars, where they appear to have knowledge of the Mexica worldview but summarily dismiss it: "He is the true God, the one you call Ypalnemoani but never actually knew" (Sahagún [1564] 1944: 67).[6]

Viewed in terms of communication theory, this attitude can be seen as part of a massive and totalizing reframing project: the beginning of a spiritual erasure. The context of the 1524 "dialogue" and the spiritual crusades and military campaigns it inaugurated was disappointment: the conquistadores had come looking for mythical cities of gold. Frustrated in that search, they turned to forced labor to extract riches, which arguably required a "tame" labor force—thus the need for mass conversion. In keeping with this need, the well-coordinated objective of the Spanish priests in New Spain was to continually and systematically demean and destroy all vestiges of Indigenous thought, religion, spirituality, and culture, having determined it to be demonic or witchcraft, while imposing a "God-inspired" worldview and world order upon Indigenous peoples (Séjourné 1962). During this era of colonization, the church and crown had unprecedented access to Indigenous peoples; they were considered the crown's physical property (for its economic interests) and the church's spiritual property (as souls). The priests were encouraged by their belief that Indians were the perfect specimens for conversion, that "they were docile and child-like" (Florescano 2002: 155). Despite this belief, the peoples of Mesoamerica were subjected to quite forcible evangelization during three hundred years of colonial rule, a long time for the church to try out its varied conversion and catechizing methods. That massive reframing project or spiritual colonization continues to reverberate throughout the continent to this day.

Forbes points out in *Columbus and Other Cannibals* (2011) that the key to colonization was an ingenious dual strategy: the soldiers were the brutal enforcers whereas the priests were brought in to purportedly plead for the lives of Indigenous peoples—the equivalent of a good-cop-bad-cop routine. Forbes quotes Antonio Zaldívar, part of the Oñate expedition into New Mexico: "In this manner they will recognize the friars as their benefactors . . . and come to love and esteem them, and to fear us" (123).

The Reframers of the Continent

One of the major accomplishments of those priests during the colonial era was to impose a radical reframing—an alien worldview or cosmovision— upon this continent. In effect, they took one axis mundi and replaced it with a Christian one. They believed they were on a mission from God to convert the "godless natives" who had been under the dominion of the devil himself. It was not until the eighteenth century that scholar Francisco Saverio Clavigero finally wrote *Historia Antigua de México* ([1826] 1964), a secular history of Mexico, which Florescano described as "a story of the Mexican people devoid of the satanic and providential stigmas disseminated by religious chroniclers" (2006: 226). Previous to Clavigero, it was through the Christian lens of the devil that Europeans interpreted the religion of Indigenous peoples. The Spanish priests involved in this reframing endeavor included the well-known sixteenth- and seventeenth-century chroniclers Pedro de Gante ([1558] 1970), Andrés de Olmos ([1547] 1992), Fray Toribio de Benavente Motolinía ([1555] 1971), Durán ([1581] 1967), Juan de Torquemada ([1615] 1975), José de Acosta ([1604] 1970), Diego de Landa ([1566] 1938), Sahagún ([1590] 1997), Juan Bautista Pomar (*Relación de Tezcoco* [1500s] 1941), Antonio de Herrera ([1605–1615] 1945), Vasco de Quiroga ([1535] 1974), Alonso de Zurita ([1500s] 1909), Gregorio García ([1500s] 1981), and Juan de Zumárraga ([1544] 1928). Zumárraga and Olmos (the continent's first anthropologist) were sent to Mexico by King Charles V to assist in the great mass conversion; the Inquisition was initiated there in 1537 (Olmos [1547] 1992). Their task was to prevent the resurgence of pre-Columbian knowledge and spirituality. Ironically, many of the Spanish priests ended up preserving Indigenous knowledge in their writings, which were written in justification of the mass-conversion project but which they often never saw published. León-Portilla wrote this about the chroniclers: "What they rescued in the sixteenth century was little known to most of their European contemporaries. A fear of revival of idolatry prevented its diffusion. It was not until the late 19th century that the ancient manuscripts have begun to be rediscovered in the archives and libraries of Mexico, Guatemala, the United States, Spain, the Vatican, Italy, France and Great Britain" (1980: 34). Their systematic study has only begun to take place recently. This is important because while the colonial-era writers dutifully demonized Indigenous culture, their writings were considered a potential bad influence on Indigenous peoples.

The relative exceptions to the satanic narrative of the early colonial period were Bartolomé de las Casas ([1552] 1974, [1559] 1990, [1500s] 1985) and Francisco de Vitoria ([1500s] 1980). They both believed in the full humanity of Indigenous peoples, though dependent upon their conversion.[7] In defense of native peoples, in 1520, Las Casas complained in a letter to King Charles about the conquistadores: ". . . for which scabrous and bitter reason no word can be more hateful to the Indians than the word

Christians, which, in their language, means demons. And without doubt, they are right, because the actions of these Governors are neither Christian nor humane, but are actions of the devil" (quoted in Berger 1991: 6). While many priests (Gante is another example) and their orders did champion the rights of Indigenous peoples and lash out against the ungodly acts of the conquistadores, they did not treat Indigenous peoples as their spiritual coequals but, at best, as children.[8]

Las Casas advocated forcefully for the Indians and while he won legal concessions, the greed of the conquistadores overwhelmed the declarations from the King of Spain. Their only apparent goal was gold. For example, Cortés said this to the first Aztec ambassador he met: "We have a disease of the heart that can only be cured by gold" (Gómara [1500s] 2000).

While children of the Mexica *pipiltin* (nobility) were encouraged to read and write, the church and the crown specifically forbade them from the Catholic priesthood. Mendieta ([1595–1596] 1997: 86) wrote, "they prefer to be ordered and told what to do." The Colegio de Tlatelolco was created at the site of the Aztec/Mexica calmecac (school of higher learning), where the nobility had been educated. The new college trained them in Latin, Spanish, and Nahuatl, but expressly not for the priesthood. Also, in 1555, the First Mexican Provincial Council banned sermons in native languages, also forbidding "the sale to Indians of a book of fates that was circulating in the Castilian" (Gruzinski 1993: 56).

Added to the list of those who participated in reframing the narratives of this continent were Catholicized Indigenous and mestizo writers who lent their knowledge to the mass-conversion project. After the invasion, European priests sought out the most educated Indigenous peoples to serve as "informants." These informants translated materials for the priests into Latin, Spanish, and Nahuatl, as well as Otomi and Maya. It was not until the twentieth century when they were finally recognized as writers themselves (Galarza 1992). Several of the known informants who assisted Sahagún include Antonio Valeriano, Alonso Vegerano, Martín Jacobita, Pedro de San Buenaventura, and Andrés Leonardo (León-Portilla 1985). Another native scholar, Hernando Ribas, assisted Fray Motolinía in the compilation of his Nahuatl dictionary.

Some sixteenth-century Christianized Indigenous writers were acknowledged for their role in support of the mass-conversion project. A few of these are Fernando Alvarado Tezozomoc (*Crónica Mexicáyotl* [1576] 1998), Fernando de Alva Ixtlilxochitl (*Historia de la Nación Chichimeca* [1610–1640] 2000), Cristóbal del Castillo ([1606] 1991), Martín de la Cruz (Baldiano Codex [1552] 2002), Guaman Poma (1500s; see Adorno 2000),[9] Domingo

Francisco de San Antón Muñón Chimalpahin Quauhtlehuanitzin (Codex Chimalpahin [1621] 1997), and Garcilaso de la Vega ([1609] 1976). Garcilaso was the only native writer who saw his work published during that era (Mignolo 2006).

A War over Images

The mass forced conversion lasted throughout the Spanish-colonial era (1521–1821), and can rightly be viewed not as one event but as a three-hundred-year process or project.[10] It can perhaps also be viewed as a communications laboratory experiment in conducting a war of imagery, as imagery is the primary means by which European friars communicated their evangelization messages.[11] Although Bonfil Batalla (1996) posited that the colonizing project failed, it actually never ceased. Serge Gruzinski wrote in *Images at War* (2001: 2):

> The image exerted a remarkable influence on the discovery, "conquest" and colonization of the New World in the sixteenth century. Because the image—along with written language—constitutes one of the major tools of European culture, the gigantic enterprise of Westernization that swooped down upon the American continent became in part a war of images that perpetuated itself for centuries and—according to all indications—may not be over even today.

Other scholars have also examined the mass-conversion project, including this war over imagery, and likewise perceive it as a continuous event or process. Florescano (1994, 2002, 2006), D. Carrasco (1990), Anzaldúa (1987), Bonfil Batalla (1996), Gruzinski (1993, 1994, 2001), Mundy (1996), Galarza (1992), Broyles-González (2001a), Mignolo (2006), and P. Gonzales (2007) all posit that the legacy of the mass-conversion effort is still with us today. Their work reveals the colonial origins of the view that sees Indigenous peoples from the south as aliens in the United States.

Some scholars (Arnoldo De León 2002, Santa Ana 2002) track the precise origins of those ideas to the nineteenth century. These ideas/images represent Mexican men as lazy, violent, and bloodthirsty; Mexican women as easy; and both as drunkards, foreigners, backward people, obstacles to progress and civilization. In their totality, the images depict Mexicans as less than human, not deserving of full legal rights, not belonging. And even though not all Mexicans are immigrants to this country, they are often framed as such by U.S. media, to great negative effect. Literature on media stereotypes suggests that projecting Mexicans as immigrants activates negative ideas about them: "Immigration is not simply an issue regarding migration but about preconceived ideas of Mexicans (Hispanics)" (Domke, McCoy, and Torres 2003: 126). This study found that if immigration is framed as an ethical and human-rights issue, people respond more positively; if it is framed as a resource-competition issue, the response is always more negative (130).

A similar formulation can be observed in the 1500s debate regarding whether Indigenous peoples were human. If the question was "Are they demonic?" the cause was lost and it was determined that Indigenous peoples were not entitled to human rights. But if it was framed as "Can they be saved?" that presumably favored the humanitarian position. However, both frames were still European. The shared assumption was that the devil—a concept that did not exist in pre-Columbian America—had dominion over the people and they needed to be saved (Vento 1998).

Arguably, those preconceived ideas about Mexicans and Central Americans in the United States are associated with many of the same frames and metaphors that project Indigenous peoples as savages as a way to keep them/us in the past. As Cynthia-Lou Coleman noted in "A War of Words" (1996: 189), some metaphors or stereotypes associated with American Indians are that they are thieves and interlopers, irrational, unlawful, undemocratic. This may help to explain why even in the modern era, depictions of women or men with brown skin—something associated with Indigeneity—are rare in Latino media and virtually absent in Latina beauty magazines (Johnson, David, and Huey-Ohlisson 2003: 167).[12]

Thus, while negative ideas/images of Mexicans can be found as part of U.S. media stereotypes traceable to the 1800s, they are virtually the same as the images and stereotypes of Indigenous peoples formulated by Spanish priests in the early 1500s, including the belief that Indigenous peoples were illiterate. These images were unquestionably part of a larger framework or project, backed up by the use of force during the colonial era. The Spanish-colonial war of images, which was copied, in effect, by later European colonizers, arguably is what made it possible to portray Mexicans and Central Americans as aliens and invaders today.

Reframing Tools: Indigenous-Style Communications

In examining the tools that were used to impose or reframe the story of the continent in this mass-conversion project, one becomes cognizant that they are generally Indigenous media. Examples are post-Cuauhtemoc codices created in the style and manner of pre-Cuauhtemoc ones, and *lienzos* (painted linens) used as teaching instruments for the propagation of the Christian faith.[13] With regard to the use of these and other media, the writings of the Spanish priests of the colonial era provide ample proof of their assumptions and intentions. For example, Diego Valadés, in *Retórica Cristiana* ([1579] 1989), wrote that it was the Franciscans who first used imagery/paintings for religious instruction because Indians did not use letters. Thousands of churches and chapels were painted for such purposes, predicated on the misguided belief that Indigenous peoples were illiterate.

This massive and totalizing project also included the construction of churches (utilizing forced Indian labor) with the stones of Indigenous temples and pyramids—and on the very same foundations. Huge books filled with imagery were also a means of instruction. Yet mass conversion wasn't a matter of propaganda alone; it was assisted by the use of force. A message was being communicated, particularly with the churches atop the pyramids: the Christian church is superior to the Indigenous demonic temple.

Relatedly, the media described above came to be associated with a specific physical place where religious instruction occurred, namely the atrium of the monastery, the church, the religious school. The use of thousands of religious paintings and imagery that imitated Indigenous methods and styles of communication "was the method by which Indians were Christianized" (Florescano 2002: 157). At religious schools, children learned catechism through songs and Christian psalms, danza, theater, and Western musical instruments, "which they fused with Indigenous music and traditions" (160).

The church, which saw devils everywhere, continually imprisoned, tortured, hung, and executed suspected idolaters throughout the colonial era. This repression precipitated constant rebellions throughout the continent.[14] Even "humanist" priests, such as Sahagún and Las Casas, were convinced that the native codices and calendars were demonic.[15] The priests forced a new calendar on the people, which was the most radical change they implemented because its primary objective was the erasure of memory. The Indigenous calendars were useful for predicting rains and regulating planting and the (maíz) harvest, calendars that had been developed over thousands of years in the Americas. They were replaced by a religious calendar (first the Julian, then the Gregorian) developed over millennia on another continent that commemorated European actions and doings that had little to do with the Americas (Florescano 2002: 164–66).

Oral Traditions and the Public Square

The attempt by Spanish priests to convert the Indigenous peoples of the continent en masse started with an effort to destroy pre-Columbian knowledge while at the same time making use of the very same media that Mesoamerican peoples had been utilizing to perform their agriculturally based ceremonies. Prior to the arrival of Europeans in Mesoamerica, danza, ritual dancing, was part of an integrated system, which also included music, poetry, and song, that was used to communicate the culture, including creation, origin, and migration stories and historical events. The primary function of these public rituals and ceremonies, which were connected to the uniform calendars, was to ritually govern peoples' births, lives, and deaths. Instructions were recorded on the amoxtlis or codices, which communicated culture, preserved memory, and helped to unify the many diverse populations. Added to these media were the huehuetlahtolli or the ancient word, a guide for moral instruction. These elements together represented what Carey describes as "ritualized communication," in which the emphasis is not simply on communicating a message but on representing "shared beliefs" (1992: 18).

What changed after the arrival of the Spanish friars is that these public media were used for the purposes of mass conversion.[16] The communication of Christian teachings was highly visual and symbolic and manifested even in the architecture: temples/pyramids, the most public and visible symbol of Indigenous religion and spirituality, were destroyed and churches built atop them. These and other efforts were designed to publicly communicate the message that Christianity was superior. To ensure that the people did not completely reject the message of the friars, syncretized communication and ceremonies were used to communicate the compatibility of the old religion with the new.

Syncretism and Semiotics

In examining the tools used for mass conversion, one can also see (modern) visual-communication theories at work. The use of these devices, which relied heavily on Indigenous imagery, for the purposes of mass conversion involved a semiotic process that incorporated signs and symbols that were familiar to Indigenous peoples (Jensen 1995).[17] In this case, the priests who had become familiar with the meaning and importance of Indigenous imagery and history exploited that knowledge. Gruzinski (2001) has noted that since the arrival of Columbus, a war over images has been waged. Part of the reason for the contentiousness of this ongoing war is the issue of syncretism.[18] This issue is directly tied to the war over imagery, particularly in Mexico. During the repressive colonial era, for obvious reasons of survival, oppositional narratives took the form of syncretic communications, much like the messages used for mass conversion. The principal example of syncretic communication is the mutual attempt to link Christianity with the ancient spirituality of the continent, including the idea relayed in the Testerian Codices that Jesus ate tortillas with his disciples at the Last Supper (Galarza and Monod-Becquelin 1992: 48–49).

The image of Tonantzin or Guadalupe is the consummate icon in the struggle over images. Chicana scholar Broyles-González wrote that Tonantzin/Guadalupe represented a monumental struggle beyond imagery:

> The peoples that were being subjected to mass-conversions had to relate to the images, and in that sense, the image of the Virgen de Guadalupe—a brown virgin—was the quintessential or crown jewel of images. (2001a: 657)

It was not until 1531 and the purported appearance of the Virgen de Guadalupe, on the same hill where Tonantzin (Earth Mother) was venerated, that the peoples of Mexico purportedly adopted the new religion en masse.[19] As Rudolfo Anaya also noted in "Aztlán: A Homeland Without Borders" (1989: 239), the linking of Guadalupe and Tonantzin, viewed as a subversive act, became the most important aspect of syncretism.[20]

The literature regarding la Otra Conquista informs us that syncretism was a two-way street, creating a space for Indigenous peoples, oftentimes in the very place of Christian instruction (churches and monasteries). An example of this is manifested in the Codex of Tlatelolco, the Codex Mexicanus, "which discreetly marked the correspondences, in the secrecy of memories, under Christian images or by the re-use of old symbols" (Gruzinski 1993: 62). Another example is the hiding of ancient Indian narratives in the *cantares* or religious songs: "Indians preserved the songs in writing, sprinkling them with Christian terms to thwart the censors" (57).

In the Other Conquest, the church was not unaware of the pitfalls of syncretism. This syncretic project certainly created a space for Indigenous resilience, yet the church tolerated it for fear that a total rejection of things Indigenous would cause Indigenous peoples to completely reject Christianity. Ultimately, the driving force making syncretism sustainable was that the Spanish friars were always ready to subject Indigenous peoples to the whip to regulate which forms of syncretism were permissible.

Gruzinski wrote:

> These inflections, these displacements, were not mind games or products of an abstract confrontation between great entities that for convenience we call cultures, but concrete outcomes of practices as diverse as the painting of glyphs, writing, map-drawing or plastic creation. By means of these practices the revolution of modes of expression and communication launched by the Spanish colonization took place. (1993: 69)[21]

For Gruzinski, Guadalupe also functions as the ultimate justification for la Otra Conquista. He construes the use of her image as the exploitation of Indigenous prior knowledge. After many years, the image itself transforms into prior knowledge, becoming, on the surface, the counterstory of the continent.

I describe the image—which I consider to be an amoxtli itself—metaphorically in the following manner: Maíz is the story. Guadalupe is the counterstory. She is alien, and yet she is also native: Tonantzin. Maíz is Quetzalcoatl and, in her *tilma* imagery, Guadalupe triumphs over the serpent. Yet Quetzalcoatl, the feathered serpent, is also the morning star that appears in the east, and may be Saint Thomas. And the triumphant Guadalupe/Tonantzin is brown. Maíz is not rejected but instead utilized as the Holy Eucharist. And thus the story and counterstory are fused. The original story and frame reside inside the counterstory and the counterframe. This is a deep story—an historia profunda.

Maíz as Civilizational Impulse

Numerous scholars of Mesoamerica agree that maíz was its civilizational impulse: Mexican scholars Bonfil Batalla (*México Profundo*, 1996), Florescano (*Memoria Indígena*, 1999; *National Narratives in Mexico*, 2006), and Martínez Parédez (*Un Continente y Una Cultura*, 1960; *El Popol Vuh Tiene Razon*, 1968) contextualize the Indigenous roots of Mexican peoples and the Mexican nation as the living presence of Mesoamerica. In this sense, the people themselves, from Mexico and Central America, are Mesoamerica today.[22] They represent the resilience of maíz culture. The above-named scholars' examination of stories, myths, and narratives, and of identity formation, indicates that maíz was the civilizational impulse that created the continent's maíz-based cultures, including Mesoamerica. Bon-fil Batalla's work led him to conclude that surface Mexico, that which was European, foreign, and imposed, was part of an imagined Mexico. *México profundo*, on the other hand, continues to be Indigenous. Mexico, he posits, cannot be analyzed without understanding the process of de-Indigenization: "De-Indianization is not the product of biological mixture, but the product of ethnocide" (1996: 17). He further argues that throughout history, de-Indigenization has forced Mesoamericans to renounce their collective Indigenous identities: "Separation from cultural patrimony is the final process of de-Indianization" (18). We are left to wonder: what kinds of human beings result from this process?

Florescano's work buttresses the argument that maíz and Mesoamerica continue to be a part of the living culture of most Mexicans and Central Americans.[23] Many scholars, such as Ramón Gutiérrez (2000), scoff at the notion of unity and continuity between Mesoamerica and present-day Mexico and Central America, particularly in regard to mestizos. This is countered by Martínez Parédez's primary thesis, one continent and one culture united by belief in a serpentine philosophy manifested by the concepts of Quetzalcoatl, Kukulkan, Gucumatz, Viracocha, and so on. This culture was created by a people called the Tamoanchanes or Toltecs (1960: 35), who were the predecessors of the Olmecs, the Maya, and the later Aztec/Mexica.[24] The Tamoanchanes/Toltecs, according to him, were learned peoples and possessors of all the arts of civilization. Their religion-philosophy, made possible by the development of maíz, was mathematical and scientific, and was not polytheistic, as claimed by the Spanish priests. In spreading their knowledge, they learned Nahuatl in the process. Their teachings can nowadays be considered Maya-Nahuatl, an ancient synthesis of Toltec-Mesoamerican culture, whose influence extended from Alaska to Patagonia (Martínez Parédez 1960: 54). While the works of Martínez Parédez are not common knowledge to Mexican Americans, they did form part of the core philosophy of Teatro Campesino in the 1960s–1970s, particularly in Luis Valdez's *Pensamiento Serpentino* (1973).

Along with the aforementioned works, a basic examination of migration codices is crucial and includes the seminal *In Amoxtli, in Tlacatl* (Galarza 1992) and *Para Leer la Tira de la Peregrinación* (Galarza and Libura 2000). Galarza's recent decipherment of the amoxtlis is monumental in that it potentially affects virtually all the literature on Mesoamerica. His work has begun to take the guesswork out of the escrituras-pinturas.[25] Prior to his work, the Aztec/Mexica codices of ancient Mexico had long been considered illustrations, as opposed to precise writings. As such, much of what

Western society knew about the Aztec/Mexica and Mesoamerica was/is marred by misinterpretation, framed by colonial Spanish priests. Arguably, little good can be learned regarding Mexican Indigenous peoples, cultures, and narratives if the five-hundred-year-old good-versus-evil/God-versus-the-devil frame or lens is utilized.

It was precisely this biased frame that prevented the earlier decipherment of the Maya and Aztec/Mexica codices, along with the seeming inability to comprehend the cultural significance of Teotihuacan. In *Memoria Indígena* (1999), Florescano revealed that to understand the maíz-based civilization of Teotihuacan is to understand the Americas. Teotihuacan, he asserted, is actually the ancient Tollan of the Toltecs, long thought to be a mythical city in the sky. Tollan/Teotihuacan is where Mesoamerica's philosophy and culture congealed, and from there, they spread throughout the continent. Understanding this has partly come about through the recent decipherment of Maya writings long thought to also be pictographs/hieroglyphics or illustrations rather than a language with precise meanings; but this information is also to be found in the *Popol Vuh*, the most ancient book of the Maya. Through Galarza's work, we are now learning the actual writings of the tlamatinis (wise ones). In the classic dialogue between the Franciscans and the Indigenous elders of Anahuac in the early 1520s, the elders informed the Franciscans that they themselves were but functionaries or bureaucrats and that only the tlamatinis, many of whom already had been killed, could adequately answer their questions because they had been trained to read the ancient books and had the requisite knowledge about the nature of the universe (León-Portilla 1985). Florescano (1999: 35) also refers to them as the Amoxhuaque, that is, scholars learned in the ancient codices.

Scholars have actually long been aware of the misinterpretations of Mesoamerican written languages. As Gruzinski notes: "The conquest forced them [Indigenous peoples] into a space entirely invented by western Europe, imposed by the Spanish and labeled with superimposed terms and concepts—superstitions, beliefs, cults, sacrifices, adoration, gods, idols, ceremonies, etc." (1993: 15). As part of this inventing and labeling, peoples were divided into literate and illiterate categories. It is this artificial division that later resulted in historians studying lettered peoples and anthropologists studying those purportedly without letters.

The works of the aforementioned (Indigenous) Mexican scholars, as well as the oral traditions of Indigenous elders, ensure that Mexican narratives and non-Indigenous counternarratives are discussed with the benefit of Indigenous epistemologies, research methodologies, and paradigms, and of insight from living Indigenous peoples.

The Fluidity of Identity and an Evolving Indigenous Identity

In *Voices in the Kitchen* (2006), Meredith Abarca understands the centrality of food and the kitchen to Mexican and Mexican American women and culture; while she acknowledges pre-Columbian connections, she does not explicitly explore those deep connections.[26] Although Broyles-González does not focus on food or maíz per se, in her essay "Colonizing the Colonizer: The Popular Indianization of Catholicism" (2001a) she asserts that native/Chicana/Latina women, not men, have been instrumental in passing along both Indigenous spirituality and native traditions in the Mexican community.[27]

Like other scholars, Chicana/Chicano scholars have generally framed and examined Mesoamerica as a civilization from the past, not as their present reality. Through this backward-looking frame, Chicanas/Chicanos (as well as Mexicans and Central Americans) are perceived as the descendants of Mesoamericans, not as part of live and dynamic Indigenous or maíz-based cultures. Due to the policies of de-Indigenization, they have generally not been recognized by society, or by themselves, as Indigenous, though this is now changing, as evidenced by the works of Patrisia Gonzales (2012), Juan Gómez-Quiñones (2012), and others mentioned in this chapter.

The controversial issue of Mexican American identity, fluid, evolving, and at times contradictory, informs the literature about the resilience of maíz culture. The era of the late 1960s and early 1970s was a time when many Chicanas/Chicanos viewed themselves as having inherited a "glorious Aztec past." On the other hand, some simply saw themselves as mestizo, not Indigenous—at least not in the present tense. A few Chicana/Chicano scholars saw these same peoples as Indigenous and generally as part of Mesoamerica, albeit de-Indigenized. How scholars identify these groups (or themselves) has implications relative to cultural resilience and the survival of (maíz) stories and narratives.

During the 1960s–1970s, Chicana/Chicano popular culture was typified by expressions of Indigeneity but not within the framework conceived by Florescano, Bonfil Batalla, Broyles-González, and others. Most accepted the Bering Strait theory or narrative—of peoples having migrated from Asia to this continent some twelve to twenty thousand years ago.[28] In this schema, the ancestors of Indigenous Mexican peoples slowly migrated southward into Mexico, eventually developing into the Olmec, Mayan, and Toltec civilizations, with the Aztecs/Mexica arriving in Mexico later from Aztlan.[29] Chicanas/Chicanos became the inheritors of this timeline/framework and narrative. They were not contextualized as Indigenous peoples but rather as "descendants of" Indigenous peoples. Even when they were conceived of as mestizos, the Indigenous part of the equation was relegated to the past.

Aside from Armando Rendón's *Chicano Manifesto* (1971), many scholars point to Rodolfo Acuña as having originated this view of Chicano history as continuous and unified. However, in this initial period, virtually all Chicana/Chicano writers and scholars were associated with this narrative and contextualization, a narrative that included the story of the ancestors of Chicanos leaving Aztlan.[30] While Acuña is known for his widely heralded *Occupied America* (1999; first edition 1972), it was his earlier work, *A Mexican American Chronicle* (1971), that put forth the Aztlan narrative.[31] Later scholarship by Chicanas/Chicanos began to move away from the idea that all Mexicans had migrated from Aztlan. Indigeneity was brushed off as romanticized or culturally nationalistic history, or as applying only to Mexico's culturally isolated populations.[32] This paradigmatic shift resulted in a dramatic de-emphasis of Indigeneity within Chicana/Chicano studies. Recent exceptions include the works of D. Carrasco (1990), Anzaldúa (1987), Elizondo (1988), Broyles-González (1994), Vélez-Ibáñez (1996), Vigil (1998), Menchaca (2001), Maestas (2003), Hernández-Ávila (2000), and P. Gonzales (2007, 2012).

Anzaldúa, in *Borderlands/La Frontera* (1987), and Elizondo, in *The Future Is Mestizo* (1988), have been instrumental in speaking to notions of an Indigenized *mestizaje*,[33] a concept of racial and cultural mixture far different than José Vasconcelos's (1920) concept of *la raza cósmica* (the cosmic race).[34] Angie Chabram-Dernersesian has argued in "I Throw Punches for My Race" (2006) that Vasconcelos's concept, while seemingly inclusive, was anti-Indigenous. It helped to obliterate contemporary Indigenous-mestizo peoples and their cultures. This, she posited, was accomplished through the romanticization of the pre-Columbian Aztecs-Mayans-Toltecs (not the nomadic Apaches or Comanches), and by contextualizing Indigeneity as something disconnected from contemporary reality. In "Refiguring Aztlan" (2001), Rafael Pérez-Torres argues that (1960s–1970s) Chicanos owe their nationalism to Vasconcelos and post-Revolutionary Mexico.[35] Not all Chicanos subscribed to Vasconcelos's ideas, as evidenced by the above-named scholars. Elizondo (1988) predicts that in the future, the whole world will be mestizo. Anzaldúa (1987) argues that in the future, Mexicans will once again recognize their Indigeneity. Anzaldúa, in particular, is also credited with empowering Chicanas/Chicanos to embrace multiple and fluid identities, an idea that is seemingly antithetical to nationalist ideas that permeated the 1960s–1970s (Davalos 2001).[36]

In *Aztecas del Norte* (1973), Forbes's primary thesis is that Mexicans are *Anishinaabe*, or Indigenous to the continent,[37] and that many Mexican Americans in the U.S. Southwest, given their long residence there, are also part Pueblo, Hopi, Navajo, Apache, and so on. What Forbes (1961–1962, 1973), Vélez-Ibáñez (1996), Vigil (1998), Menchaca (2001), and P. Gonzales (2007, 2012) all argue is that culturally, Mexican Americans are part of the same continuum that created Mesoamerican civilizations, thus Indigenous. From various standpoints, scholars have, in the past, argued that most Mexicans are actually mestizos, though Forbes has long argued that so is everyone else . . . that the whole world is mestizo, and that mixture cannot be a disqualification from being Indigenous (Forbes 1973).[38]

While initially criticized as essentialist by postmodern scholars, Vigil's *From Indians to Chicanos* (1998) is now recognized for formulating Chicanas/Chicanos as Indigenous peoples, not descendants of them, as many of the early Chicano scholars claimed.[39] He connects Chicanas/Chicanos to maíz, with its seven-thousand-year legacy, and to four historical stages: the pre-Columbian period; the Spanish-colonial era; Mexican Independence and nationalism; and the Anglo period—"from Indians to peasants to migrants to immigrants" (4).

The work of Vélez-Ibáñez (1996) asserts minimally two-thousand-year-old connections between the cultural regions of central and northern Mexico and the U.S. Southwest. The connecting thread, he notes, is agriculture, namely maíz, beans, squash, and chile. He also noted that the kiva, the ball game, Quetzalcoatl, platform mounds, maíz, and the Katsina—all associated with the ancient Hohokam, Mogollon, and Anasazi in the U.S. Southwest—have roots in or connections to Mexico or Mesoamerica. He argues that there never was a cultural desert between the regions: "The border is in the mind. In the minds of many, the maíz, the obsidian, the turquoise, the macaw feathers, the shells, the hides and the parrots are a testament that there have never been borders" (267).

Insurgent Metaphors

In *Brown Tide Rising* (2002), Santa Ana examines how the lives of Mexicans and Latinos[40] are debased through metaphors or frames. His book is a study of textual metaphors in the (Los Angeles) media during the mid-1990s in relation to immigration. Here, he documents how the media aided in the construction of Mexicans and Latinos as alien intruders invading the U.S. house. The primary media images to emerge from this era are of Mexicans running across the border, including traffic signs that project illegality and illegitimacy of human beings. All this amounts to a metaphoric mapping. What is projected is that all Mexicans and Latinos are illegal and that immigrants are to be equated with animals. And because civil and human rights pertain only to human beings, one cannot be racist against animals. While Santa Ana concludes that these metaphors can be traced to the Manifest Destiny era of the 1830s and 1840s, one can again argue that images of this nature can be traced back further, to the Spanish-colonial era of the 1500s–1800s. The "God-inspired" master narratives of Manifest Destiny and Spanish colonialism end up clashing on the same geographic landscape in the nineteenth century. However, the Spanish/Hispanic[41] and Anglo narratives agree with respect to Indigenous/Mexican peoples: both continue to see them as outsiders and peoples to be culturally dominated.

Santa Ana's analysis and that of frame theorist George Lakoff are useful for analyzing the frames created by the sixteenth-century-era Spanish priests, particularly in their war against Satan and his allies. In *Moral Politics: How Liberals and Conservatives Think* (2002), Lakoff notes that the demonic is used today as a metaphor for both liberal and conservative politics. In the eyes of the Spanish priests, the holy-demonic distinction was a literal divide between the Euro-Christian world and Indigenous America.[42] The narrative they created may be the source of current stereotypes of Mexican/Indigenous peoples as not fully human, not deserving of full human rights, not possessing rational minds, being backward, lacking history, and being demonic.[43] The existence of such negative imagery may help to explain why peoples search out their own stories and their own metaphors. As Linda Tuhiwai Smith noted in *Decolonizing Methodologies* (1999: 35): as human beings, "the need to tell our stories remains the powerful imperative of a powerful form of resistance."

Santa Ana (2002) addresses the issue of countering the hegemonic master narrative of history with insurgent narratives. He writes that countering the master narrative is done by presenting facts, then creating insurgent metaphors (312). In this respect, the continent's maíz stories produce alternative metaphors, but they do not constitute counternarratives. Instead, they are their own narratives. Lakoff (2002) wrote that reframing is a necessary tool when countering opponents. For Lakoff, reframing is not rebuttal but rather the use of higher-level frames. At the same time, he argued that the problem is not the lack of a common vocabulary with which to counter master narratives by engaging in political discourse: "The vocabulary exists. It's the concept/vision of co-equalness that doesn't exist" (384). In a later work, *Don't Think of an Elephant* (2004), he asserted that the most powerful words/ideas and the frames that stick are the ones that conjure fear.[44] Fear works because it affects "the cognitive unconscious—structures in the brain that we cannot consciously access. . . . We also know frames through language. All words are defined relative to conceptual frames. When you hear a word, its frame is activated in your brain" (xv). In this respect, one can see the sixteenth-century priests as masters of reframing in that they created a world that was not only completely alien to Indigenous peoples but ensured that to maintain the old ways was to be in league with the devil.

For Linda Tuhiwai Smith (1999), reframing (in the modern context) begins with rejecting colonialism and imperialism as the primary marker by which nations, peoples, and civilizations should be defined. Not to do so privileges European contact (24).[45] Similarly: "The project of reframing is related to defining the problem or issue and determining how best to solve the problem. . . . Reframing occurs in other contexts where Indigenous people resist being boxed and labeled according to categories which do not fit" (19–21). This is also, she argues, why colonizing vocabularies, colonizing frames, Western conceptions of time, and Western categorizing schemas are rejected. Countering those frames, she argues, is a centering process in which Indigenous research and theory are no longer marginalized, erased, or trivialized.[46] However, according to Smith, decolonization is not simply about reframing or retelling stories/narratives, it also includes rehumanization, what Paulo Freire, in *Pedagogy of the Oppressed* (1970), simply terms humanization. Rejecting notions of authenticity, Smith writes, is also critical in reframing and decolonization; it is usually government authorities who determine who is Indigenous and a citizen and who is not. Part of reframing, in this context, because it is part of decolonizing work, is conducting research that claims and names. It is also conducting emancipatory social research that encourages specific action to resolve specific issues. Her research has found that the reason Indigenous issues do not get addressed appropriately is that governments generally frame Indigenous issues and peoples as problems. She wrote: "Many Indigenous activists have argued that such things as mental illness, alcohol and suicide are not about psychological and individualized failure but about colonization or the lack of collective self-determination" (1999: 153). Similarly, her research indicates that framing and media stereotypes cannot adequately be addressed without first examining their colonial roots in relation to pre-1492 cultures.[47]

American Indian Views of Myth, History, and Memory

On the topic of writing, history, and memory, many U.S. Indigenous scholars limit their scope to North America, specifically the parts of it north of

Mexico. They generally affirm that native peoples did not record time or history in the same manner of Europeans. Instead, there was a greater reliance on collective memory, particularly through the memorialization of events that had a profound effect on the "psychic life of a community" (Deloria 1973).[48] In the south, Indigenous peoples utilized both written and oral traditions but began to rely more heavily on the oral after Europeans began to destroy Indigenous forms of writing.

In *A Forest of Time* (2002), Peter Nabokov wrote that Europeans have always questioned the capability of American Indians to store history and to recall it accurately. As cited in Nabokov (6), Dr. Samuel Johnson asked: "What can a nation that has not letters tell us of its origins?" It is virtually the same question that José de Acosta asked Joan de Tovar several centuries earlier in the 1500s: "How could the Indians, without writing, remember so many things?" (Florescano 2006: 73). Anishinaabe activist and author Walt Bresette answered the first question in *Walleye Warriors* (Whaley and Bresette 1994: 12) by pointing out that "the United States has great libraries but poor memories; the *Anishinabe* the reverse." For Nabokov, the literature indicates that from the very beginning of European contact, Europeans have in effect reduced Indigenous history to myth/legend/folktale, "etic categories imposed by outsiders" (2002: 65) and equated with falsehood, even though it is clearly established that myth and chronicle both contain history. Where and how history is stored is, in effect, irrelevant; no one methodology is necessarily superior to another.

In *The American Indian Mind in a Linear World* (2003), Donald Fixico observed that the Indigenous methodology is story and narrative concerned with morality and future. This methodology, argues Fixico, is not concerned with when but rather why and how (24–25).

In *Native Science* (2000), Gregory Cajete observed that the metaphoric mind "communicates and relates to the world in the more holistic structures of oral stories, linguistic metaphors, images and intuitions" (29). Stories, he asserted, are science. In a later work, Cajete observes that myth and story form the nexus for historical information. In *Spirit of the Game: An Indigenous Wellspring* (2005: 42), he affirmed these ideas: "Story is a primary structure through which humans think, relate and communicate." He added that story is both content and oral tradition, and the primary vehicle for communicating the culture.

Related to how memory is stored and communicated, particularly in regard to maíz narratives, the work of Joseph Campbell is important. His ideas are relevant to pre-Columbian times, as he notes that all peoples employ myths to make sense of the world. He also noted the following, in an interview with Bill Moyers, about ritual: "A ritual is an enactment of a myth. By participating in a ritual, you are participating in a myth" (Moyers and Campbell 1991: 103). Ritual and ceremony, he noted, are but a collective manner of storing and communicating memory.

In *The Myths of the Opossum* (1993), López Austin's primary thesis is that the foundational knowledge of the continent is preserved within the knowledge of the foods, plants, medicines and animals that inhabit the world of Indigenous myths. In a later work, included in *Sin Maíz No Hay País* (Esteva and Marielle 2003), he is more specific about the centrality of maíz. In his essay, "Cuatro Mitos Mesoamericanos del Maíz" ("Four Mesoamerican Myths About Maíz," 2003: 29), he simply writes: "Humans domesticated maíz. In turn, maíz domesticated humans." He further posits that everything about humans and maíz is intertwined with myth, including creation, history, writing, music, dance, and spirituality.

The Aztlan Narratives and the Map Literature

While much has been written on the possible location of Aztlan, the discussion between 1961 and 2000 took place without the benefit of maps. While there is a long tradition of locating Mexican Indigenous peoples in what is today the United States on 1500s–1800s-era maps, there is scant mention of these maps when discussing the purported pre-Columbian migrations.[49] This question formed part of my original research and is relevant not because the maps locate the, or an, actual homeland but rather because this nationalized migration narrative has been permanently etched into the Chicano psyche, so much so that it comes close to eclipsing the much older maíz narratives.

Some early chroniclers who traveled to what is now the U.S. Southwest cite codices and Indigenous sources in their claim that New Mexico was where Aztlan was located (Villagrá [1610] 1933). Jerónimo de Zárate Salmerón ([1626–1627] 1966), writing from New Mexico, pointed northward towards Lake Copalla (purportedly the Great Salt Lake in what is now Utah) as the Aztec point of departure. This coincides with the idea of a departure from a lake, a story also told in the Aubin Codex ([1576] 1963), the Boturini Codex ([1530–1541] 2000), and the 1500s Sigüenza map.

In regard to maps, only one modern scholar, Joseph Sánchez in *Explorers, Traders, and Slavers: Forging the Old Spanish Trail, 1678–1850* (1997), acknowledges their existence. Although he dedicates a chapter to this topic, he engages the theme not in terms of possible Indigenous migrations but rather in terms of legendary places, including Teguayo Lake (the Great Salt Lake). Regarding Teguayo, Alonso Posada wrote in 1686 (as cited in Thomas 1982: 42):

> Beyond this nation from seventy leagues, in the same northwest direction one enters afterwards between some hills at a distance of fifty leagues more or less, the land which the Indians of the north call Teguayo and the Mexican Indians call Copola. . . . The same old tradition states that from the region came not only the Mexican Indians, who were the last, but all the rest of the nations which in different times, were settling in these lands and kingdoms of New Spain.

Posada clarifies his meaning on the topic: "They mean that this applies to Guatemala and all the rest of the kingdoms and provinces of Peru and those which are contiguous on the mainland." Whether Posada's account is true or not is not at issue here; what it simply affirms is that there is a substantial literature—including maps—over a span of centuries that generally points to what is today the Great Salt Lake region or other points north as the point of origin of Indigenous peoples of Mexico and Central America.

Indigenous narratives on origins and migrations are generally remanded by non-Indigenous scholars into the realm of fable. This includes discussions regarding Aztlan. In *Mapping the Transmississippi West, 1540–1861* (1957), Carl Wheat discussed citations on several maps of a place called the Antigua Residencia de los Aztecas (Ancient Dwelling of the Aztecs). Other maps he cited point to the Great Salt Lake as the place of origin of Mexican Indigenous peoples. The maps include the 1847 Disturnell map, the 1804 Humboldt map, the 1768 Alzate map, and the 1729 Barreiro map (see appendix 2).[50] Wheat dismissed as fabrication the maps' information about origins and migrations. However, though he was dismissive of the idea of Aztlan or Teguayo, he also wrote about the Sea of the West and ancient organized societies in California: "This is why our ancient Spaniards, from the time of Don Fernando Cortés down to the present, have longed to discover and settle the coast of California, because of many of the reports they had of the people who lived in those places, and the fact that the Mexican nation emerged from them" (101). The belief that these ideas are but fabrications could explain why modern scholars, including Chicana/Chicano and Indigenous scholars, have stayed away from the subject. The irony, given the centrality of Aztlan in the Chicana/Chicano 1960s–1970s imagination, is that these maps did not contribute to that same imagination.

Indigenous and Western Mapping Traditions

An examination of the conceptual difference between Indigenous and Western mapping is enlightening in regard to how worldview shapes mapmaking. Writing in *Painted Books and Indigenous Knowledge in Mesoamerica* (2005), Boone posited that unlike Western maps, Indigenous maps contained not simply geography but story, history, and narrative. For this reason, it is difficult to distinguish escrituras-pinturas from maps. Nevertheless, as Boone noted, it is known that conquistador Hernán Cortés was given maps by the Aztecs/Mexica; apparently no such pre-Columbian maps have survived. Mark Warhus, in *Another America* (1997), noted that not all Indigenous maps were printed or designed in the form of European-style cartography, nor were they all terrestrial in nature (Keski-Säntti et al. 2003).

While the maps were the route by which I indirectly came upon my maíz research, Martínez Parédez in *Un Continente y Una Cultura* (1960)[51] and Girard in *Los Mayas* (1966) suggest that embedded within the thousand-year-old Aztlan migration story is a much older story, a deep story involving a bird and serpent and the maíz-based culture of the Toltecs/Tamoanchanes. This appears to be the historia más profunda (most profound story), relative to maíz, of this continent.[52]

Maíz Culture in the Twenty-First Century

There is no question that despite industrialization, high technology including genetic modification, and unfair trade practices by global corporations, maíz culture is alive and well among Indigenous and Indigenous-based peoples throughout the continent. *Iroquois Corn in a Culture-Based Curriculum* (1999), by Dr. Cornelius, and *Indian Corn of the Americas* (1989), edited by José Barreiro, provide evidence of this claim. Those two books, written by Indigenous peoples, along with *The Gift* (1998), a documentary directed by Gary Farmer, are prime examples of native peoples telling their own stories about maíz, without other peoples' interpretations. Whether maíz is central to Indigenous peoples or not has never been in question. Whether maíz culture and maíz narratives are also present in "mestizo" communities or de-Indigenized communities in the United States is generally the question I ask in my research.[53] Bonfil Batalla (1996) argues that even if maíz-based calendrical ceremonies are missing and even if most Mexicans are separated from the *milpa* (cornfield), the answer is still yes. Maíz, culture, the people, and society, he argues, cannot be separated.

Miguel Ángel Asturias ([1949] 1988) is credited with putting into words the idea that the people of Mesoamerica are people of maíz. For him, the concept is the main staple of Mesoamerican codices. The idea that people are made from maíz is also what undergirds the anthology *Sin Maíz No Hay País* (Esteva and Marielle 2003). The book is emblematic of this relationship, as each author emphasizes the centrality of maíz to the nation. While Anzaldúa's (1987) work is not centered on maíz or maíz culture, she does assert that the mestiza is similar to Indigenous corn, the product of crossbreeding.

Despite this, other Chicana/Chicano scholars have made the observation that the maíz diet of corn, beans, and squash, plus chile, generally continues to be a part of their family's daily lives. Scholars D. Carrasco (1990), Vigil (1998, 2012), Vélez-Ibáñez (1996), and Abarca (2006), along with the several other Chicana/Chicano scholars listed above, see continuity of Mesoamerican culture in the United States, or at least traces of it. Vélez-Ibáñez sees the annual *tamalada* (tamale party) as a secular ceremony.[54] It is not simply a communal meal, it also involves the communal preparation of the tamales and the sharing or exchanging of stories over the preceding twelve months. Other similar lay holidays that have spiritual pre-Columbian counterparts include Día de los Muertos (Day of the Dead) and the *quinceañera* (*Xilonen*; see chapter 5). These ceremonies have also become secularized and highly commercialized. In their pre-Columbian context, virtually all ceremonies are connected to maíz.

Several scholars, including Turner, Florescano, and Francisco de la Peña, examine how and why it is that Mesoamerican culture translates into an emphasis on specifically Aztec/Mexica culture in the past few centuries amongst Mexicans. Following the tradition of Eric Hobsbawm and Terence Ranger (1984), de la Peña, in *Los Hijos del Sexto Sol* (2002) views the grasping for Aztec/Mexica culture as part of invented traditions. In disagreement with Bonfil Batalla (1996), he states that *la mexicanidad* (Aztec/Mexica culture) is more the product of an imaginary Mexico than a México profundo.[55] Several Chicano scholars concur, including Genaro Padilla (1989), Jorge Klor de Alva (1997), Emma Pérez (1999), Pérez-Torres (2001), and Virginia Fields and Victor Zamudio-Taylor (2001).

Florescano, in *La Bandera Mexicana* (2004), sees the desire to identify with Aztecs/Mexica as part of an effort to attain authenticity or principio. Turner, in *Dramas, Fields, and Metaphors* (1974) sees it as part of a *primary process*. Both reflect a desire to return to the root during times of uprising against oppression. As noted previously, this arguably occurred during both the Mexican Revolution and the Chicano Movement. In *Religions of Mesoamerica: Cosmovision and Ceremonial Centers* (1990), Davíd Carrasco sees Mesoamerican (not necessarily Aztec) culture among Chicanos, but he does not attribute it to a principio or a primary process. He wrote: "Mesoamerica's pre-Columbian traditions have continued to play a vital role in the colonial and post-colonial communities. Meaningful traces of these traditions can even be found in the Chicano communities in the United States" (125).

Joseph Campbell would see the phenomenon of Chicanos identifying with Aztec/Mexica culture simply as an effort to make sense of the world. It can be argued, extending Lakoff's ideas, that this phenomenon is part of a metaphoric mapping. Similarly, such assertions of Indigeneity can be seen as an application or example of Santa Ana's insurgent narrative. Many Chicano scholars agree that invoking an Aztec/Mexica narrative is not so much about accuracy as about responding to a hostile environment that tells Mexicans to go home.

Aside from danza, much of Mesoamerica's history and traditions are stored and communicated in the huehuetlahtolli. Several of the 1500s-era priests (Olmos and Sahagún) collected huehuetlahtolli, otherwise known as the ancient word or ancient words of wisdom. In *Huehuetlahtolli: Testimonios de la Antigua Palabra* (1991), Librado Silva Galeana criticizes Olmos and Sahagún for Catholicizing the huehuetlahtolli; however, they acknowledge that the Indigenous spirit of the guidances and admonitions still comes through.

The other great repository of maíz culture is Mexican/Indigenous cuisine. In one respect, this is where maíz culture is transmitted to its greatest extent, and much of the communication or transmission is thousands of years old.

Conclusion

The literature on maíz and maíz narratives is rich. It includes Indigenous pre-Columbian codices and post-Columbian codices. The weakness of the literature is that the pre-Columbian codices continue to suffer from biased mistranslations. A further weakness is that we do not yet have access to the works of non-Christianized Indigenous writers. At the moment, we at least know that through syncretism, much Indigenous knowledge was "hidden" and thus conserved. However, because the Spanish priests believed that the escrituras-pinturas, the images that accompanied the European post-Columbian codices, were illustrations as opposed to language, a mistake that is only now being unlearned, it is possible that Indigenous oppositional writing may yet surface. That would be an invaluable contribution to understanding Indigenous mindsets and worldviews during the colonial era, which might vary.

In analyzing the resilience of maíz culture, several Mexican scholars, including Bonfil Batalla (1996) and Florescano (1999), have argued that Mesoamerica is not a process from the past but continues to be at the root of México profundo, including and principally its culture. While the ideas of these Mexican scholars have not typically extended to Mexicans and Central Americans living in the United States, Chicana/Chicano writers have generally treated this topic. However, while some have romanticized the connection to Mesoamerica, others have almost completely rejected Indigeneity as something confined to the past. And yet a whole cadre of scholars, many of them young, have begun to argue that Chicanas/Chicanos and Mexicans and Central Americans in the United States are not merely the descendants of Indigenous peoples but Indigenous peoples themselves. Many of them do specific research, not on the heritage of Aztecs or Mayas but on other specific tribal peoples. While this form of scholarship is the antithesis of romanticizing Indigenous roots, it opens up a space for my work on story and narrative in regard to de-Indigenized peoples. Most de-Indigenized peoples are not connected to tribes, due to a number of factors, including de-Indigenization projects from the colonial era to the present. Current scholarship also opens up an examination of this de-Indigenization, which, in effect, is separation from culture, kinship, ceremonies, story, and narratives. It also lends itself to the study of cultural resilience. Despite hundreds of years of attempts to destroy the maíz narratives of the continent, they are still present, which brings to mind the words of Nez Perce–Chicana scholar, Inés Hernández-Ávila, speaking of the insight of an elder:

> Many Native American people who have been cut off from their traditions are hungry to recapture their ways or, at the very least, have a sense of what they have lost. Grandpa Raymond always said: "The ceremonies, the language, the songs, the dances are not lost. We are lost; they are where they have always been, just waiting to be [re]called." (2000: 16)

It is critical *how* one recalls or accesses these stories and other cultural elements; in my work, it has been through elder epistemology.

Figure 4. Corn Mother by Pola Lopez. This corn mother is an example of how the Virgen de Guadalupe is thoroughly associated with maíz culture. Courtesy of the artist.

Zazanil Xilotl Huehue Tlahtolli

Tata Cuaxtle Félix Evodio

Tata Cuaxtle is a Nahuatlahtoltemaxtiani, *a Nahuatl educator, for Xinax-calmecac-Anahuacalmecac in El Sereno, California. He is a respected Nahuatl-speaking elder from Copalillo, Guerrero, Mexico. This maíz story, a shortened version, was passed on to him by elders from his village, and is relayed specifically for this book.*

In zazanil Huehue Tlahtolli yehyectica, Copalillo, Guerrero, Mexico. Ihuan oh cahuilihtehqueh huehuetqueh Tata Cuaxtle. Ihuan pehua ihquin:

Nemia ceh to Nana Lamatzi ihuan ceh ih telpoca-ixhui; on ih ixhuitzi mohmoztla nochipa quih palehuiyaya ih Cihtzi campa tlacual-yehc-chihua, ihcon ixpan nozcaltihtia ih telpoca-ixhui ihuan cuahc ocaxilte mahtlactle ihuan yeye xihtle, opeh quih nohnotza, opeh quilia Huehue Tlahtolli.

Noh nequiliz telpocatzi, noh nequilz ixhuitzi aman nih mitzilliz ceh tlahtolli ixnex caque, iti huehueictzi qui pia tlin tih cahzicamatiz, quih pia tlin tih huelliz ihpan tlalticpac tih tequipanoz ihcon tih huelliz tih yehc nemiz ihpan Nemoani, tih huelliz tih tocaz, tih huelliz tih tlacolloz, tla yoh tih tlacollo tih huelliz tih tlacohcoyoniz ihuan tih tlatepehuaz; tih tepehuaz ih huachio to nacayotl chilli, ih huachio tomatl ihuan tic matiz quenihque tih huelliz tih cocolliz chihlli tlinon noh tlalilia ihca tih cocolliz, tlinon hualnanti ihpan tlalticpactle on ihca noh cocollia chihlli, aman ixcaque nih mitzilliz noh nequilliz ixhuitzi "noh cocohllia ihca tzonacapahtli,

55

notzo quillia tzonaca cuitlatl" ihcon huahllo in Huehue-tlahtolchictle, incon in tlahtol huehuetqueh, noche tlin tih cuah tlin ihca tih nemeh yaha tonacayotl tlin ihca tih yoltoqueh, noh tequipanoa, noh cuitlahuiya, noh tlazohtla, noh tlahtlane ihtex to Nantzi Tlalticpactle ihtex to Tahtzi Tonatio, ihtex Tlatque-Nahuahqueh yahameh on tequipanoah nochipah ihca tonalli ihuan ihca yahualli, yahameh ihtex onnoh tlahtlaneh tlin tih cuah ihpan huehueimeh tepemeh campa noche huehuetqueh, lamatzitzintin yohue on "Tlacahcahuah" onpa noh tlatlactillo, note ixpantia noh tlahtlane, noh pohcuiya xinaxtle campa nih tohoah teoyomeh, campa nih tohoa nihcan Omeyocan, campa tex yolmacatica to Tahtzi Tonalli ihuan to Nantzi Tlalticpactle ixcaque ixtlalle impan moh tzontecon yaha ihna Huehuetlatoltzintle tlin to Huehuetquemeh oquin tlacuanahuatihqueh mah quehyehuacan ihpan in tlanemilliz, ihpan in tlamachilliz ixcahce nih miztlatzoca mahtilia noh yehc telpoca-ixhuitzi.

Tlatzohcamate to máhuiztahtzi, to mahuiznantzi.

Ometeotl.

Historia Antigua del Nacimiento de Elote

Esta historia antigua está aguardada en Copalillo, Guerrero, México. Y dejaron los ancianos esta historia a Tata Cuaxtle. Y empieza la historia así:

Había una abuela muy anciana y también un hijo nieto. El hijo nieto, al diario, siempre ayudaba a la anciana donde acostumbraba hacer la comida. Y así su presencia, el joven iba creciendo y desarrollándose. Y cuando cumplió trece años, la anciana empezó a darle consejos y amonestar. Empezó a decirle la antigua palabra.

Mi apreciable hijito, mi apreciable nietecito, te diré una palabra—escúchame, ya estás grandecito y debes de entender qué debes de saber de la tierra, a trabajar. Así puedes vivir y no sufrirás en esta vida. Conocerás como sembrar, conocerás como desmontar donde vas a sembrar el maíz. Y si ya desmontaste y limpiaste, harás el trabajo de hacer hoyos en la tierra donde vas a exactamente a sembrar el maíz. Y también conocerás la siembra de transplante. Regarás cuidadosamente la semilla de chile donde temporalmente está sembrado, y también la semilla de tomate. Y conocerás el conocimiento de hacer más picoso el chile. Qué es lo que se le echa para hacerlo picoso. Qué es lo que se le viene usando en la tierra para hacer más picoso el chile. Ahora escúchame apreciable nietecito. Se hace picoso con la medicina del estiércol del murciélago. Así viene este antiguo hecho. Así es la palabra de los ancianos. Todo lo que comemos y es el sustento para nuestra vida, eso es lo que nos mantiene vivos y se trabaja. Se quiere y se aprecia y se cuida. Se pide ante de nuestra Madre Tierra y se pide ante nuestro Padre Tonatio. También se le pide al Tlatquenahuahqueh, que es la energía del agua, el fuego, el aire y la tierra. Ellos son los que trabajan siempre de día y de noche (dualidad). Junto a ellos se pide en las montañas donde todos los ancianos y ancianas van a hacer ofrendas. Allí se llora, allí se pide, allí se presenta, allí se asoma la semilla y también se hacen los rezos. En este lugar es donde todo trabaja en dualidad. Nuestro gran Padre Sol y nuestra Madre Tierra representan la dualidad y el origen de la vida. Ahora escucha todo este consejo y mantenlo en la memoria. Esta sabiduría es la antigua palabra que los ancianos encomendaron que aguardemos en la vida. Te lo doy cuidadosamente, mi muy apreciado nietecito.

Gracias gran padre y gran madre.

Ometeotl.

Ancient History of the Birth of Maíz

This ancient (and abbreviated) history is kept by the peoples of Copalillo, Guerrero, México. And the elders left this story in the hands of Tata Cuaxtle. This is how the story begins:

There was an elderly grandmother and also her grandson. The grandson would help his grandmother every day where the meals were prepared. That is how the young boy kept growing and developing. When he turned thirteen years old, his grandmother began to give him advice and words of caution. She began to teach him the huehuetlahtolli or the ancient word.

My precious little one, my precious grandson, I want to give you some advice—listen to me, you are now a little older and you should understand the things you need to know about the earth and how to work it. This way you can live and you will not suffer in life. You will know how to plant, you will know how to till the soil and where you will plant the maíz. Once you till the soil and have cleared it, you will make the holes in the earth where you will know precisely where to plant the maíz seeds. And you will also know how to transplant seeds. You will water the chile seeds where they are already planted and also the seeds of the tomato. And you will learn the secrets of how to make the chile hotter. You will know what to add that makes it hotter. You will know what you need to do to the earth to make the chile hotter. Now listen to me my precious grandson. The chili becomes hotter with the medicine of bat manure. This is an ancient practice. That is the word of the elders. All that we eat is our life sustenance, it is what keeps us alive and thus we work. We care for it and appreciate it. We offer prayers before Mother Earth and we offer prayers before our Father Sun. We also offer prayers for the Lord of the Near and Nigh, who is the energy of the water, the fire, the air, and the earth. They are the ones that work by day and by night (duality). Along with them we offer prayers in the mountains where all the elders make offerings. There, one cries, one prays, one presents oneself; that is where the seeds present themselves and where one offers prayers. In this place is where everything works in duality. Our great Father Sun and our sacred Mother Earth represent the duality of the origin of life. Now listen to this guidance and keep it in your memory. This wisdom is the ancient word that the elders entrusted to us to keep for life. I give it to you cautiously, my precious grandson.

Thank you great father and great mother.

Ometeotl.

Maíz Narratives and Counternarratives

When "Our Story" Begins

When Don Felipe "read" me the story of Quetzalcoatl being assigned by the Lords of Tamoanchan to find food for the people (see prologue), he enacted or reenacted a story that has been handed down for perhaps several thousand years. Since then, I've heard similar stories recounted by several other elders. About fifteen years ago I saw a play about the ants of Quetzalcoatl at Nahuatl University in Morelos, Mexico. In many of the ancient stories, humans, Quetzalcoatl, and ants are intertwined. In the *Popol Vuh*, the ants permit the hero twins—Hunahpú and Xbalanqué—to escape certain death at the hands of the Lords of Xibalba by performing a task (cutting flowers) designed to kill them. This was part of a battle that the twins eventually won and that resulted in the creation of humans and maíz.

In ancient times, ants were not seen as enemies of the milpas but as family. Rather than kill the ants, people directed incantations at them. For example, here, as related by the Spanish chronicler Hernando Ruiz de Alarcón ([1629] 1984: 110–11), is an incantation from Martín de Luna of Temimilzinco, who was 110 years old (the interpolations in brackets are the translators', not mine):

> Come on now, uncles, possessed ones or foreigners . . . with your veiled eyes or faces, and with teeth like sharp points. Why are you doing harm

to your sister, the white woman [the sown field], and [why] have you lost respect for her? . . . Let it be soon! Oh my various uncles, priests, oh people from Popotlan, *Nahualli*-eyes-owners, *Nahualli*-obsidian-teeth-owners [i.e., the ants] . . . Will you sweep for her, will you respect her? If you will not accompany her [i.e., do her honor], I will tear down that by means of which you are [i.e., the ant hill]. If you do not obey me [you will regret it].

Ancient stories of ants, humans, and maíz abound, and they are not confined to the past. In 2003, I gave an assignment to students at UCLA to look for something Indigenous within their homes. The instructions were, if they were told there was nothing, to persist, to look in the kitchen, in photographs, in stories, and so on. One student related that her parents told her that there was nothing Indigenous about them. She persisted and was told to speak to her uncle. Initially, he too denied there was anything Indigenous within the family. In fact, he took umbrage. He told her: "Indigenous? We're not savages!"

Due to her persistence, he eventually relayed the following story: In Mexico, their family had the best milpa in the whole village because when it was time to plant, they took a statue of Tlaloc (a Nahua spirit of rain and maíz) to the fields. They placed it on the earth and then pounded the earth. Wherever it would jump the highest, that's where they would bury the statue, and thus they produced the best milpa.

These stories illustrate that the maíz narratives of the continent often reside in our memory and are alive.

While the story of Quetzalcoatl and the ants can be seen as an antithesis to the Western master narrative of history, like the *Popol Vuh* it is not a counternarrative, for it predates the western narrative on this continent. This is true of most if not all Indigenous creation/origin stories on this continent. Together, the maíz narratives tell the story of this continent—a continent that does not figure meaningfully into the Euro-American time-line until 1492.

The stories of resistance to Columbus, Cortés, Pizarro, and other conquistadores can perhaps properly be seen as counternarratives, but the maíz stories preexist and exist outside of that framework.

For Indigenous peoples, they are not simply other narratives but part of a different axis mundi. López Austin, in *Tamoanchan, Tlalocan: Places of Mist* (1997), wrote: "One of the basic reasons for the historical unity of Mesoamerica was the universal cultivation of maíz. The cosmovision that developed over thousands of years was based on agricultural production. Despite the social and political peculiarities of the different Mesoamerican societies there was one strong common denominator, the growing of maíz, which allowed cosmovision and religion to be a means of privileged communication" (11).

It is also what informed that axis mundi. For many peoples from maíz-based cultures, maíz or the maíz tree—often represented as the foliated cross—is the axis mundi (Schele and Freidel 1990). It is the frame through which life is viewed. For Westerners—who generally look to the Bible as their axis mundi—to acknowledge maíz as the Mesoamerican axis mundi would be to seemingly reject their own axis mundi and their own narrative, which has misinformed the world that there was no credible or coherent history outside of Europe prior to 1492. This helps to contextualize why, after more than 520 years of attempted destruction of virtually all pre-Columbian communication systems, including the codices—along with attempts to erase and rewrite the knowledge within them—the seven-thousand-year maíz narratives still survive. López Austin explains: "The early colonial destruction of the institutions that supported its beliefs and rituals were [*sic*] not enough to prevent its persistence. In spite of the disappearance of the political mechanisms—the intellectuals, priestly organization, and the calendar—the tradition continues to flourish among the farmers" (1997: 11). In reality, the calendar has survived beyond its agricultural function and continues to this day to inform ceremonial cycles of peoples in cities, even in the United States.[1]

In examining the predominant Western narrative, one can observe that the language of domination and dehumanization and of superiority and inferiority has not yet been remanded to the past. It is not atypical to read assigned books in undergraduate courses or graduate seminars at major universities in which non-Western peoples are referred to as heathens, savages, primitives, uncivilized, undeveloped, and backward and their beliefs referred to as pagan, heathen, or superstitious. This is part of the reason for the development of standpoint theory—which determines how we view and examine the world—and even more broadly, it is also why the fields of feminist and ethnic studies developed in the 1960s and 1970s (Harding 1987). One of the accompanying features of Spanish colonialism in the Americas was the attempt to decimate Indigenous languages, along with Indigenous philosophy, thought, and culture, this while imposing colonial/Christian worldviews, culture, and languages. At times, Indigenous languages and Indigenous forms of communication, the literary and oral traditions, were employed as part of missionization. This syncretic process, in effect, amounted to attempts to spiritually kill Indigenous peoples and create Christians.[2] This was not a by-product of the church's mass-conversion project but its objective.

During this era, a political language of superiority and inferiority was created and employed by Spanish friars to aid the imposition of Western culture and religion. While most of the Americas have been free of European political control for some time now, colonialism is very much alive in the realm of religion, culture, and language, and with respect to the cultural values attached to the imposed language of domination. This legacy is everywhere. Perhaps nowhere is it better illustrated than in the usage of the term *indio/india* (Indian) in the Spanish-speaking Americas; this term represents the consummate Western reframing of the original peoples of this continent. Aside from being wholly inaccurate to describe the autochthonous peoples of this continent (Indians are from India), throughout history *indio/india* has, ironically, been pejorative. In the eyes of non-Indigenous peoples, *indio* is the lowest insult one can hurl at someone, connoting a brute, uneducated "savage." There is a direct relationship between the tendency to use it and the user's color: the light-skinned population directs its vitriol against the dark-skinned population, though the brainwashing has been so thorough that even members of the dark-skinned population will use it against others who look like themselves. Many also use it against the rural population, the campesinos, or against people labeled "*nacos*" (tasteless, unsophisticated)—the equivalent of "hillbillies." The internalized hatred is so extreme that the rural population will also deny being Indigenous, reserving the term *indio/india* for those who live in Indigenous-speaking villages. Yet historically, even those who speak Indigenous languages cease being identified as Indigenous if they leave their villages, get educated, speak Spanish, and change their clothes.

This disruptive de-Indigenization process has convinced Indigenous peoples that they had no history or narrative of worth prior to the arrival of Europeans. By bringing to light the maíz narratives, my work challenges the practice of assigning "narrative" status to Western master narratives or dominant narratives while assigning counternarrative status to all others.

Centeotzintli: The Story of the Continent

The Western world does not know the name of the person or people or peoples who created maíz, nor the precise field where maíz was first cultivated. Scientists tell us that the development of maíz occurred some seven thousand years ago in southern Mexico and/or possibly Central America. They consider it one of the greatest scientific feats in human history (Fussell 1992).[3]

The day maíz was created is the metaphorical birthday of a radically new culture on this continent. It is the day that a civilizational impulse was unleashed that over the next several thousand years created many diverse cultures across the continent (Florescano 1999).[4] It is why the Maya mark the beginning of their calendar with a zero that is represented by a shell or seed. The Maya concept of zero represents germination and not the absence of value: "Zero is the concept of the origin of everything" (Martínez Parédez 1968: 9). In Nahuatl, *ce* represents the number one, taken from *cintli* or maíz.

While the Olmecs were not the first people to develop their culture based on maíz, they are the first of the known cultures that built great cities and relied on large-scale maíz production.[5] Prior to the advent of maíz and large-scale agriculture, the peoples on this continent lived for many thousands of years by hunting, trapping, fishing, gathering, and cultivating other crops. The vibrant Indigenous cultures that developed as a result of these sustenance activities remain with us to this day.

The introduction of maíz did not displace these more ancient cultures but added to them. At the same time, it transformed many of them. With the advent of maíz, peoples created more sedentary cultures, ceased constantly moving, and began to gather in more permanent villages. Eventually, they built thousands of great settlements or cities across the continent. Today, they are generally known as ruins—mounds or pyramids often reduced to tourist attractions.[6] The history of even the largest of these cities, though they are recognized as ceremonial centers and considered architectural marvels, is still framed as being shrouded in mystery. The general public knows very little about even the most well known of these centers: Teotihuacan.

The idea of these hundreds of ceremonial centers as tourist attractions is itself a frame and a distortion; it is not accidental. Conscious decisions centuries ago by Spanish friars helped to create a bias that continues to keep the public in the dark about the pre-Columbian history of this continent. This is accomplished in several ways, primarily by non-Indigenous scholars continuing to repeat the belief that Indigenous peoples did not record credible history. By commission or omission, Western scholars, particularly in the past but in the present as well, have generally kept people in the dark by dismissing the oral tradition. Oneida scholar Cornelius wrote: "Archaeological evidence does not include the beliefs of the people, thus ignoring or eliminating indigenous beliefs" (1999: 121). For example, many peoples throughout the continent, including the Oneida, a North American woodland people, consider corn a gift. They tell of receiving corn from "the woman who falls from the sky" (Barreiro 1989, Farmer 1998,

George-Kanentiio 2000). While no Western scholar has publicly suggested a direct connection with Mesoamerican cultures, the memory of *corn as a gift* may be evidence of a continental or civilizational unity that various scholars speak about (Bonfil Batalla 1996, Florescano 1999).[7]

This general lack of understanding of maíz culture on the part of non-Indigenous peoples has, through the years, fomented wild speculation about (besides the origins of the peoples of this continent) far-flung origins for corn. This question is no longer the subject of much debate. As Edgar Anderson observed in 1947 (cited in Mangelsdorf 1974), corn more than any other plant documents its own history. Paul Christoph Mangelsdorf noted that "not a single corn cob, unmistakably pre-Columbian, has yet been found in any part of the Old World" (1974: 206). For such reasons, Western scholars view maíz as an artifact of the Americas.

Many modern Western scholars have compounded this lack of understanding of Indigenous peoples and societies by continuing to afford European chroniclers the status of primary sources. Many of these "witnesses" themselves participated in mass confiscations and burnings of books, purportedly because they were demonic. This occurred throughout Mesoamerica during the three hundred years of colonialism, including the destruction of the huge library (royal archives) at Texcoco in 1535 led by Bishop Juan de Zumárraga (Florescano 2006) and the infamous 1562 *auto de fe* led by Bishop Diego de Landa at Maní, Yucatán.[8] Although it is generally acknowledged that there was pre-Columbian contact, perhaps accidental, between the continents, it is also generally accepted that this continent developed for several thousand years in relative isolation from Europe, Asia, and Africa.[9] In parallel to cultures on those continents that experienced the advent of agriculture some ten thousand years ago, the peoples of the Americas began a similar agricultural revolution at about the same time, albeit with different crops and different tools.[10] In due time, ancient Mexicans developed the style of agriculture known as *chinampa* (floating gardens), astronomy, mathematics, science, large-scale architecture, writing, calendars, and other technologies. Most of the well-known ancient cultures of the Americas are associated with maíz, including the Olmec, Maya, Teotihuacano, Mixtec, Zapotec, Toltec, and Nahua, plus the Andean cultures in South America, and Chaco, Cahokia, and other Mound cultures in the United States. Unquestionably, maíz spread for thousands of years in all directions, radically changing the continent. Maíz made its way into what is today the United States several thousand years ago, including via the Hohokam.[11] The Hohokam, peoples that came from Mexico two thousand years ago into what is today the U.S. Southwest, built impressive irrigation canals for maíz that are still in use today (Forbes 1973). Cornelius (1999: 121) pointed out that there is indisputable evidence that corn was growing in Illinois and Ohio long before the arrival of Europeans.

Scientists tell us that maíz is one of the few crops that cannot grow by itself; it requires human intervention. Thus, its movement, and the transmission of knowledge of how to cultivate it, certainly occurred through human contact. This is why scientists know that there was diffusion of maíz from southern Mexico and an attendant cultural and civilizational impulse that spread in all directions, including into what is today the United States. It is also why scientists agree that maíz and maíz culture did not exist outside of the Americas, prior to 1492. Virtually all maíz-based cultures of the Americas record, in song, art, ritual, dance, and ceremony, how maíz came to them.

By the time of European arrival, maíz had already made a major impact upon the continent and its peoples, generally everywhere except the coldest regions. Yet maíz culture did not replace hunting, fishing, and gathering. If anything, it supplemented it. While some cultures on the continent were only minimally impacted by maíz, on the whole, most were greatly affected. This contradicts notions of an empty continent and roaming Indians, particularly in what is today the United States (Deloria 1973, Blaut 1993, Mann 2005).

Maíz narratives are part of the oral traditions—based on experiential knowledge—of virtually all maíz-based cultures on this continent, with all or most viewing maíz as sacred. Some hold that "we are made from maíz." This is the meaning of the Nahua concept of centeotzintli or teotl cintli.[12] The import of this concept is that maíz culture is not lost or dependent on ancient romantic cultures. Instead, it is alive and can still be seen throughout the continent on a daily basis.[13] To speak of maíz culture invokes the larger maíz-based food complex that includes beans and squash as well—the "Three Sisters." In Mexico and Central America, the complex in its fullest form is what instructors at Nahuatl University dubbed the "Seven Warriors of Nutrition": corn, beans, squash, chile, nopal (cactus), amaranth, and chia.

The Erasure

The 1492 narrative, the narrative that injects "the Old World" into the American landscape, did not necessarily have to be a counternarrative, but many Indigenous peoples see it as such. This is primarily because in effect, Euro-Americans have proclaimed their story to be official history, or the universal story of humanity. This narrative is not a history of the world or encounters between civilizations but a story told from only one perspective. Instead, this imposed master narrative is backed by military force and occupation and is dependent upon the erasure of other peoples' stories, thousands of years of histories of the many cultures and civilizations of the planet, including this continent. To tell this story, to continue with this master narrative, requires reciting history through a biased Western prism.

The means of erasure of the maíz narratives included the literal destruction of native histories, both in North and South America. This was done by confiscating or destroying books (codices), paintings, or the *quipus* (knotted strings) used in Andean record keeping, or by claiming that native peoples were illiterate, didn't possess either "true" writing or any writing at all—and thus no history, no nations or civilizations, nor knowledge itself (Galarza 1992, Mignolo 2006, Florescano 2006). The oral tradition, meanwhile, was belittled as somehow less reliable or credible than European texts.

Boone's primary thesis in *Stories in Red and Black* (2000) is that Europeans reduced differences in writing to a matter of superiority and inferiority. This biased and superstitious fanaticism did not go unchallenged as the debate regarding the "superiority" of European texts and the validity of Indigenous knowledge began in the early 1500s. Consider Manqu Inka's assessment, as recalled by his son, Titu Cusi ([1570] 2005: 170–71), a native writer from the Andes:

> The first thing you will do is not believe a word of what those bearded men say. . . . What you can do is give outward signs of obedience to their orders. . . . When you cannot resist any longer, make the motions before them but never forget our own ceremonies.

The above quote affirms that Indigenous peoples already were aware that their knowledge and narratives and humanity were in question and that they therefore designed ways to counter these hegemonic efforts.

Similarly, in the first documented intellectual exchange between Spanish missionaries and Indigenous peoples, held in Mexico City in 1524 between twelve Franciscans and a group of Mexica civic leaders, the latter revealed that their knowledge was already being lost: those charged with understanding the ancient knowledge, the tlamatinis (who could rebut the Franciscans), had been killed. The Mexica representatives explained the tlamatinis' role: "Our priests keep the books of our ancient knowledge in which they leaf through and read day and night regarding the calendar" (Sahagún [1564] 1944: 52).

Another aspect of this erasure is continued historical justification for the extreme violence associated with the Spanish/European colonization of the Americas, of which the aforementioned book burnings and other forms of erasure were a part. Justification of this violence forms part of the Western master narrative and comes in many forms, including claims that Spanish/European brutalities either are exaggerated or were not substantially different from the violence that native peoples inflicted upon each other in the pre-Columbian period.[14] These denials partly revolve around intra-European debates as to whether the Spanish or the English were more brutal. Those who defend the offending Spanish from that era do so by claiming that the notion that they were more brutal than the English constitutes a "Black Legend" against Spain. For many Indigenous peoples, the question of which European power was more brutal is less than irrelevant; it is a meaningless debate.[15]

The topic of erasure of the histories of this continent is not incidental; it goes directly to the credibility of early colonial sources, which academic scholars worldwide have been dependent upon for five hundred years. During a time of brutal conquest and Inquisition, nothing was written or published that did not conform to one of the primary objectives of the Spanish project: the Christianization and de-Indigenization of the Americas. Writings that did not support that project were subject to censorship and deemed unpublishable. Even many of the writings of the priests were edited by censors to the point that what was published did not correspond to what they had written.[16] It was for the same reason that virtually every pre-Columbian text was destroyed. It is appropriate to be skeptical of the priests'/chroniclers' version of Indigenous history, in which everything Indigenous is dismissed. It is not unreasonable to assess their view of history as but part of their good-versus-evil/God-versus-the-devil reframing. Useful things can be gleaned from their accounts, but regarding Indigenous ways of life and beliefs it is not unreasonable to question their accuracy, given their creation of clearly libelous legends of rampant cannibalism, massive human sacrifice, demonic idol worship, illiteracy, backwardness, and subhumanness.[17]

All of these erasures and all the irrelevant debates are in the service of justifying hundreds of years of colonization, land theft, slavery, and genocide (Deloria 1973). Worse, however, is that they permit the disappearance of Indigenous history and narratives. They also allow Euro-American nation-states, including the United States, to impose their Columbus-and-the-Pilgrims narrative on the rest of the world. This manner of framing the world contributes to notions of Providence and Manifest Destiny and eventually to the "American Dream." All is predicated upon erasure and demonization, and a fictionalized and romanticized narrative of the spread of European civilization.[18]

J. M. Blaut wrote this about European beliefs in *The Colonizer's Model of the World* (1993: 60): "The matrix of implicit beliefs about historical non-Europe includes ideas of alienness, savagery, cruelty, cannibalism, deceitfulness, stupidity, cupidity, immodesty, dirtiness, disease, and so on—a matrix firmly supporting the general belief that non-Europe cannot have been progressive." In this Western narrative about non-Europe, as recounted today, whatever violence occurred upon first contact or subsequently was necessary and justifiable to bring Christianity and civilization to uncivilized ruthless savages. As Arturo Aldama states in *Disrupting Savagism* (2001: 10), the objective of Europeans, in their own minds, was to humanize Indigenous peoples, to take them from the category of animal to that of human. This was accomplished by teaching and evangelizing them, by converting "savages" into Europeans.[19] Essentially this is how the history of Europeans and their colonizing efforts on this continent is interpreted by many Europeans and Euro-Americans; simply as an effort to civilize and save the natives.[20] Contrarily, it can also be seen as but a sublime effort to deflect the hundreds of years of atrocities that Europeans wrought upon this continent, and as the justification for how Westerners continue to perceive Indigenous peoples (Pewewardy 2005, Aldama 2001, D. Carrasco 2000, Nabokov 2002, Blaut 1993, Martínez Parédez 1968).[21]

In many non-Indigenous narratives, neither the word *genocide* nor *land theft* appears. Instead, the decline of Indigenous populations is attributed to the effects of disease—as a result of the poor immune system of Indigenous peoples, as opposed to conditions of war, famine, starvation, brutality, and exploitation. Even writers favorable to Indigenous peoples continue to overemphasize disease, Blaut, for example: "The Americans were not conquered; they were infected" (1993: 186). In examining colonialism in the Americas, Blaut also creates a linkage between colonization, imperialism, civilization, westernization, modernization, and globalization, treating them as parts of a single process. This is a frame that many scholars do not utilize, though it generally fits with Indigenous views of the continent. What differentiates the parts of this continuum is simply speed and a change of international actors. The first dominant globalists were the Spanish and Portuguese, then later the English, the French, and the Dutch, and now the United States. The *Western* or *master narrative* is a general name for the effort to give a singular coherence to that continuum, that official historical worldview (Blaut 1993). It is the same process that Gruzinski describes in

Images at War (2001). Utilizing it in an uncritical way in effect reinforces the notion that the Western narrative is the true narrative of the world.

Western scholarship, which promotes the compartmentalization and atomization of knowledge—through specialization—generally discourages contextualizing this centuries-old phenomenon as part of today's explanation of reality. As Aldama noted: "The tendency in postcolonial studies to relegate the struggles against neocolonialism to a place 'over there somewhere' denies the complex power relations of internal colonies and the complexities of racial, class, and gender oppression in the United States" (2001: 19). In *Cartographies of Diaspora* (1996: 224), Brah concurs: "few canonical texts in the study of 'postmodernity' address colonialism, decolonization or racism in any systematic way." He also notes that "the colonized remains largely elusive as subject in much of this body of radical criticism" (225).

Despite these erasures, maíz culture and its corresponding narratives have survived. As León-Portilla has noted, agriculture was the key to the development of Mesoamerica: "Maíz is the first chapter of history in Mesoamerica and the Andes" (2003a: 7). And while the Spanish destroyed much of the Mesoamerican way of life, the culture itself, which was based on maíz, survives because the dependence on maíz only increased. It increased because food was needed to feed the masses toiling for Spain against their will.

Another aspect of erasure is the Western argument that prior to the coming of Europeans, there were no nations or nation-states here. If no nations existed, then no nations were disrupted or destroyed. This is a fallacious argument. It also absolves the colonizers of the harm and land theft they inflicted upon these "nonexistent" Indigenous nations.

Missing is the Indigenous frame or the Indigenous worldview of what happened as a result of 1492. It is true that the region that became New Spain during the colonial era and Mexico after independence from Spain was not the Greater Aztec/Mexica Empire or the Nation-State of Anahuac. It was not a modern nation-state or nation-states that were severely disrupted or destroyed by the conquest, it was Indigenous peoples and civilizations, particularly the maíz-based cultures of Mexico, Central America, and the Andes, and virtually all other Indigenous peoples, who were subjected to genocide, land theft, forced labor, and forced conversion. Despite this massive destruction, the culture of these peoples was resilient and survived. Thus, the notion that there is no continuity and no unity among Mexican peoples—or no basic unity between all Indigenous peoples of the continent—can be interpreted as a self-serving storyline that comports to the hegemonic Western framework or narrative, or simply another maneuver to erase this part of human history.

The Contra-Narrative

After erasure, the next step was the imposition of a new frame or a new narrative. It began with a commonly taught story, which I remember from my school days:

> *Challenging the widely held beliefs of his contemporaries, Christopher Columbus sets sail across the Atlantic Ocean on the* Pinta, *the* Niña, *and the* Santa Maria. *The objective of this commercial venture, called the Enterprise, is to find a westerly route to the Indies. After several months of sailing, on October 12, 1492, he discovers America and proves that the world is round. He not only claims the continent for the King and Queen of Spain and finds riches for them, he also begins the greatest civilizing project in the history of humanity, to bring both civilization and Christianity to the savages of the New World, and to those in Africa as well. Through this divine mission, he not only brings forth economic prosperity for the Old World but also finds and opens up "the New Promised Land" for all those fleeing oppression and bondage and seeking religious freedom, liberty, equality, democracy, and justice for all. Thus, America becomes the beacon for all of humanity.*

While this oft-repeated story regarding Columbus is an amalgam of fables and legends, it is taught as historical fact in U.S. schools. It also forms the cornerstone of the Western master narrative. In it, Columbus symbolically is the quintessential Founding Father, not simply of the Americas but of the United States itself. Metaphorically, he is America's first "Gringo." He is the person who, according to the Western narrative, symbolically connects the East (Orient) and West culturally and makes possible the unity of humanity.

Ignored in this story, besides ancient wayward travelers from other distant lands, are Indigenous peoples as human beings. Ignored are Amer-Indigenous narratives thousands of years old. They simply don't count, and Indigenous people are essentially remanded to the status of savages waiting to be discovered, civilized, and saved by Europeans on divine and commercial missions from God. Without moving, Indigenous peoples are displaced culturally and geographically, as they are not part of the West and certainly not part of the East.

Plate 1. Humans emerging from maíz. Untitled painting by Tanya Alvarez, after a thousand-year-old mural in Cacaxtla, Mexico. Courtesy of the artist.

Plate 2. *Ce Topiltzin* by Paz Zamora (Mapitzmitl). This is a depiction of Ce Topiltzin–Quetzalcoatl, a bringer of civilization to the continent. The original Quetzalcoatl is often represented as a feathered serpent. Courtesy of the artist.

Plate 3. *Corn Mother* by Pola Lopez. This corn mother is an example of how the Virgen de Guadalupe is thoroughly associated with maíz culture. Courtesy of the artist.

Plate 4. Map of Aztlán by Pola Lopez. A modern amoxtli depicting the Aztlan–
Tenochtitlan migration a thousand years ago. Hidden within this image is the
seven-thousand-year-old story of maíz. Courtesy of the artist.

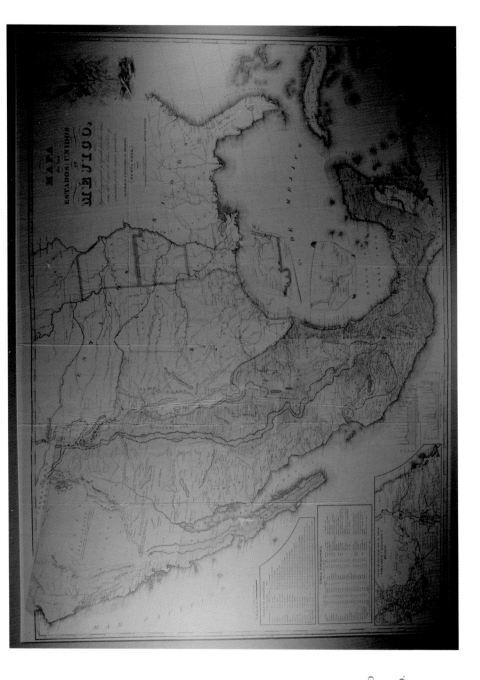

Plate 5. Disturnell map, 1847. This map was attached to the 1848 Treaty of Guadalupe Hidalgo. Courtesy of Brenda Limon.

Plate 6. *We Are Not a Minority*, East L.A. mural by Mario Torero, Rocky, El Lion, and Zade, 1978. Courtesy of Mario Torero.

Plate 7. The Ants of Quetzalcoatl by Laura V. Rodriguez. Courtesy of the artist.

Plate 8. *In Lak'ech* by Grecia Ramirez. Courtesy of the artist.

Plate 9. *Maíz Tree* by Verónica Castillo Hernández. Courtesy of the artist.

Neither the histories of Indigenous peoples nor pre-Columbian contact between the continents (Vikings, Asians, Africans) form part of the master narrative because they do not conform to the religio-vision of the conquest of the Americas.[22] Despite the Columbus story being mostly lore and fable, it survives because it is useful and helps to weave the ideas of divine mission, Providence, and Manifest Destiny into the master narrative. In this manner, as Cree scholar Sharon Venne (1998) argued, it serves to justify genocide, land theft, slavery, and the complete dehumanization of peoples that fall outside of the master narrative. In this religio-vision, she argued, Euro-Iberians were not simply entitled to these lands but, in effect, were carrying out a divine mandate to Christianize and civilize the entire world.[23] This mandate enabled Spanish conquistadores to both take lands not claimed by Christians and wage merciless war upon non-Christians, with divine right (Venne 1998, Newcomb 2008).

The mandate, which came in the form of the *Requerimiento*, a Spanish proclamation backed by papal bulls, was authorized by the King and Queen of Spain via the Catholic Pope. In this vision, violence and genocide are seen as fully sanctioned by God. First penned by Juan López de Palacios Rubios in 1513, the *Requerimiento* reads in part as follows:

> If you do not do this, and maliciously make delay in it, I certify to you that, with the help of God, we shall powerfully enter into your country, and shall make war against you in all ways and manners that we can, and shall subject you to the yoke and obedience of the Church and of their Highnesses; we shall take you and your wives and your children, and shall make slaves of them, and as such shall sell and dispose of them as their Highnesses may command; and we shall take away your goods, and shall do you all the mischief and damage that we can, as to vassals who do not obey, and refuse to receive their lord, and resist and contradict him; and we protest that the deaths and losses that shall accrue from this are your fault, and not that of their Highnesses, or ours, nor of these cavaliers who come with us. (Newcomb 2008: 35–36)

The objective of reading the *Requerimiento* was to comply with a "legal" requirement, with pardons embedded into it. It served notice to the peoples of the Americas that if they did not convert and surrender their lands, merciless war would be waged upon them. The reading of the proclamation, which was almost always in Latin, sans translation, was, in effect, all the permission required to wage a "lawful" conquest. Las Casas ([1500s] 1985), "defender of the Indians" in the 1500s, thought it was a complete scam.

Yet it conformed to the narrative being woven by those representing both church and crown, and one that, as Vine Deloria Jr. points out in *God Is Red* (1973), was necessary in order to depict the continent as empty of civilized human beings.

The Master Narrative

In relating the history of humanity, Western scholars have generally placed themselves in charge of writing official history. The long march of this history begins in the "Old World" and then reaches the "New World" via Columbus in 1492. This narrative myth today is told in both secular and religious paradigms. Regardless of whether this story begins with the Garden of Eden or the Western secular "march of progress," they both form part of the Western narrative. Columbus's story is an example of the merging of these two worldviews.

In the modern era, it is non-Western, insurgent, or oppositional scholars that refer to this worldview as "the master narrative."[24] They get to name it, but generally they do not get to contribute to it. This is the centered narrative that all other narratives revolve around or are subordinate to.[25] In this schema, the oppositional views are those of feminists, leftists, non-Western scholars, Indigenous scholars, or scholars of color and are considered the counternarratives. Despite challenging the master narrative, counternarratives can inadvertently still privilege "the master narrative" because it is kept in the center.[26] The Columbus story could just as easily be conceived of as a counternarrative rather than part of the master narrative. Failure to reject that centering outright can actually reinforce or further privilege the Western narrative. This is why, for many Indigenous and other non-Western scholars, the history of this continent does not begin with Columbus or the Vikings or with contrived links to Biblical stories.

Indigenous worldviews generally challenge and reject that schema altogether. For instance, the maíz cultures of this continent were profoundly affected by the events of 1492, yet the maíz narratives and other origin/migration stories did not disappear. In this view, what comes post-Columbus on this continent is viewed as but an interruption or simply as the beginning of the counternarrative, or what I term the "Contra-Narrative." Because of the profound effect of 1492, the maíz narratives become resistance narratives, an example of cultural resilience. The stories and the ancient narratives are resistance. The foods, particularly the tortilla within U.S. culture, are also resistance.

The maíz narrative does not deny the existence of a dominant Western narrative. It recognizes the Western narrative's dominant and hegemonic status and the need to challenge its place in history. Many Indigenous peoples simply seek the maíz narrative's rightful place as a valid narrative for peoples that come from living, maíz-based cultures or from other cultures Indigenous to this continent.

Some scholars maintain that the maíz narrative is but a metaphor that helps to tell the (nonhegemonic) story of not only the continent but humanity itself. Truthfully, all narratives are metaphoric. They constitute not history per se but the stories we choose to remember, and forget. That is what creates or gives meaning to our lives and our constructed narratives. As Boone reminds us: "Just as all maps are selections and condensations of the features of an area (there are no maps that show everything at the original scale), there are no memories or recollections of the past that do not select and omit. It is impossible to speak of all of the past. Instead, when we think about the past, we organize and structure events to create threads of comprehension" (2000: 13). This is also a basic definition of media framing.

Black-White Narrative

The current master narrative, as crafted in the United States, is unique in that it is most often framed in black-and-white terms, primarily through white eyes (Wilson and Gutiérrez 1995). Both mainstream and oppositional scholars often speak of the nation being founded upon slavery. While this is true, the nation was also built upon an earlier foundation: land theft and the dehumanization and attempted elimination of Indigenous peoples. This omission or blind spot—also a frame—generally precludes discussion of the morality of the foundation of the United States itself. This is what permits U.S. history to be framed as a black-white narrative, generally bypassing this earlier truth. Instead, at best, Indians are but the backdrop for Pilgrims and Thanksgiving. At worst, they are remanded to museums, or nowadays, casinos.

Absent as well in the telling of this master narrative is an Indigenous seven-thousand-year-old maíz narrative or narratives (the centeotzintli narratives), told in Indigenous languages and through Indigenous eyes. Neither the color red or brown nor a racialized Spanish tongue computes.[27] The maíz narrative, like the peoples who come with it, is viscerally rejected by a large portion of the population who appear to feel that their carefully crafted civilizational story or historical project is being interfered with, contaminated, or undermined. This may help to explain the nation's anti-immigrant and anti-bilingual-education movement. Santa Ana (2002) argues that the careful crafting of the master narrative includes framing peoples from the south as either vanquished or mongrels; never as U.S. citizens, never as part of the present, never as full human beings. It is this framing imperative that precludes a full discussion about the possible Indigeneity of some fifty-five million red-brown-black residents of the United States (i.e., "Latinos"), most of them of Mexican or Central American, and Indigenous, origin. Such a discussion would disrupt the master narrative that has essentially eliminated Indigenous peoples from the pages of U.S. history. Scholars such as Vivian Delgado in *You're Not Indian, You're Mexican* (2007) interpret this dynamic of exclusion as part of or a continuation of the policy of Indian removal (which might more aptly be called termination). A discussion of Indigeneity would also challenge the acceptability of remanding Indigenous peoples in the United States to unseen places (reservations, barrios, and urban ghettos). Through narrative exclusion, these brown populations from Mexico and Central and South America have been de-Indigenized and converted into Hispanic/Latino populations, in effect framed as non-Indigenous populations (Delgado 2007). A common characteristic of this process is promoting the notion that Hispanic/Latino and even Chicano history began when Europeans set foot on this continent.[28]

The Rise of Ethnic, Indigenous, and Feminist Studies

The establishment of ethnic-, Indigenous-, and feminist-studies departments in this country in the 1960s and 1970s was a direct challenge to the master narrative. In effect, all these fields of study challenged the narratives and invisibility of women and Indigenous peoples and other peoples of color. Within this context, Chicana/Chicano studies or Raza studies was also created. Within these disciplines, the idea arose that their challenges to official history constituted counternarratives. Those opposed to these disciplines merely viewed them disparagingly as revisionist histories and the scholars as revisionists.

In the United States, the establishment of these disciplines was generally part of civil- and human-rights struggles that were in turn part of, or coincided with, great anticolonial struggles worldwide. One can also argue that it was simply an effort to be heard and counted and included as part of humanity, the expression of a desire to unleash long-suppressed voices.

Mainstream scholars sometimes criticize and frame these disciplines and their scholars as being part of identity politics. Within this realm, there are no legitimate grievances nor is there a need for restitution.

The maíz narratives come out of this context, from both Indigenous and Chicana/Chicano studies, though the maíz narratives are no recent phenomenon but rather part of a seven-thousand-year-old narrative. Through elder epistemology, the argument is made that the maíz narrative does not constitute revisionism. The same can be said about feminist, ethnic, and Indigenous studies and other resistance or oppositional disciplines. Far from revisionism, the maíz narrative is an acknowledgment of an ancient narrative that is documented in both ancient codices and the living and dynamic oral traditions of maíz-based peoples.

Conclusion

After decades of research, it is now known that most Chicanas/Chicanos are probably not of Aztec/Mexica ancestry per se, as Hernández-Ávila comments in the *Amoxtli San Ce Tojuan* documentary (R. Rodríguez and P. Gonzales 2005). Yet in a symbolic sense, modern Mexicans have indeed inherited Aztec/Mexica culture because it has been nationalized by the nation-state of Mexico. And because that same nationalized Aztec/Mexica culture has been imported into the United States, it has become part of the culture of Mexicans living in the United States. That does not detract from the fact that the participants in this culture are actually part of much older and still-living maíz-based civilizations—multiple ancient Indigenous cultures, not just the Aztec/Mexica, including civilizations and cultures of what is today the United States. In the face of a dominant global culture, maíz cultures continue to be resilient.

Figure 5. Map of Aztlán by Pola Lopez. A modern amoxtli depicting the Aztlan–Tenochtitlan migration a thousand years ago. Hidden within this image is the seven-thousand-year-old story of maíz. Courtesy of the artist.

¡Qué Buenas las Gorditas Rellenas!

Maestra Angelbertha Cobb

Maestra Cobb is from the Nahuatl pueblo of Xiloxixico, at the highest point of the Sierra Madre in the state of Puebla, Mexico. She now lives in Sacramento. She is a lifelong educator and teaches this song to pre-K–6 children about the importance of maíz. It is sung and danced to the "Macarena." She is responsible for introducing many Aztec/Mexica ceremonies into the United States, particularly women's ceremonies, such as the coming-of-age ceremony the Xilonen.

El maíz es la base
la base de nuestra cultura
porque quita todo el tiempo el hambre
y a tu cuerpo te le da figura
bien bien buenas que se ven rellenas
bien bien buenas que se ven rellenas
las gorditas hechas de maíz
porque dicen tienen mucho calcio
ese calcio que me falta a mi

bien bien buenas que se ven rellenas
bien bien buenas que se ven rellenas
a los niños siempre les encantan

las actividades hechas de maíz
porque disfrutan al explorarlo
y se sienten mucho muy feliz

bien bien buenas que se ven rellenas
bien bien buenas que se ven rellenas

con frijoles y con salsita
pero recuerdas que si comes muchas
se te agranda la pancita

bien bien buenas que se ven rellenas
bien bien buenas que se ven rellenas
con papitas y verduras
un poco de carnita
son sabrosuras

bien bien buenas que se ven rellenas
bien bien buenas que se ven rellenas
con lechuga y pollo
con queso, rabanitos y repollo
a todos nos gusta eso

bien bien buenas que se ven rellenas
bien bien buenas que se ven rellenas

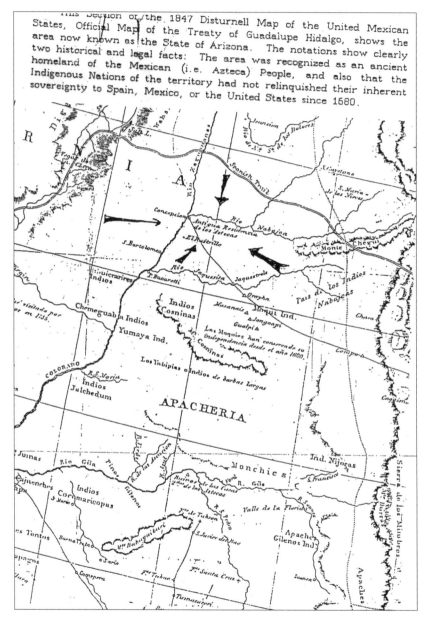

Figure 6. Portion of 1847 Disturnell map showing Antigua Residencia de los Aztecas. Courtesy of Tupac Enrique Acosta.

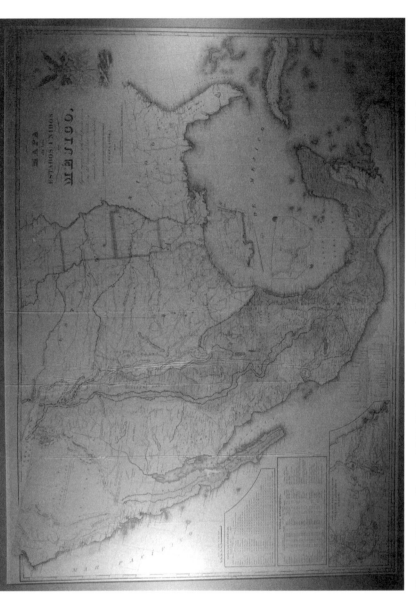

Figure 7. Disturnell map, 1847. This map was attached to the 1848 Treaty of Guadalupe Hidalgo. Courtesy of Brenda Limon.

CHAPTER THREE

The Aztlanahuac Maps

The maps from the 1500s to the 1800s that I uncovered in my initial research on origins and migrations appear, on paper, to buttress the thousand-year-old Aztlan–Tenochtitlan-migration story. It is the search for these maps that steered me to the older maíz-Quetzalcoatl narrative, which arguably is ensconced inadvertently within many of these same maps.

My primary map research was triggered by my receipt in the mid-1990s of a small portion of the 1847 Disturnell map.[1] It showed a region in which the map noted two salient things: (1) that the Hopi of Arizona had been independent since 1680, and (2) that the ancient homeland of the Aztecs (Antigua Residencia de los Aztecas) lay north of the Hopi. The notation regarding 1680 is relevant to Hopi land claims: it is offered as proof that they have never surrendered their sovereignty to anyone. The other notation seemed to indicate that, at one point, the Aztecs lived in the U.S. Southwest. This little photocopy functioned as both story and media, as it was being circulated in underground circles in the technology of the time, prior to the widespread use of the Internet. Neither was it published in book form. Its circulation was limited to being passed around at gatherings and conferences, in effect, just below official radar. While the map's existence was not a secret, it had not been circulated in the mass media prior to the late 1990s. Upon receipt of the photocopy, I followed up by conducting research for my column, determined to find the source of the information given by this map. To my knowledge, research on this topic, even during the Chicano Aztlan-consciousness era, had not been previously published. While conscious of the Aztlan-migration story, I did not presuppose that my research entailed looking for Aztlan, though many people made that assumption. My research revealed that in the many years of engagement with the topic of Aztlan, maps had not been part of the discussion. It was not until after the initial map research was complete that I determined that several of the maps were indeed attempting to track the Aztlan-migration story. Because some of the maps were but copies, the publishers of the copied maps may have been unaware of the narration or the source of the narration on the maps.[2]

The importance of these maps, given that they were generally out of the public eye during this time, is that they contain citations related to not just the Mexica migration but also more ancient migrations. To contextualize these hidden transcripts and hidden narratives, I examined the differences in approach and content between Indigenous and European mapping, discovering in part that Mesoamericans had a long tradition of recording not simply geography but their origin/migration stories on maps.

The U.S. Master Narrative: Mexicans as an Unwanted Population

The U.S. master narrative is the same in relation to Mexican peoples in the United States as to other Indigenous peoples; Mexicans too are framed as defeated and conquered nonwhite peoples in the way of progress and civilization. Along with other Indigenous peoples and wild beasts, Mexicans stand between a God-chosen people and their divine purpose of spreading freedom and heaven on earth over the entire continent.[3] From this point of view, Mexicans do not belong in the United States; they are aliens, foreigners, and mongrels, the epitome of the "other" and "enemy," and their very presence represents a threat to U.S. expansion. This is where Mexicans have traditionally fit into the U.S. master narrative. As Menchaca argued in "Chicano Indianism" (1998), Mexicans in the United States in the 1800s, especially the dark ones, always functioned as a subservient population, segregated, discriminated against, and subjected to extreme violence, including lynchings, often in connection with expropriation of land.[4] However, as Balderrama and Rodríguez argued in *A Decade of Betrayal* (1995), it is the twentieth century that creates the frames or media tropes regarding Mexicans that are prominent today. Anti-Mexican messages resonate during periods of economic instability, contributing to periodic mass-deportation/ repatriation campaigns between 1910 and 1920, and again in the 1930s; Operation Wetback of the 1950s;[5] and the mass-deportation raids of the

1970s and 1990s (Balderrama and Rodríguez 1995). The anti-Mexican hysteria has also intensified in this century.[6]

The Aztlan Insurgent Narrative

Responding to the notion that Mexicans did not belong in the United States, Chicanos in the 1960s proclaimed that the lands that were formerly Mexico—the U.S. Southwest—were in fact the ancient Aztlan of the Aztec/Mexica. Prior to 1969, the theme of Aztlan was not generally a serious topic of discussion among Mexican Americans. While Mexican writers on both sides of the border wrote about the U.S. Southwest as the land lost by Mexico in 1848, it was Chicano scholars, writers, and poets who politically equated the purported former homeland of the Aztec/Mexica with the lands formerly belonging to Mexico with the Southwest. In this manner, they argued that Chicanos could not be alien to lands that belonged to their ancestors.[7] In *The Decolonial Imaginary* (1999), scholar Emma Pérez noted that poets "literally and symbolically chiseled the Chicana/o nation—Aztlán" (59). She continued: "Aztlán, when taken out of the past, becomes a culturally constructed nation written into the present imaginary by poets, historians, and social scientists" (60). Though not all Mexicans or Chicanas/Chicanos descend from the Mexica, the terms *Mexica*, *Mexican*, and *Chicano* became conflated during this time. Thus, Chicanos claimed the geographical space of the Southwest as part of their purported Aztec/Mexica heritage and ancient homeland. This narrative has several contentious variations. My research here does not attempt to ascertain whether these narratives are factually based; they are noted, in an effort to understand why Chicanas/Chicanos believe themselves not to be alien to what is today the U.S. Southwest, and also because it is virtually impossible to understand the much more ancient maíz narratives without first understanding these Aztlan frames. They include:

* Aztlan as the Aztec/Mexica homeland
* Aztlan as the land that was formerly Mexico
* Aztlan as the U.S. Southwest
* Aztlan as the spiritual homeland to Chicanos
* Aztlan as part of a bronze/Indigenous continent

All the Aztlan stories, as used by Chicanos in the 1960s–1970s, are, in effect, counterframes that conform to narratives of belonging. The

countered frame is that of Mexicans as an illegal, illegitimate, and alien
population (Santa Ana 2002). Aztlan upsets that media frame, and the
name itself becomes a trope as it connotes Indigeneity, resistance, and a
claim to lands where Chicanos are viewed as foreigners and invaders. These
claims are not without merit. They are what Broyles-González (2001a)
refers to as symbolic resistance narratives. The hidden transcript, the whis-
pered stories of Aztlan being in "the north" (specifically in New Mexico or
Utah, as will be shown shortly), emerges from colonial chronicles of the
1500s, written by both Indigenous writers and Spanish priests, utilizing
ancient written and oral traditions.

As utilized by Chicanas/Chicanos in the 1960s, these frames, tropes, and
narratives emerged within a highly charged political environment. Many
Mexicans and Central and South Americans had long internalized the
belief that they were an unwanted population in this country, particularly
since this attitude was regularly articulated in the media.[8] This attitude
was rooted in systemic violence in the 1800s and it manifested as periodic
repatriation/deportation campaigns throughout the twentieth century.

As Lakoff noted in *Don't Think of an Elephant* (2004), frames that acti-
vate fear and lead to demonization are those with which many mainstream
Americans are most comfortable. Because the scapegoating of foreigners is
a well-embedded frame taken for granted in American society, it must be
activated for it to work, especially when it involves Mexicans.[9] Fear-based
mass deportations—immigration enforcement is nowadays conflated with
anti-terrorism—serve as useful triggers, producing calls for bigger walls, mili-
tarization of the border, and anti-immigrant laws and ordinances nationwide.
In Arizona, the governor signed the anti-immigrant legislation SB 1070 amid
her own invented claims of beheadings in the Arizona desert.[10]

The Aztlan-Consciousness Era

While some have characterized the idea of Aztlan as an expression of
romantic nationalism or ultranationalism (Cheng 2004), the Aztlan narratives of the 1960s–1970s can also be seen as a defense mechanism in
response to U.S. ultranationalism. Michael Billig wrote: "This nationalism,
above all, has appeared so forgettable, so natural, to social scientists, and
today is so globally important" (1995: 6).[11] One response to anti-Mexican
and anti-immigrant hysteria was the explosion of the Chicano/Chicana
Movement. It was a political movement akin to the Black Power and American Indian movements. One product of it, according to some scholars, was

the reinvention of Aztlan and the creative construction and comprehension of new ethnic origins "as a self-conscious maneuver aimed at propagating symbolic forms of separatist nationalism" (Klor de Alva 1997: 56).

This movement came with many new signs, symbols, images, and frames. The signs were pre-Columbian, while the frames connoted Indigeneity—the antithesis of alien and foreign. Poet Alurista (Alberto Urrea)[12] is often credited with associating the idea of Aztlan with the U.S. Southwest because in 1969, at the Chicano Youth Liberation Conference in Denver (a foundational gathering for the Chicano Movement), he penned "El Plan Espiritual de Aztlan" (1970). However, it was Rodolfo "Corky" Gonzales of La Raza Unida Party–Crusade for Justice who was most associated with the idea of attaining an Aztlan-Chicano homeland (R. Gonzales 2001). While land-grant-rights activist Reies Lopez Tijerina and labor leader Cesar Chavez were never associated with Aztlan, young Chicanas/Chicanos identified with their movements partially because many of their symbols broadcast Indigeneity.

The struggle for land was associated with Mexico's Indigenous leader Emiliano Zapata. During that era, the portrait of Zapata holding a rifle, with the words "Tierra y Libertad" (Land and Liberty), was one of the primary images associated with the Chicano Movement. This message connoted Indigeneity. Other portraits of Zapata carried the words "It is better to die on one's feet than to live on one's knees." The farm workers' struggle in the United States—which was symbolically connected to Zapata's struggle—was about the land and the people, represented by the United Farm Workers (UFW) flag, which featured a black eagle.[13] When turned upside down, that same eagle took the shape of a pyramid. Both symbols have long been associated with Indigenous Mexico.

Jack Forbes, in 1961, may have been the first modern U.S. scholar to make the connection between Aztlan and the U.S. Southwest. In that year in southern California he helped establish the Movimiento Nativo Americano (Native American Movement), a precursor to the Chicano Movement. Writing nearly ten years before Alurista, in "The Mexican Heritage of Aztlán" (1961–1962), Forbes wrote on behalf of the organization. He argued that:

> Prior to 1821, the word Mexican referred to persons who were Nahuatl-speaking (that is, to those, such as the Aztecs, who spoke *el idioma mexicano o Nahuatl*), or who were of Nahua ancestry. . . . Thus when we refer to the Mexican heritage before 1821 we are referring primarily to the Nahua (or Aztec-Toltec) heritage, although the word

can also be extended to include non-Nahua peoples who have since 1821 become part of the Mexican republic of Mexico (Tarascans, Mayas, Mixtecs, Zapotecs, Yaquis, etc.).

Forbes continued, "Aztlan is the Aztec (Mexican) name for their original homeland far to the north of the Valley of Mexico." He located it in the U.S. Southwest and northwest Mexico, "both of which are part of a common geographical-cultural-historical unit" (1)—north of what traditionally has been considered Mesoamerica. The Movimiento Nativo Americano promoted the idea that Mexican Americans were native or Indigenous peoples of the Southwest, as part of an Indigenous continent. The Southwest, he posited, was culturally Mexicanized in ancient times via maíz, as well as in historical and contemporary times. He posited that the barrio of Analco in Santa Fe, New Mexico, the barrio where the Nahuatl-speaking Tlaxcalteca first lived when Spaniards brought them there, was the birthplace of the Chicano (R. Rodríguez and P. Gonzales 2002, 2005).

While Forbes and his ideas were influential in the early Chicano Movement of the 1960s and 1970s, his work is generally not cited by current Chicano and Chicana scholars, who instead credit Alurista with both anchoring the idea of a Chicano Aztlan and giving the Chicano movement a nationalist bent and an Indigenous character. Only Daniel Cooper Alarcón in *The Aztec Palimpsest* (1997) and Sheila Marie Contreras in *Blood Lines* (2008) seem to be aware of Forbes's role in this discussion. Cooper Alarcón posited that Aztlan was constantly being rewritten and that when understood as a palimpsest, "Aztlan ceases to be ahistorical and insists upon an examination of the past, a study that will reveal not only the complexity of Aztlan, but of the Mesoamerican history that was used as a resource by Chicano nationalists" (11). *Palimpsest* is another term for rearticulation, a process that has seen Mexicans in the United States view themselves differently through the generations.

Also associated with Aztlan is the late Luis Leal, who came to the United States in 1927 actually looking for Aztlan in what is today the Southwest (R. Rodríguez and P. Gonzales 2005). After the 1970s, when most scholars no longer wrote about Aztlan as an actual physical location, Leal wrote: "Whosoever wants to find Aztlán, let him look for it, not on the maps, but in the most intimate part of his being" (1989: 13). Alurista had been one of his students in the 1960s, a fact that points to the possible influence of Leal on the young insurgent artist (R. Rodríguez and P. Gonzales 2005).

Forbes's (1961) essay and Alurista's (1970) manifesto, bracketing the 1960s, may indicate that the idea of Aztlan was germinating in Mexican

American activist circles throughout that decade. At the same time, Leal's research, decades earlier, demonstrates that such discussions were certainly taking place throughout the twentieth century in Mexican American circles, even if there is no public documentation prior to 1960. In Mexico, published discussions took place throughout the colonial era and in the nineteenth and twentieth centuries, particularly among influential writers such as Manuel Orozco y Berra ([1880] 1954), Alfredo Chavero (1884), and Eustaquio Buelna (1887).

The Aztlan-consciousness era had many naysayers, and a short shelf life among intellectuals—the late 1960s through the mid-1970s.[14] However, Aztlan as a concept did not withdraw from the Mexican American political lexicon and landscape altogether, though it ceased being the overarching metanarrative of a generation. Ironically, Aztlan as a subject of study has a longer tenure in the academic world. There, Aztlan goes from "representing nation, unity, and liberation" to an atomized Aztlan. One of those articulations includes the idea of Aztlan as "the borderlands"—a concept often associated with Anzaldúa—representing a shift of focus from origins to identity (Pérez-Torres 2001: 234).[15]

The shift occurred as the number of Mexicans/Chicanos more than doubled from the previous generation. This population ceased being associated strictly with the Southwest and has now spread throughout the country.[16] Ironically, this spread is one reason for the general disuse of the Aztlan concept; it arguably does not resonate with peoples outside of the Southwest. This is particularly true for people born since the 1970s.[17] Yet, like a calendar stone, its memory is ever-present, particularly in the Southwest, where the majority of Mexicans and Central Americans in the United States in fact continue to live. For many of those who continue to use the Aztlan concept, Aztlan is not a geographical entity but a spiritual homeland without borders. Others relate Aztlan not to the U.S. Southwest but rather to the entire continent.[18]

Aztlan as Aztec-Homeland Narrative

The "Aztec homeland" or Aztlan is the purported place of origin of the Mexica and point of departure for their migration, an event associated with various dates including AD 1064, AD 1116, and AD 1160.[19] On 1500s-era maps, the name is given as Aztalan or Aztatlan. Nuño de Guzmán reached a town called Aztatlan in 1530. John Chávez wrote: "This locale was situated in northwest New Spain when the Spaniards began to associate

Figure 8. Tira de la Peregrinación: the Boturini Codex. Depiction of the Aztlan–Tenochtitlan-migration story.

the Seven Cities with the Seven Caves of the Aztecs" (1989: 58).[20] When Guzmán reached Aztatlan, he determined he had not found Aztlan and razed it, and thus the search for Aztlan shifted further north (Buelna 1887). He moved on because, like other explorers, he was expecting to find a land of riches.[21]

The basic story of the Aztec/Mexica migration is found in several codices, including the well-known *Tira de la Peregrinación* or Boturini Codex ([1530–1541] 2000), written some ten to twenty years after the initial Spanish invasion. The migration story is also part of the Mendoza Codex ([1541–1542] 1992), which depicts the end of the journey, culminating with the founding of Tenochtitlan in AD 1325. While the narrative is contained in these codices, written in a pre-Columbian style, only the Aubin Codex ([1576] 1963, 1980) actually contains the word *Aztlan*, which was added in European letters.

The basic migration story found in the *Tira de la Peregrinación* and the Aubin Codex is also a feature of virtually all sixteenth–nineteenth-century European chroniclers and writers. Many relate it to the origins of the Aztec/Mexica or other Nahuatl-speaking peoples or the origins of Indigenous peoples in general. Most point to the north, with almost all of them naming the location of Aztlan as New Mexico. Indigenous writers from that era, most prominently Fernando Alvarado Tezozomoc (*Crónica Mexicáyotl* [1576] 1998), also pointed to New Mexico. During the 1500s, New Mexico encompassed what is today the greater U.S. Southwest. On maps, the land to the east was Florida. However, Tezozomoc was not definitive in regard to the location of Aztlan. He wrote: "The Mexicans left from the place called Aztlan, which is in the middle of waters. . . . The Aztlan of the ancient Mexicans is what is today called New Mexico" (15). He later wrote that they lived in "the great city of Aztlan, Chicomoztoc, more or less; in the city of Aztlan, Aztatlan, the land of herons, which is why it is called Aztlan; it was a place that perhaps is close to the extensive coasts, with extensive waterways, a place that nowadays the Spaniards call New Mexico, Aztlan, Chicomoztoc" (21). He further wrote that they left from "Quinehuayan, in the year 12 Cane; this is how they came, the ancient Aztecs, Mexicans, Chichimecas, from Aztlan, from what is now called New Mexico" (22).

Other Indigenous writers from the 1500s–1600s who wrote on this topic include Diego Muñoz Camargo ([1585] 1998), Cristóbal del Castillo ([1606] 1991), the author of the Ramírez Codex ([1500s] 1944), and Domingo Francisco de San Antón Muñón Chimalpahin Quauhtlehuanitzin (Codex Chimalpahin [1621] 1997). Muñoz Camargo, from Tlaxcala, Mexico, wrote that the ancestors of virtually all Mesoamerican peoples had crossed a body of water, then settled at the site of the Seven Caves, with the Chichimecas being the last peoples to arrive and migrate south. Del Castillo wrote that the Mexica were not the first to cross the waters to reach Mexico. He also noted that they left Aztlan, near a lake, due to oppression from the Chicomoztocas (115). While the author of the Ramírez Codex is unknown, Orozco y Berra (1944) posits that it was likely an Indigenous writer. This codex locates Aztlan in New Mexico. Written in the late 1500s, the Ramírez Codex is derived from Crónica X, written around 1525. Chimalpahin Quauhtlehuanitzin also locates Aztlan in New Mexico, but adds that it was actually the original or Old Mexico and that the Aztecs had been there for 1,014 years before migrating. He also identifies it as Aztatlan. The basic storyline is this: guided by Huitzilopochtli, the Aztecs/Mexica departed in the eleventh or twelfth century, from an island in a lake, somewhere in the north. A variation is that after leaving, they arrived at a cave (Chicomoztoc or Seven Caves), then continued on their journey. After many years of migrating and settling new towns, they came upon an eagle devouring a serpent. It is there that they established

their new home of Tenochtitlan/Mexico City in AD 1325. This is the story
that is emblazoned on the Mexican flag.

The story as given by non-Indigenous writers is a much more detailed
narrative, and is recounted in various codices, including the Florentine
Codex ([1577] 1961, 1976) of Sahagún.[22] The longer version—which can
also be considered an historia más profunda, rarely mentioned in the context of the Aztlan-migration story—is of a journey from across the oceans
several thousand years ago. When the people landed, they arrived with
wise elders carrying books that taught about architecture, astronomy, and
mathematics, along with the arts and sciences. Not long thereafter, some
of the elders returned with their books across the ocean to the land from
which they originally came. Of those peoples that remained, some went
south, toward Guatemala. Others went north. They remained there, and
then much later began a series of southerly migrations. The last of them
was the Mexica in AD 1064 (Florentine Codex ([1577] 1961). The more
well-known and truncated Aztec/Mexica version is a one-thousand-year-
old story of coming from the north, from Aztlan/Chicomoztoc. It is this
version, associated with Mexico's flag, that has been inscribed in the nation's
history and psyche. Neither the date of the migration nor the exact point
of departure is as important as the narrative that Tenochtitlan/Mexico City
was founded as a result of a southerly migration, long before the arrival of
Europeans.

The Toltec migration story is also different, reputedly made much
earlier than the Aztec/Mexica story. The Toltecs of Tollan/Teotihuacan
are credited with bringing coherency, via their stories, to Mesoamerica's
Quetzalcoatl-maíz culture (D. Carrasco 2000, Florescano 2006).[23] The
Toltecs are viewed by many of the colonial chroniclers as having migrated
not from across the oceans but from the Middle East, via China, after
the Great Flood or the Tower of Babel, arriving first in California, then
Huehuetlapallan, then migrating south (Boturini 1746b, Clavigero 1964,
Sánchez Lamego 1955).[24]

Despite the many varied migration stories, the basic trope of emergence
from a place called Seven Caves (Chicomoztoc for the Mexica) is one that
is common to many, if not most, Mesoamerican peoples. The *Popol Vuh*
of the Quiché Maya depicts the people emerging or migrating from Tulan
(Seven Caves), a place sometimes identified with Tollan/Teotihuacan
(Florescano 1999). There is no scholarly consensus as to where these
Seven Caves were, nor the location of Aztlan/Chicomoztoc. There is
also no consensus as to whether Seven Caves even existed on earth; the
argument is made that they existed in the mythical realm (López Austin

1997). Some scholars say that the Seven Caves simply represent seven peoples, lineages, or clans. However, in many Indigenous cosmologies it is commonly believed that caves are a source of power, often identified with places of creation/emergence.

Cecilio Orozco posited in *The Book of the Sun, Tonatiuh* (1992) that the word *Nahuatl* (Four Rivers) originates in the U.S. Four Corners region. In a later work (Rivas Salmón and Orozco 1997), Orozco and Mexican scholar Alfonso Rivas Salmón favor Mezcatitan (Mexcaltitan) in the Mexican state of Nayarit as the site of Aztlan. Other Mexican scholars concur.

Mexican Indigenous scholar Arturo Meza Gutiérrez argued that the nationalized Aztec/Mexica migration story is European fiction, designed to invoke Biblical stories of promised lands (R. Rodríguez and P. Gonzales 2005). Meza Gutiérrez's hypothesis is that the migration of the Aztec/Mexica—who were mathematical and scientific peoples—was guided by astronomy, not visions or gods. He argues that peoples with that kind of advanced knowledge did not have to propitiate gods with human sacrifice to assure the proper functioning of the universe. A similar idea has been proffered in a different context by Steve Lekson in *The Chaco Meridian* (1999). He argues that the migration of the Anasazi, ancient peoples of the Southwest, was based on astronomical alignments. Neither Lekson nor Meza Gutiérrez has suggested that the Mexica and Anasazi were the same peoples. Lekson's theory is that the migration of the elites (engineers, architects, scientists, and mathematicians) would have occurred from Chaco to Aztec, New Mexico, then to Mesa Verde, Colorado, and then southward to Paquime, Mexico. All of these sites are aligned astronomically on the same meridian, as is Culiacán, Mexico. The timeline and the geography generally coincide with the Aztec/Mexica migration of the eleventh or twelfth century. Culiacán, coincidentally, is also featured prominently in the purported Aztec/Mexica migration journey. It is the first stop after Chicomoztoc (Lekson 1999).

Taking a differing view, Carrasco, Jones, and Sessions (2000: 51) argue that the Mexica were neither nomads nor migrants to Mesoamerica but simply feigned foreignness to associate themselves with the advanced Toltecs.

Maps: Charting Myth, Legends, and History

Without question, the 1500s–1800s-era maps that my research uncovered point to ancient Mexican Indigenous migrations from what is today the United States. Despite this plethora of maps, there was an absence of discussion of them by Chicana/Chicano and Mexican scholars during the time when Aztlan was central to the discipline of Chicana/Chicano studies. The maps I examined appear to allude to the Aztlan–Tenochtitlan-migration story, along with the deeper and hidden maíz narratives.

While the basic Aztlan-migration story is taught as legend or fable in Mexican schools, the story points to many recognizable geographic locations in Mexico. Therefore, throughout the years, many people have attempted to locate Aztlan somewhere on the continent, especially using maps. The first known attempt to locate Aztlan, long before the arrival of Cortés, was purportedly ordered by Moctezuma I of the Mexica, who was interested in finding the location of his ancestors. In this endeavor, he commissioned a legion of magicians (Boone 2000: 19).

Before continuing this discussion, a word of caution regarding cartography is necessary. Prior to the twentieth century, although maps contained useful information, they also contained distorted and even fanciful information. Aztlan falls into this category somewhat, as it was initially confused by Europeans with Cíbola. Another word of caution comes from López Austin (1997). Searches for origins have often suffered from a European inability to distinguish myth from history, and he notes that "migration routes were frequent examples of that confusion." Cities like Tenochtitlan/Mexico City and Culhuacan were modeled after "the ancestors' place of origin" (51). Other names of mythical places of origin are: Tlalocan, Tamoanchan, Aztlan, Chicomoztoc, and Teoculhuacan. Still others are Tula, Tollan, and Huehuetlapallan. Some but not all of these names can be located on maps.[25]

Several 1500s-era maps, including the 1531 Oronce Fine map, may illustrate López Austin's point about confusing myth and history. It marks a place called "Ta-ma-cho," located in the Gulf of Mexico, near what appears to be the mouth of the Pánuco River. Phonetically, it resembles Tamoanchan, the name of the place from which maíz, and the ancestors of the Maya-Nahuatl-speaking peoples of the continent, purportedly originated several thousand years before the arrival of the Spaniards (Florentine Codex [1577] 1961). Moctezuma reportedly related this story to Hernán Cortés. It was also recounted by several chroniclers, with some accounts locating Tamoanchan in Morelos.

López Austin (1997) argued that while there may be several earthly Tamoanchans, the original model—paradise, where Quetzalcoatl first took maíz—is not to be located on a map.[26] Perhaps affirming this tendency to locate mythic places on earth and on maps, the 1656 Sanson map—which depicts California as an island—also locates a Tula (associated with the

Toltecs) in the vicinity of Florida. There are in fact many Tulas in Mexico (another form of the name is *Tule*) and others in the United States as well.

Yet another caution regarding Western mapping comes from elders who say that Indigenous peoples have lost more land through mapping than through actual war. Corbin Harney of the Western Shoshone nation helped to contextualize this idea. He said: "My people, the Shoshone people, they're connected with what's over there in Mexico." Looking at the Disturnell map, he said: "The whole continent belonged to us. At one time we roamed the whole thing." Maps, he observed, were like photographs, capturing but a moment in time (Aztlanahuac interview, August 19, 2001: in R. Rodríguez and P. Gonzales 2004). He concluded that Western mapping is the quintessential frame-up: who belongs and who doesn't. Information in maps shifts with power relations; consider the Antigua Residencia de los Aztecas, which appears for several centuries on Spanish/European and Mexican maps but disappears from U.S. maps after the Treaty of Guadalupe Hidalgo. Another example of such framing is a 1998 *Newsweek* map—distributed to high schools nationwide—that shows North America as "Anglo America."

Mills College geographer Deborah Santana comments on the power of maps, specifically the 1847 Disturnell map that contains the Antigua Residencia citation:

> Maps really are important not only in what they say, but what they don't say. The mapmaker has a tremendous amount of power, not only to show things, but also to hide things. We so often assume that a place or process is really the way it's portrayed in a map and yet a map can be mistaken either accidentally or intentionally. Maps have a tremendous amount of power and often determine how people feel about places. (Personal communication, September 3, 2001)

Commenting on the map, she argued that it confirms what many Chicanos and southwestern peoples have said for centuries; that Aztlan is not simply folklore, for "the map is a visual representation and acceptable proof that as of 1847, that location of the Aztec homeland was accepted by the mapmaker as being a real part of history." Santana noted that she uses the map in her classes and that it creates a shock among the non-Latino students.[27] Santana concluded:

> It goes against everything that they've been taught. I don't think that it would have so strong an impact if I just sat there and told them. I could

tell them all the history and all the questions about maps that have been
found and about the traditions of the people of the Southwest and the
connection between Nahuatl and Uto-Aztecan languages and I don't
think anything would impact them like this map does.

As the views of Santana show, whether the information on the Disturnell
map is accurate or not, it has nowadays taken on a life of its own in the
post-Aztlan-consciousness era.

Aztlanahuac: Mesoamerica in North America

Of the nearly two hundred maps from the 1500s–1800s that I initially
located that reference north-south connections, most of the relevant information regarding the primary Aztec/Mexica migration story can be gleaned
from three main maps (see appendix 2): the 1804 Humboldt map, the 1768
Alzate map, and the 1728 Barreiro map. They plot a point of origin and
three other points of a southerly migration route that eventually reached
Tenochtitlan/Mexico City. They agree on: (1) the region around the Great
Salt Lake as the point of departure; (2) the first stop on this migration
journey as the confluence of the Colorado and Green Rivers; (3) the second stop as Casa Grande, near Tucson, Arizona; and (4) the third stop as
Paquimé, near Casas Grandes in Chihuahua, Mexico.[28]

The Disturnell map is a fourth map in this group. While it leaves out
the point of departure, it does note the same three migration stops as the
earlier maps. It appears that the Barreiro map plotted the Mexica migration
story for the first time on a non-Indigenous map, serving as a template for
subsequent mapmakers.

Other maps (Miera y Pacheco from 1778 and García Conde from 1845;
see appendix 2) appear to show the first stop on this route, after departure
from the Great Salt Lake, not on the confluence of the Green and Colorado Rivers but at a point to the east of that confluence. The reason for the
uncertainty or inconsistency is that maps were still inaccurate even up until
the twentieth century, and there are no major ceremonial or archaeological
sites near that confluence. However, lying to the east are the ruins at Aztec
in New Mexico and Mesa Verde in Colorado. The Miera y Pacheco and
García Conde maps most likely are pointing to Aztec.

Despite this apparent inconsistency, there is a wealth of information on
each map. Earlier maps allude to the same information. My map research

indicates that the material for the Disturnell map—including the Antigua Residencia de los Aztecas citation—was copied from earlier maps. Moreover, the idea of ancient Mexican migrations from the north, beginning from a body of water, did not originate with any European map. Instead it comes from pre-Cuauhtemoc codices and chronicles that recorded those oral traditions. They may, in addition, correspond to the stories of Indigenous peoples of the U.S. Southwest, who speak of a large lake as the point of origin of Mexican peoples (Sánchez 1997). The idea of having migrated from a lake or body of water may be part of a much older, primordial story of origins for Indigenous peoples not only in the south but also in the north.

Much of the information on early colonial maps of the Americas came from native sources. Some of it corresponded to ancient Indigenous stories. Some was accurate, some was not. In many instances, the information given about sites may have been accurate but then written down incorrectly. This is understandable given mutually unintelligible languages and inept, or biased, translators and translations. The oft-cited case of Yucatán is the best example. Hernán Cortés himself related the story ([1500s] 1990) that when Europeans landed in Yucatán, they asked the native people where they were. The people responded, "Uic athan." This meant "We can't understand you." The Spaniards thought the response to their question *Uic athan* was the name of where they were and thus inadvertently christened it Yucatán. What is now Yucatán is reputed to have been known as the "land of the turkey and the deer" (D. Carrasco 1990).

It is highly likely that the mapmakers indeed were attempting to locate Aztlan and other Mexican Indigenous points of origin on these maps. However, of the hundreds of maps in archives across the continent, only Humboldt mentions Aztlan by name. While his information seems to have come from the Alzate map and/or the Barreiro map, neither of them mentions Aztlan.

Many maps of the 1500s to 1700s cite, not Aztlan, but Aztatlan—and not in the Great Salt Lake region but in the northwest part of modern Mexico, possibly in Nayarit. This actually may be an early cartographical representation of where Aztlan was supposed to have been and corresponds to the point that many Mexican archaeologists cite: Mexcaltitan in Nayarit (Orozco y Berra 1944).

Many Mexican Indigenous elders, including Don Aurelio (personal communication, August 11, 2005) and Maestra Cobb (February 20, 2007), also point to this location. It is often said that the reason that Spanish explorers kept looking to points further north is that (1) they were convinced that

Aztlan was a place of riches; and (2) native peoples kept pointing them north, either toward the Seven Cities that explorers were looking for, or toward a lake, or simply away from them.

Other maps from the 1500s and 1600s may allude to older Toltec migrations, reportedly involving Huehuetlapallan, Tula, and Tollan/Teotihuacan. Without question, more recent maps do show Toltec migrations coming from what is today the United States, including points outside the Southwest. A twentieth-century map, *Mapa General de las Grandes Inmigraciones*, depicts Nahoa, Olmec, and Otomi peoples all coming from the north. Nahoa (Nahuatl) migrations are shown down the U.S. California coast. The Otomi are depicted as coming from the Southwest, whereas the Olmec are depicted as coming from the Great Lakes region, down the Mississippi. One Olmec branch migrates toward Florida, then on to the Caribbean, whereas another travels down the Gulf of Mexico into Mexico (López Rosado 1940).

While future research may arrive at more definitive conclusions regarding Mexican Indigenous migrations, there is an undeniable cartographic tradition of attempting to chart migrations from what is today the United States into Mexico.

The Hidden Narratives

There appears to be a hidden relationship between these maps and the centeotzintli or maíz narratives of this continent. It bears repeating that there is incontrovertible evidence of maíz migrations from southern Mexico into what is today the United States several thousand years ago. However, beyond scientific evidence, there is the narrative that, Martínez Parédez (1960) argued, united the entire continent through maíz. He also argued that the ancient story of Quetzalcoatl, the bringer of maíz and civilization, is the hidden narrative on the Mexican national coat of arms and the Mexican flag. He wrote:

> The national coat of arms obeys an idea precisely derived from the Tamoanchan, the Place of the Feathered Serpent, because what the Aztecs found at Lake Texcoco, perched atop a cactus, was precisely an eagle and a serpent, the same symbolism, the same concept that the Proto-Mayas proclaimed when they migrated to these lands thousands of years earlier. . . . This is precisely what the Aztecs had been looking for. Once organized, they accepted Quetzalcoatl into their pantheon. (90)[29]

In *Los Mayas* (1966), Girard saw a relationship between the eagle and serpent of Mexico's flag and Quetzalcoatl—represented by the bird and serpent glyph for Tamoanchan, found in the pre-Columbian Dresden Codex. Further, Girard affirms that the glyph represents the creation of human beings in Tamoanchan—also the birthplace of maíz—from the blood of a serpent, brought by a bird and mixed with *masa* or corn dough (391–92).

This same hidden narrative undergirds the migration story found on the Disturnell, Humboldt, Alzate, and Barreiro maps, which appear to reference the Aztlan-migration story. The older maps from the 1500s and 1600s also appear to track or allude to the even older Toltec migrations. Various maps note a Tolm, Tolman, or Toliman, and even Tamoanchan; this may be an attempt to chart the migration of the Tamoanchanes/Toltecs.[30] As Martínez Parédez (1960) noted, the eagle-and-serpent imagery is much older than the Aztecs and resonates beyond Mexican borders, all the way to Peru. The Mexican flag, he posits, depicts not simply the Aztec/Mexica migration story but, hidden within it, the serpentine philosophy of the Toltecs, which spread in various forms throughout the continent and was embraced by the peoples who came to be the Nahoa-Chanes, Nahua-Maya, Quechua-Maya, and others.

According to this narrative, the eagle-and-serpent trope—Mexico's meta-cultural root paradigm—actually contains the more ancient maíz narrative of the continent. It has been hidden, they argue, behind the eagle-and-serpent symbol since it was adopted by the Aztec/Mexica.[31] Many elders throughout the continent tell a similar story. In *Iroquois on Fire* (2006), Mohawk writer Doug George-Kanentiio wrote about an Indigenous conference on migration held in Denver in the 1990s at which most of the participants from throughout the continent were in agreement with the narratives of Indigenous peoples having come to the Americas from across the oceans, though not from Europe (8–9). George-Kanentiio noted that the Maya are generally considered the "grandparents" of other Indigenous peoples. These ideas of common stories and common origins are not isolated. They are also told by campesinos regarding their connection to corn. In *1491: New Revelations of the Americas Before Columbus* (2005), Charles Mann asked Héctor Díaz Castellanos of Oaxaca what kind of Indian he was. He responded: "Somos hombres de Maíz"—"We are people of corn" (221). Mann relates that he was miffed by the expression "Somos hombres de Maíz," unable initially to comprehend how people could identify, not with an ethnicity or nation-state, but with something that people eat, and believe themselves to be made from it.

The idea of common origins, or at least of a common connection, is mapped by many of the oral traditions of Indigenous peoples throughout the continent. In 1990, at an Ecuador Indigenous summit, the Prophecy of the Unity of the Eagle and Condor—North America and South America—was revealed and made public. It predicted that just as the continent was once one, it would be so again. It reinvigorated an Indigenous movement that views the continent as ancient and unified, and it also set in motion the Peace and Dignity Journeys held every four years since 1992 (Gustavo Gutierrez and Tupac Enrique Acosta, Aztlanahuac interviews: in R. Rodríguez and P. Gonzales 2004).[32]

Maestra Cobb asserts that there are cultural-linguistic links between southern Mexico and the U.S. Southwest. She commented that years ago, while attending a ceremony in Hopi, she became aware that she was able to understand Hopi elders in her Nahuatl language (R. Rodríguez and P. Gonzales 2005). Linguists have long known that the Hopi and Nahuatl languages are both members of the Uto-Aztecan language family (Forbes 1973). Yet scholars posit that the distance between the communities is so great (Puebla and Hopi are more than two thousand miles apart) and the separation would have occurred so long ago that they should not be able to comprehend each other today.[33] Cobb's testimony that she held many conversations with elders over the course of two weeks is, for some academic scholars, something of a linguistic mystery. However, her testimony contributes to a ceremonial discourse that many elders throughout the continent speak of—about being one people and being united by maíz (R. Rodríguez and P. Gonzales 2005). Cobb's story suggests continuous north-south cultural connection over thousands of miles.

Mapping a Story or Mapping the Land

My discussion of map research thus far has emphasized the different traditions and competing cosmovisions of the Indigenous and Western colonial worlds. This section compares and contrasts the ways Western-constructed maps and Indigenous maps portray and represent cultural landscapes or places, and the ways in which these maps shape social memory and narratives and counternarratives of belonging and identity. It is the Indigenous traditions and narratives, the same ones used on maps, that have helped shape Mexican/Chicana/Chicano identity and spiritual and geographic consciousness—including the notion of being Indigenous to what is today the Southwest. Two representative maps help to illustrate these points:

the Cortés map or Nuremberg map from 1524 and the Indigenous map of Tenochtitlan also known as the Mendoza Codex ([1541–1542] 1992). They demonstrate the different worldviews that went into the construction of European and Indigenous maps.

In *The Mapping of New Spain* (1996), Barbara Mundy argued that the 1524 and 1541–1542 maps are representative of the differences between Indigenous and European cartography. Both were understandable to their respective audiences, but were most likely indecipherable to each other's. She argued that they were made at a time when Europeans were creating maps in earnest. Indigenous peoples were also making maps. Both represented spatiality, but utilized different concepts, reflecting their different worldviews.

For the peoples of Mesoamerica, European maps would have been wholly insufficient, as their emphasis was primarily on geography and cultural hegemony, whereas Mesoamerican maps were more concerned with narrative history, origins, and ceremonial discourse. In *Writing Without Words* (1994), Boone and Mignolo argued that Aztec/Mexica mapmakers placed Tenochtitlan at the center of the universe, that their maps were used for purposes of war, and that they were also useful to *pochtecas* or merchants. Post-Cuauhtemoc Indigenous maps or lienzos, on the other hand, were used to claim land or settle land disputes. During the early Spanish-colonial era, these were considered legal documents.

The 1524 map of the Aztec capital of Tenochtitlan/Mexico City is typical of European maps of the time, and is based on the contemporary account of Hernán Cortés. The viewer sees the Valley of Mexico with the city of Tenochtitlan at center, including its canal, a lake surrounding the city, and adjacent towns. Mundy (1996) notes: "At center, the European viewer would see the city's dark heart, for here lay the main temple precinct of Tenochtitlan, with its temples and skull-racks, where human sacrifice was once celebrated." Two systems of projection were employed in combination, Euclidean and Albertian, the objective of the mapmaker being to give a model of the entire city, "since the city [itself], like the larger world, was visible to the human eye only in parts, never in its entirety" (xiii). Put another way, the map looks like a (distorted) aerial view of the city.

In contrast to the European map, the 1541–1542 Indigenous map is rectangular, divided into four quadrants enclosed by a larger rectangle, though it "is not based on a geometric projection like the Euclidean one we saw guiding the Cortés map. Perhaps it is better thought of as being a humanistic or social projection—that is, the physical space of the city has not been filtered through and reduced by an overlying graticule; rather, its

structuring device is the human or social layout of the city—four constitu-
ent parts, populated by the calpolli of ten founders" (Mundy 1996: xvi). It
is also a historical projection. The map depicts the city of Tenochtitlan in
1325, and not just the city itself but also the event of its founding. It is part
of the Aztlan-migration story and perhaps also the more ancient Toltec/
Tamoanchan migration story.

In regard to this same map, Galarza (1986) says it can be completely
read and is much more complex than he or other scholars had imagined. It
can also be read in connection with the *Tira de la Peregrinación* or migration codex: the *Tira* purportedly, as discussed above, relates the Aztlan–
Tenochtitlan-migration story, and the Mendoza Codex is essentially the
end of that story, depicting, in map form, the founding of Tenochtitlan.
However, in regard to the *Tira*, unlike what has been repeated by scholars
for centuries, Galarza and Libura (2000) posit that the Mexica departure
with which it begins most likely is not from a place called Aztlan. They note
that Aztlan's glyph does not appear in the *Tira*. Instead, they write, *Aztlan* is
a name that was most likely created by either Europeans or Europeanized
scholars. According to Galarza and Libura, what does appear in the *Tira*
as the point of departure is a place called *Ce Acatl Ameyalco*: One Reed,
Flowing Waters. They note that the *Tira* does mention the Mexica leaving
from Chicomoztoc. That the *Tira* does not mention Aztlan does not mean
that they necessarily discount it; they simply say they cannot find it in this
codex. They also believe that much of what is known about the Mexica
from the codices will have to be discarded and that it will take researchers
at least two generations to correct all the misinterpretations.[34]

Returning to the Aztec/Mexica-migration story and its corresponding
eagle-and-serpent symbol, its use as a national symbol is problematic
because there were/are hundreds of Indigenous nations in what is today
Mexico. As such, there is not one Mexican migration story but hundreds.
The Aztec/Mexica-migration story as depicted in the above-named codices
became Mexico's official migration story when those who fought in the
Mexican War of Independence of 1810–1821 nationalized it. In part, this
nationalization came about because of the importance of Tenochtitlan/
Mexico City to the psyche of the new insurgent nation. During the colonial
era, Spanish administrators attempted to de-Indigenize New Spain, particularly Anahuac and its capital. This happened at all levels, including an
assault on Indigenous imagery. Early Spanish administrators attempted to
impose the image of a lion and a castle as the seal of Mexico City. However,
the local population managed to replace it with the symbol of the eagle

holding a serpent perched on a nopal (cactus), the same symbol that is today found on the Mexican flag (Florescano 2004).

This dynamic, in which Spanish signs, symbols, stories, and narratives were imposed upon Indigenous peoples, was constant throughout the colonial era; it included the imposition of the name "New Spain." Florescano in *La Bandera Mexicana* (2004: 39) wrote that Mexico/New Spain was in a never-ending battle over identity, imagery, symbols, and even its very name. This battle laid the seeds for the New Spain–Mexico antagonisms, with the Indigenous name eventually winning out. It is a point made by scholar David Buisseret (1998) that Mesoamerican influence on modern mapping, as in other endeavors, can still be seen wherever Mesoamerican peoples survived. Thus, with the advent of the War of Independence, the liberators saw themselves as restoring the ancient Aztec/Mexica nation or empire, even though the eagle-nopal symbol was not initially familiar to the rest of the peoples of New Spain or Mexico. Or, if they were familiar with it, it was as the Mexica migration story, not, apparently, the story of all Indigenous Mexican peoples (Florescano 2004).

Returning to the discussion of the maps, what distinguished most Mesoamerican maps (escrituras-pinturas) from European ones is that they recounted events such as their origins, migrations, and the founding of their cities and communities (Mundy 1996). Indigenous maps told stories, not simply providing a geographical snapshot of the landscape. Indeed, these are two radically different mapping concepts. Malcolm Lewis wrote that Indigenous maps, particularly Mesoamerican maps, shared another feature: they were indistinguishable from codices or text. "For the Aztecs and their neighbors prior to the Spanish conquest, there was no such distinction between map presentations and 'written' presentations" (1998: 113).

That Lewis places *written* in quotation marks speaks to the continued theme, the "modern" bias that is still seemingly difficult to erase. Although Mesoamerican scholars now acknowledge that the Maya had a complex written language, they still exhibit a Western bias toward Aztec/Mexica writing (Boone 1998).[35]

Virtually all surviving escrituras-pinturas tell the story of maíz — creation myth, cosmic myth, historias profundas. They represent another form of mapping. For example, the Borgia Codex ([pre-Columbian] 1993) is a map of "cosmology," containing several pages of maíz, including one in which maíz is the axis mundi (25). Other codices with corn symbology include Codex Borbonicus ([pre-Columbian] 1979), Codex Cospi ([pre-Columbian] 1994), Codex Zouche-Nuttall ([1300s] 1992), the Mendoza Codex

([1541–1542] 1992), the Dresden Codex ([pre-Columbian] 1972), the Florentine Codex ([1577] 1961, 1976), and Codex Vindobonensis Mexicanus I ([pre-Columbian] 2007). For Nahua-Maya peoples, cities themselves also constituted cosmogonic mapping (López Austin 1997).

This is why the significance of the book burnings conducted by Spanish priests cannot be overstated. While it is highly likely that Spaniards used Mesoamerican maps for purposes of war and to obtain riches, it is also apparent that many were destroyed because they did not appear to be Western-style maps. Yet precisely because Indigenous maps were not recognized as maps, many are believed to have been placed (hidden) onto the codices written by Spanish priests—as "illustrations."

Nabokov (1998) notes another commonality among Indigenous mapmakers. He contends that although Indigenous peoples had always had maps of one sort or another (petroglyphs, hides, and so on), the importance of these maps heightened with the invasion of Europeans because Indigenous peoples were forced to prove land claims. Maps became indispensable to them for this, though their claims were often still not respected.

Conclusion: Aztlan/Maíz: Hidden/Open Transcript

The complex and multilayered story of Aztlan can, in part, be understood in the language of Scott's (1990) "hidden transcripts." Aztlan to peoples in Mexico means one thing—legend—but to Chicanas/Chicanos in the United States, it is an open declaration of defiance of the U.S. master narrative.

When "El Plan Espiritual de Aztlan" was revealed in 1969 (Alurista 1970), it was a symbolic declaration of political and cultural insurrection—akin to Scott's "rare moment of political electricity" when the hidden transcript becomes an open record (1990: xii–xiii). For Chicanos/Chicanas, the declaration liberated an ancient narrative about ancestors descending from the Southwest and invigorated a political movement that did not simply demand justice and equality but proclaimed Indigeneity in lands in which Mexicans had traditionally been framed by the U.S. master narrative as aliens and unwanted strangers. The 1500s–1800s maps, independent of accuracy, appear to buttress the narrative of "El Plan" and also to contain the hidden maíz narratives related to the Toltecs, maíz, and Quetzalcoatl. This synergy of ideas, stories, and proclamations has created a new narrative and a new identity for peoples who, a generation ago, still accepted the imposed alien frames of mainstream society and in many cases even saw themselves as white and Spanish. However, this new story is actually an ancient one, a narrative about the unity of the continent based on maíz. This story—of being "gente de maíz"—appears to also resonate with de-Indigenized peoples of the Americas because in times of high conflict, it too functions as a "belonging" story. And unlike the Aztlan story, it is not seen by many native peoples of the north as an encroachment on native lands (cf. note 18).

Saramamalla (Ñukanchik Mamashina)

Luz María de la Torre

"Runakuna kawsashpa katikpika Saramamalla kawsakunkarakmi tukuy Allpamamapak runakunata mikuchinkapak."

Willka kawsaypika Saramamamantami muyuntimpi katinata ushanchik. Ñawpa pachamanta, Kunan pachamanta, kipa pachamanta samaykunawan tinkirinata ushanchik. Chashnami tukuy ayllukunawan, llaktakunawan, apukunawan, tukuymanawan shukllashina tantarishkami kanchik. Shinami sara muyukunawanka wañuykunapipashmi mutsunchik. Chay muyukunawan pukllakpillami wañushkataka shuk chakapishina yallichinkapak nishpami pukllanchik. Saramama chaymantachari kunan pacha, tukuymana pachapipashmi kan. Chay samaytami kay tukuy llaktakunapak runakunaka wiñarishkanchik.

Saramamalla muyuka
Abya-yalamanta,
Amaru-Kanchamanta
America shutiwan riksishka allpamanta
runakunata mikuchishpa kawsarka.

Ñukanchik karapak shanulla tullpuka
Saramamashinami kan.
Ñukanchik yawarpash,

Ñukanchik yuyaypash,
Tukuy ñukanchik kawsaymi
Sara mishkillami kan.
Andesmanta runakunaka
Saramantami rurashka kan.

Hatun-mamakuna, mamakuna, ushikuna,
Tukuy Andesmanta Runakuna
chay tawkasami sarakunatami
mirachishpa katinakun:
shinami:
yana, yurak, killu, puka,
shanu, kullkiyashkalla sarakunawampash;
paykunawanmi
sumaychay, chikankunatami kuyanchik.

Saramamalla (Madrecita Maíz)

"Mientras el *runa*[1] viva, seguirá existiendo la Saramamalla para nutrir al mundo."

El maíz visto desde lo sagrado ha constituido la voz de la conexión entre el pasado, el presente y el futuro, ha unido a las generaciones, los pueblos, los espíritus, las Diosas y Dioses, en fin con todo cuanto sea posible vivir en armonía e interrelación colectiva. Por eso que las semillas de maíz obrando como puente espiritual están también presentes en los juegos funerales porque la semilla ayuda al difunto a hacer esa transición de este mundo a la energía infinita. De modo que maíz significa presencia y permanencia, y de esa energía estamos nutridos todos los runas de este continente.

Saramamalla
alimentó al ser humano
de Abya-yala,
Amaru-Kancha
o conocido como América.

Nuestra piel dorada
como el color de maíz.
Nuestra sangre,
nuestro pensamiento,

nuestra palabra,
toda nuestra vida,
tienen sabor
de maíz.
El ser humano andino
está hecho de maíz.

La abuela, la madre, la hija,
el runa andino
sigue acrecentando
esa grán variedad de maíces:
negros, blancos, amarillos, rojos,
cafés, plateados;
y con ellos hemos aprendido
a respetar y amar la diferencia.

Our Sacred Maíz Mother

"As long as the runas[2] live, our sacred maíz mother will exist to feed the world."

Sacred Maíz has been the voice and connection between the past, present, and future, it has united the generations, the peoples, the spirits, the gods and goddesses, and finally all things that make it possible to live in harmony and in collective relations. That's why the seeds of maíz function as a bridge between the spiritual and are present during funeral rites because the seed helps the deceased make the transition from this world into the infinite energy. In other words, maíz signifies presence and permanence, and from that energy all of us human beings are fed on this continent.

Our Sacred Maíz Mother
fed human beings
of Abya-yala,
Amaru-Kancha,
also known as América.

Our golden skin
like the color of maíz.
Our blood,
our thoughts,

our words
all of our lives
have the taste
of maíz.
The Andean human being
is made of maíz.

The grandmother, the mother, the daughter,
the Andean human being
continues to eat
from the great varieties of maíz:
black, white, yellow, red,
brown ones, and silver;
and with them we have learned
to respect and love the difference.

Figure 9. Woman using a metate, Borgia Codex (143). This image of a woman with a child on her back grinding corn is found on various pre- and post-Cuauhtemoc codices. It is also found on many tortilla wrappers. Courtesy of Foundation for Advancement of Mesoamerican Studies.

Maíz as Civilizational Impulse and the Tortilla as Symbol of Cultural Resistance

Hoping it would facilitate the mass conversion of the continent's Indigenous peoples, Spanish priests, as Chimalpahin Quauhtlehuanitzin reveals (Codex Chimalpahin [1621] 1997), used tortillas as communion. Early on, the priests understood the sacredness of corn. For instance, Chimalpahin wrote this about the Last Supper: "And when our Lord Jesus Christ had spoken, he took tortillas and gave them to the apostles" (173). Here are instructions found in the Codex Chimalpahin for someone fifteen or older during Lent:

> First of all it is necessary that you believe that the most holy sacrament is made with wine and with tortillas. But it is the office only of the priest, the clergyman, to make it; no one else. And when the priest has uttered the word of God that is called consecration over the tortillas and the wine, then the tortillas are changed into the precious body of our Lord Jesus Christ and the wine is changed into his precious blood. They are no longer in any way tortillas. (179)[1]

Framing Maíz: The Past or a Seven-Thousand-Year Continuity?

Before maíz was created and domesticated here on this continent, the peoples of Mexico, Central America, and the Andes were already planting cotton, beans, and other crops.[2] However, it was maíz that not only

109

transformed but also created many societies on this continent. Virtually all societies were affected. And while maíz is associated with Indigeneity—because it has been a staple of AmerIndigenous peoples for thousands of years—it is also associated with migration because maíz cannot grow by itself. Ronald Wright in *Stolen Continents* (2005: 98) wrote that the path of "agriculture [maíz] spread north from Mexico to the Pueblos [New Mexico], then to the South, and finally to the Great Lakes."[3]

Despite this, tortillas are almost singularly associated with Mexico. For people of Mexican descent, the tortilla or *tlaxcalli* is unrivaled in its centrality to the diet. Archaeological evidence suggests that while the tools for making tortillas, the *metate* and *mano*, have been used for many thousands of years, maíz did not immediately become central to the Mexican diet until several thousand years after its initial domestication in Southern Mexico (Tapia 1997).[4] Regardless, embedded in Mexicans' psyche is the narrative that their/our diet is at least seven thousand years old. Maíz possesses a complex meaning for Indigenous peoples, and while the Spanish friars of the colonial era understood its sacredness,[5] the other Spaniards generally viewed it as food for Indians and animals. Despite this, the corn tortilla has always occupied a special place in history, particularly in times of war and famine.

In the United States, maíz has often been instrumental in reinforcing a sense of identity among Mexicans and Central Americans, positively or negatively. On the negative side, maíz plays a part in denigrating stereotypes that associate Mexicans/Indigenous peoples with the past; the positive identity stems from the assertion that these people are "gente de maíz" or people of corn (Asturias 1988). As the above frame suggests, association of Mexicans/Indigenous peoples with the past, and marginalization of them as something other than integral members of today's society, is itself a misinterpretation. Where outsiders see "the past," Mexicans/Indigenous peoples read continuity.[6] It is this frame, with its underlying tension, that courses through this chapter.

Tortilla as Symbol and Metaphor

Some of Mexico's leading Mesoamericanists posit that Mesoamerica—via maíz culture—is very much alive among Mexico's Indigenous and Indigenous-based populations. This conservatively amounts to about 90 percent of Mexico's population (Bonfil Batalla 1996, Florescano 1999, López Austin 2003). This idea runs contrary to the trend of Western scholarship that discourages seeing unity, singularity, and continuity when it comes to peoples and cultures.[7] Bonfil Batalla further argues that the notion of a lack of continuity is a function of colonialism and that current identities are products of colonial imposition. He wrote that during the colonial era, Indian identity was atomized to the local level, and as such, no national identity was permitted, adding that Mesoamerican identity equals a civilizational and national identity, which was not permitted under colonialism. He asserted that this atomization process, which he described as ethnocide, continues to this day, asserting that the dominant colonial ideology robs Mexico of its Indigenous roots, bequeathing them only to those populations known as Indians. A continental identity, I would add, is also discouraged.

I argue, and several other Mexican American scholars also argue, that Mexicans in the United States are part of, or an extension of, maíz civilization (Vélez-Ibáñez 1996, Vigil 1998, Menchaca 2001). While this idea is part of a contentious debate, what is not in dispute is that maíz culture undergirds almost everything that is considered Mexican or Mexican American. Corn, beans, squash, and chile continue to form Mexico's basic diet. To say Mesoamerican culture, maíz culture, culture of the poor, Indigenous culture, campesino and Mexican culture, is to be redundant. In Mexico, the distinctions are often blurred and difficult to discern.

It can be argued that the round corn tortilla unites all the above Mexican cultures.[8] At a metaphoric level, the tortilla can be viewed as representing these cultures, as the circle has traditionally been associated with Indigenous peoples. Another highly recognized symbol associated with Mexica culture is the round "Aztec Calendar," whose technology is based on maíz. They are two of Mexico's most recognizable cultural root paradigms.[9] The others include Tonantzin or the Virgen de Guadalupe; the eagle and serpent associated with Mexico's flag; Cuauhtemoc, the last defender of the Aztecs; and the nation's pyramids. They are the images, icons, and ideas that are most associated with Mexico, primarily with Indigenous Mexico.[10] These images were not handed down by Western and "official" historians but instead are the product of hard-fought battles over what constitutes Mexico: a culturally European colony or part of an Indigenous civilization. And while many will accept a fusion, the root remains Indigenous (Bonfil Batalla 1996). This is not to negate cultural mixture or mestizaje, which is very real; it is but an observation regarding the imagery associated with Mexico's cultural root paradigms.

In the United States and its culture wars, the corn tortilla is metaphorically counterposed to white bread.[11] In a visual sense, they form the quintessential civilizational binary: corn versus wheat, round versus rectangular.

Tortilla equals Indigenous equals Mexican; bread equals American. In these wars, American symbolically equals white and wholesome, whereas Mexican equals brown and impure. And in an ironic twist of history, brown is alien while white equals native. It is similar to the American Indian–white binary (Coleman 1996), except Mexicans are viewed as mongrel, never noble. It is also similar to the white-nonwhite binary as traditionally showcased in many U.S. museums, where Westerners (whites) are the future and everyone else is the past: museums "are where the nation reifies its mythic past and creation. It is where the nation collects its heritage and beauty and where it exhibits its wholeness (Davalos 2001: 53).[12]

While the two foods are different, they need not be confined to that binary. They are seemingly placed there only because U.S. politics, as many scholars contend, is fueled by hypernationalism, particularly in these times of rising anti-immigrant fervor (Billig 1995). This dynamic includes the belief in the superiority of the Western world. Within this context, the United States is a "First World" nation and the world's sole superpower. Mexico is "Third World" and shares its two-thousand-mile border. As Santa Ana (2002) notes in his study of immigrants and metaphors, the United States is "house," while Mexicans are immigrants, and immigrants are animals invading the house. In that context, Americans want nothing to do with intruders, with beans or tortillas or red-hot chiles, invading their house.[13] The distorted logic also asserts that immigrants, being animals, cannot be afforded human rights.[14]

Vigil in *From Indians to Chicanos* (1998: 228) notes that mainstream society's view of Mexicans has always been embedded in language and imagery: "Claims to superior status are often accompanied by a vocabulary of insult to flaunt and fortify the power dominant groups have amassed." Part of that vocabulary is slurs such as *greasers*, *Meskins*, *beaners*, *wetbacks*, *chili chokers*, *taco benders*, *chukes*, and *half-breeds*. Many of the insults are related to food. Beans, chile, and maíz, and the corn tortilla specifically, have often been racialized and associated with peoples from the south.[15]

Stories abound regarding the denigration of Mexicans because of their foods.[16] The disdain of Mexicans and Mexican food may be due to ingrained media stereotypes. Clint Wilson and Félix Gutiérrez trace the history of negative stereotypes of Mexicans to the time of the Alamo (as in "Remember the Alamo"). As cited by Wilson and Gutiérrez (1995: 66), George Wilkins Kendall said: "Give them but tortillas, frijoles and chile colorado to supply their animal wants for the day and seven-tenths of the Mexicans are satisfied." The disdain of Mexican food may also be due to the fact that historically, colonizers have generally ranked their own foods, like their language, communication, and religion, higher than those of other peoples.[17]

The contempt of Mexican/Indigenous foods was more prevalent prior to the Chicano movement of the 1960s–1970s. It is seemingly less pronounced today as many Indigenous foods are seen as healthy, particularly in an era of obesity, heart problems, and diabetes. However, some healthy Indigenous foods—such as spirulina, huitlacoche, amaranth, and quinoa—tend to be found at expensive health stores or served as delicacies at upscale restaurants.[18] These health-conscious stores and upscale restaurants also promote these foods by touting their ancientness, a marketing practice that arguably separates ancient Indigenous peoples from their living descendants at the cash register.

The Tortilla as Civilizational Marker

Given the social-political realities of our times, it appears that maíz and the round corn tortilla in particular communicate culture in several ways:

* **Civilizational Marker**: Being part of maíz culture identifies one with the civilizational impulse that created Mesoamerica some seven thousand years ago. It is a culture that is shared by hundreds of Indigenous peoples, tribes, or nations across the continent, including the Caribbean. While it should be a source of great pride for all the peoples of this continent, as a result of intentional erasure, most people are unaware of the history of this civilization. For similar reasons, including notions of superiority and inferiority, people associate Mexico with tourist destinations and museum cultures, and also defeated cultures (Davalos 2001), and nowadays, runaway immigration and drug-cartel violence.
* **Racialized Identifier**: In the United States, the tortilla, like the Spanish language, is associated with Mexico and connotes a racialized nonwhite Mexican identity. In U.S. society, nonwhite has historically meant peoples outside the mainstream, peoples in the way of progress and civilization, and peoples subject to legal and extralegal violence, segregation, and discrimination. While most Mexicans are Indigenous, de-Indigenized, or Indigenous-based mestizos, close to 10 percent are European-based mestizos (Aguirre Beltrán 1946). The pioneering works of Aguirre Beltrán (1946, 1958) reveal that most Mexicans also have a trace of African blood, the "third root of the Americas."

* **Cultural Identity**: Many Indigenous and Indigenous-based peoples from Mexico and Central America identify, as do I, as "gente de maíz" or people of corn (Asturias 1988). That identity extends to people in this country. However, given the geopolitical context, Mexican identity in the United States is not simply "other" but, in times of anti-immigrant hysteria, "enemy." That identity, I maintain, is related to their Indigeneity, which, on this continent, has meant "enemy other" since 1492.

* **Place**: Maíz signifies a rootedness to this continent. If anything, it is the quintessential symbol of Indigenous America. Whereas a connection to maíz culture should identify peoples with the ancient cultures of the Americas, maíz is often identified by Western society with alien cultures from the south. While anthropologists view maíz as the impulse that replaced hunter-gatherer societies and fishing societies, most Indigenous peoples do not see maíz as a replacement but as a complement (Menchaca 2001, Maestas 2003). U.S. popular culture does look to the Midwest as the nation's "Corn Belt."

* **Memory/Roots**: Maíz is the basis for Mesoamerican calendars. In Nahuatl, the numeral one is *ce*, which comes from *cintli* (maíz) or *centeotzintli* (sacred maíz). Scientists peg the date of the birth of maíz at 7,000 years ago; Indigenous stories peg it from 5,113 to 10,000 years ago. The Aztec/Mexica calendar equates the dawn of the fifth age with the birth of maíz. Each age corresponds to approximately 5,113 years. Don Aurelio (R. Rodríguez and P. Gonzales 2005) and Maya writer Victor Montejo (2004) state that maíz was created some ten thousand years ago in southern Mexico or Central America, respectively.[19] However, in regard to maíz and the Maya, Montejo wrote: "Five thousand years after the counting in our calendar began, our culture is still here and flourishing once more" (71). The Maya begin their calendar at 3112 BC.[20]

* **Narrative/Worldview**: Maíz is not simply sustenance. It is beyond the notion of "We are what we eat." It is "This is who we are—this is what we are made of" and "This is where we come from" (Martínez Parédez 1968: 62). Martínez Parédez argues that maíz is also what formulates the Mayan concept of *In Lak'ech*: "The ethos or philosophy of In Lak'ech means that there is no I (and there is no you and no 'other'). Instead, there is You Are My Other Self" (19). This philosophy, he wrote, comes directly from "the cereal that was created by the ancient settlers of the continent: maíz—yes, the maíz, that creation of the savage beasts, in which, thanks to them, lies the hope

for humanity" (13). He calls this philosophy the hope for humanity because if peoples or nations were to adopt it, war would no longer be viable: it is difficult to war against oneself.

Here, we have seen two diametrically opposed views regarding maíz and the tortilla: food for animals or the hope for humanity. In many industrialized nations, animals are considered lower than human beings. In many Indigenous cultures, animals are not ranked below humans but are considered part of the same creation. In fact, in many Indigenous cultures, a *nagual* or companion spirit is usually an animal. Despite this, this conjured-up dichotomy has become real through the ages. One view sees food as, at best, a commodity, whereas the other view sees food as sacred sustenance.

Memory and Place in a Tortilla

Beyond viewing tortillas in the United States as a symbol and metaphor for Indigenous/Mexican peoples and as a racialized identifier, we can also view them as a place where memory, culture, and place are stored. An examination of the imagery on tortilla packaging reveals it to be a place where Indigeneity, via maíz, is communicated by these industries. Even the shape of the tortilla conveys cultural meaning, that is, who "we" are, Indigenous authenticity, and Mexican food as Indian food.

An analysis of the imagery associated with corn tortillas and tortilla wrappers, which is covered in the next section, also includes an examination related to memory and place, permitting the observation that place does not appear to always correspond to a fixed physical location.[21] Memory is not always or uniquely stored in stationary locations, and food can be considered a principal place where memory is also stored and where community is built. This is especially true for people of Mexican and Central American descent, living in the United States, estranged from their beloved families, culture, and countries.

Most of the tortillas and their packaging that I analyze are bought by people of Mexican and Central American origin in small *mercaditos* (grocery stores) that cater to migrants who find themselves many hundreds, if not thousands, of miles from home. In some communities, tortillas are also bought at *tortillerías* (tortilla storefronts) and *panaderías* (bakeries), which are not restaurants yet often provide the space for people to eat. Some of these busy marketplaces eventually do expand and add a restaurant. These spaces often function as modern *tianguis* or central marketplaces, where one does not simply gather food and other familiar products but is likely to encounter fellow displaced citizens. They are where stories are often exchanged. In mercaditos or barrio stores, one is apt to find cactus and *pencas* (leaves of the cactus, maguey, or similar plants) and spices not found or grown widely in the United States. Mercaditos in that sense fulfill the same function as the ethnic market, also found in communities throughout the United States. Many of these (Mexican) foods are nowadays also mainstream; one can find nopales at megastores such as Walmart. This next section focuses on the role of tortillas as objects of memory and cultural transmission.

The Tortilla Mapping Project

Background

This project I did while living in Wisconsin involved collecting and examining tortilla packaging from stores in Wisconsin, Indiana, Illinois, Iowa, Kansas, and Minnesota. For comparison purposes, I also picked up tortillas from the Southwest, and from Mexico, though there it is rare to find tortillas sold in wrappers with cultural images. The large supermarkets in Mexico employ generic messages, or corn imagery only, whereas the little mercaditos in villages, as with the tortillerías, do not wrap them and instead sell them in butcher paper or towels. The initial result was some 111 different wrappers and packages, primarily from cities I visited in the mid-2000s. While my methods were not systematic, I believe the images gathered constitute a good representation of those that appear on tortilla packaging nationwide.[22]

Circular Shape and Maíz Imagery

Before analyzing the packaging, one notes the circular shape of the tortilla itself. The shape, in and of itself, communicates a powerful message of Indigeneity. Of course, not all maíz products are circular in shape. The tamale (*tamalli*), for example, which is purportedly older than the tortilla, is thick and rectangular. (By the same token, not all bread is rectangular.) Beyond the shape of tortillas, in the United States, maíz has a long tradition of being advertised as being a native food product—Indian corn—to connote authenticity (Fussell 1992).

In the 1970s, Mazola advertised its corn oil through the use of Navajo imagery. A food product that many Americans are familiar with is Argo corn starch. While the company has existed for more than a hundred years, it has been using the image of an ear of corn crossed with a native woman as its logo since at least the 1920s.[23] The usage of American Indian images might seem incongruent in a country that has long been hostile to American Indians. Yet the idea of the "noble savage," the admiration of brave warriors and "earth mothers" and wise spiritual elders who are stewards of the environment, has been the underside of modernity.[24]

The results of my Tortilla Mapping Project revealed that the use of Indigenous imagery is the central feature on U.S. tortilla packaging.[25] This must be presumed to be because most tortillas sold in markets are consumed by Mexicans and Central Americans who now call the United States their home. Their presence has created a huge demand for their basic diet, that is, corn tortillas, beans, chile, and related foods. This demand is so great that there appears to be little need to advertise on the airwaves or in other public media.[26] Only chile rivals the tortilla as an essential food and it is generally not advertised either. A Mexican meal without chile is virtually unthinkable, thus the expression "A day without chile is like a day without sunshine."

Janet Long-Solís (1998: 9) argues that it is common cultural traits that form the basis for the nation: "Chile is one of those [primary] traits or attributes that identifies Mexicans." Perhaps it too qualifies as a cultural root paradigm. An examination of chile packaging shows that it does not rely on the same imagery as is associated with tortillas. The reason for not placing Indigenous imagery on chile packaging may be that many Mexicans prefer buying fresh chile, so they are not as big a part of the customer base for packaged chile. At any rate, after hundreds of years of colonization, there is nothing more Mexican/Indigenous than the food: the staples, which include the maíz and the chile, but also beans, squash and nopal. Perhaps Mexican companies in the United States take their cues from Mexico on this matter; in Mexico, there is seemingly little incentive to advertise tortillas, chile, or beans. This is because Mexicans "need" to eat them anyway with virtually every meal.[27]

Most U.S. tortilla packaging is made of clear plastic, embedded with logos and imagery—imagery that beckons or harks back to "the homeland" or, in this case, to something cultural and something ancient and ancestral (read Indigenous). In Mexico, most tortillas come in a plain plastic wrapper. Here, the wrapper seems to function as both a marketing tool and, perhaps by default, a repository of culture.

In times of ethnic or cultural stress, the imagery on the tortilla wrapper can also subconsciously communicate and affirm Indigeneity among Mexican/Indigenous peoples and their cultures. This message is often communicated through humor, such as when the tortilla is juxtaposed with bread, accentuating the above-mentioned cultural binary. Mexican food is projected as rich and ancient; American food is reduced to white bread and peanut butter. To unsophisticated Americans and many non-Mexicans, tortillas seemingly communicate another message: not American and not modern. For those who have antipathy for Mexicans, corn tortillas connote inferiority and even savagery.[28]

Examining the imagery on tortilla packaging, which has remained constant since the 1960s, one can also note the conflation of tortillas/maíz and human beings. This is not actually unique; a thousand-year-old mural image in Cacaxtla, Mexico, depicts this very idea, that human beings are maíz, growing on corn stalks (see plate 1). That is also the primary message communicated in the *Popol Vuh*. It is also the image/logo of tortillas from Hawaii. This is what the tortilla itself communicates, even without the wrappers: that human beings are maíz or made from maíz. Few if any other foods appear to connote this same message, at least in packaging or advertising.[29]

However, the wrappers communicate a message of Indigeneity, even if only in a subliminal manner and even if only for commercial purposes. University of Wisconsin scholar Sheila Reaves calls this a perfect example of "hidden in plain sight" (personal communication, September 1, 2005), which resonates with Bonfil Batalla's (1996) idea of a México profundo: both the tortilla and the imagery project things Mexican and familiarity, but at the root, they actually project Indigeneity. This projection may also be an example of an insurgent metaphor. An insurgent metaphor is not reactive or a response to racism. Instead, it functions as a preemptive metaphor, creating an image that in this case, connotes not simply Mexicanness but something even more ancient. Rather than alien, Mexican equals Indigenous (Santa Ana 2002). Thus, the corn/maíz tortilla, at both conscious and unconscious levels, becomes the quintessential embodiment and repository of ancient Indigenous memory, and in some cases, functions as a form of cultural resistance (Weatherford 1988). While many Mexican food products also appeal to ancient Indigenous imagery in their marketing, this is most true for corn tortillas. Despite three hundred years of Hispanicization, despite being subjected as well to the forces of globalization and Anglicization or "Americanization," Indigenous peoples and their/our foods are still seen as the root of Mexico and the continent.[30] The building of churches upon the foundations of pyramids, for example, metaphorically projects the idea that the culture was not destroyed but rather suppressed. As Bonfil Batalla wrote: "If the Indians had stopped being Indians in order to be fully incorporated into Western civilization, the ideological justification for colonial domination would have ended" (1996: 41). The Indigenous imagery on tortilla packaging appears to affirm his contention.

The failure to extinguish Indigenous culture may help to explain why Indigenous imagery is most pronounced on tortillas. The most common imagery on tortilla wrappers is of Indigenous women kneading the masa (cornmeal) on a metate and heating them on a *comal* (iron griddle). This imagery can be found in Mexican Indigenous codices (see figure 9). While some scholars might see this imagery as promoting stereotypes, one can also see it as acknowledging cultural connections and continuity, and, in the view of marketers, Indigenous authenticity.

Sandra Moriarty and Lisa Rohe caution in "Cultural Palettes in Print Advertising" (2005) that there is a fine line between a cultural attribute and a stereotype. They also acknowledge that that which is considered Mexican in advertising—chile, jalapeño peppers, families, pyramids, Spanish (not Nahuatl), Aztec and Maya symbols, and the sun—can either signify México profundo (deep Mexico) or more stereotypes. Southwest-specific images include circles, *sarape* designs, sombreros, swords, folkloric stamps, cactus, and saints.

In regard to stereotypes, there is a gendered component to maíz and a gendered discussion about it. Some scholars interpret the age of hunting as male-dominated and the age of maíz as a time when women became more central to food production. Even when plows or similar tools requiring force were developed, it is said that maíz became not an age for male domination but rather an age of balance or duality (Long-Solís 1998). Growing maíz is a long process that involves seed selection, tilling, planting, watering, thinning the weeds, harvesting, and seed selection once again. Aside from the corn that is set aside for seed selection, corn is also stored for food. The postharvest process is viewed as a women's technology. Once the corn has been chosen for consumption, it is women who prepare it in a variety of ways; it is primarily women who grind the corn on a metate or molcajete with a mano, in a process that is perhaps close to five thousand years old (Long-Solís 1998).

In the United States, the consumer must identify with the symbols/imagery; logic dictates that people would stop purchasing products they either do not identify with or are offended by (Moriarty and Rohe 2005). No negative reaction by Mexicans to the imagery of Indigenous women on tortilla wrappers has been detected in my analysis.[31] In fact, aside from the clear association with the metate and the comal, other packaging also involves women—mestizas or Indigenous—carrying tortillas on top of the head, or women as maíz itself. On several of the packages, a Mexican/Indigenous woman—mother, girl, or grandmother—is the central image, with or without corn imagery. Most often she is wearing traditional clothes and braided hair. This accentuates the point that Guadalupe Pérez San Vicente noted in the introduction to Echeverría and Arroyo's *Recetario del Maíz* (A *Maíz Recipe Book*, 2000):

> This recipe book shows us one of the faces of Mexico, perhaps that which most distinguishes Mexico, our flesh and sustenance, and it is important because it has come about as a result of a collective effort, created virtually in its entirety by female efforts, being that women have never ceded to men the dominion of maíz. (Pérez San Vicente 2000: 17)[32]

Virtually all tortilla wrappers depict maíz, and in many cases, the maíz stands alone. It appears that maíz itself functions as the quintessential expression of Indigeneity.[33] In *Quetzalcoatl and the Irony of Empire* (2000), Davíd Carrasco provides one reason for the inability of Europeans to dislodge maíz, maíz culture, and maíz narratives from the consciousness of Indigenous peoples. He states that in Tollan/Teotihuacan, the imagery of maíz was an expression of the cosmos (124). This city was not simply the largest and most influential in Mesoamerica; it was also the one that communicated the idea of Quetzalcoatl and maíz culture throughout its zones of influence. In "Reimagining the Classic Heritage in Mesoamerica" (2000), Carrasco, Jones, and Sessions argue that Teotihuacan itself *is* communication and represents modes of communication to all of Mesoamerica. In "Imágenes y Significado del Dios del Maíz" (2003), Florescano argues that Quetzalcoatl is the manifestation of maíz and that Quetzalcoatl is the first "god" made of the same substance as humans — maíz.

Whether intentional or not, the imagery on tortilla packaging affirms these ideas about maíz and Indigeneity and connects those who eat tortillas to the ancient expressions of these ideas. Other images that connote Mexicanness are often added, including the flag, or its green, white, and red colors; campesinos; cactus; and burros, images often associated with a rural or pre-twentieth-century lifestyle. While an outsider may see this imagery as stereotypical, most Mexicans would probably not, as the depictions are generally not caricatures or buffoons. In the end, their deep meaning appears to be, or to connote, familiarity, Indigeneity, and authenticity.[34]

Spanish Señoritas?

Despite several hundred years of colonization, few images on contemporary tortilla packaging hark back to things Spanish. This is in contrast to the

1950s, when much Mexican imagery in the United States was "Spanish." In the 1950s, many people of Mexican descent considered themselves to be Spanish (European) as opposed to Mexican (Indigenous), thus "Spanish" restaurants. In *The Language of Blood* (2004), John Nieto-Phillips argued that fear of disloyalty and fear of being branded as nonwhite is what motivated Spanish-speaking people of New Mexico to claim a Spanish lineage, this when New Mexico was being considered for statehood. Longtime Indigenous-rights activist Suzan Harjo argues that this confusion of identity is what she terms reidentification. When one people "colonizes another, it disarms and controls the population, and changes the identity of the peoples, both nations and individuals, who are being colonized" (2005: 31). During such a process, names are changed, usually to the language of the oppressor while Indigenous names are belittled by colonizers.

One store, El Mercadito in Madison, Wisconsin, advertises its Latin American foods as Spanish products. Imagery, however, is generally not Spanish. Several tortilla wrappers have a woman as the central image, and she is often an Adelita, a woman soldier and icon of the Mexican Revolution. Several of the images in this category appear to be mestizas, though arguably Indigenous; at any rate, definitely not Spanish. Other brands project a different phenomenon, sometimes known as reverse assimilation. For instance, a rooster is part of the imagery used to sell rice and a parrot is used to sell tortillas. Whereas parrots are indigenous to the Americas, the rooster is European, though nowadays thoroughly culturally Mexicanized.[35]

The Tortilla: "Who We Are"

It is tempting to see the tortilla as a literal map of "who we are": the "we" that corresponds to peoples from corn-based cultures and the "we" that corresponds to those who continue to consume, in sustenance and symbols, that ancient maíz diet. This idea is often expressed in terms of what Mexicans will do, how far they will drive, to find the most authentic of tortillas (or tamales) and the hottest of chiles.

Regardless of the imagery, what virtually all the tortilla packages and wrappers connote or attempt to connote, including in health-food stores,[36] is familiarity and culture, and, by implication, authenticity. Some scholars argue that the imagery on tortilla packaging actually does not reflect self-image but rather stereotypes (Johnson, David, and Huey-Ohlisson 2003). Imagery that is generally associated with women grinding corn on the metate sometimes goes hand in hand with adobe houses, burros, and Mexicans sleeping against a cactus under a large sombrero. Of the wrappers

I examined, I did not find one with a sleeping Mexican (one image finds a Mexican leaning against a cactus), though the image does still proliferate at restaurants and in lawn decorations.[37]

In analyzing such imagery, one also has to be conscious that blond people dominate the small and big screen in Mexico, especially in advertising, a seeming anomaly, or blatant racism, as Mexico has very few naturally blond people. Despite this, advertisers in Mexico utilize blond people with light skin to sell everything—except products associated with Indigenous peoples. Part of the rationale for this is that the corporate sector sees itself as catering to the continent's Spanish-speaking elites. The elites of these countries are either European-identified mestizos or see themselves as Spanish. This predilection for blond people with light skin is also generally found in U.S. Spanish-language media, though a greater effort is seemingly made to diversify the images than in Mexico (Johnson, David, and Huey-Ohlisson 2003).

Apparently, this anti-Indigenous media/advertising bias does not apply to the marketing of the tortilla, which is actually consistent with the above logic: the tortilla has long been associated with Indian food (Pilcher 1998). It is likely that the European-identified criollo population of Mexico does not eat corn tortillas in equal quantities as others do, as corn tortillas continue to be associated with Indians and/or the poor, and animals. The criollo population continues to favor European-style cuisine.

Regardless of the tortilla companies' motivation, it is possible that they are preventing the loss of cultural memory by the use of Indigenous-themed imagery, this in an era of globalization and homogenization when many people of Mexican and Central American descent are no longer connected directly to the milpas nor to the associated ancient ceremonies. Nor are most women in the United States making tortillas daily.

Tortillas and Indigenous Authenticity

The Tortilla Mapping Project also examined other food products such as wheat (bread), rice, lentils, and barley. This was done primarily for comparison, to see if these foods are depicted as being connected to ancient "Old World" cultures, parallel to maíz's "New World" association. From a marketing perspective, maíz appears to be unique, even though bread and rice, as cultivated foods, are actually older (reputedly by several thousand years) than maíz. Generally, one does not receive the same message of ancientness from these other packaged foods. Interestingly, the potato, though it is actually an ancient Peruvian crop, is associated with Europe, Ireland specifically, and perceived by many as being from there. The same can be said of tomatoes: they originate in the Americas, but are associated with Italian cuisine. Chocolate is associated with Switzerland. The list goes on: peanuts, avocados, and so on. A great percentage of foods eaten throughout the world originate in the Americas, but none are more associated with this continent, and none is perceived to be more ancient or more Indigenous, than maíz (Weatherford 1988).

Mexican Food as Indian Food

In examining the symbolic nature of tortillas and what they represent in this society—including the fact that most traditional Mexican food originates on this continent—it becomes apparent that Americans are unaware that that which is marketed as Mexican food is essentially Indigenous food. Although Mexican food today ostensibly does not have the same public stigma as it did prior to the 1960s, there are places in this country in which Mexican food is still sold as Spanish food. There in fact is such a thing as Spanish food and Spanish cuisine, but it generally bears little if no resemblance to Mexican or Central American food. Several national supermarkets nowadays have a "Hispanic" food section—labeled that way despite the fact that the vast majority of these food products are Mexican/Indigenous. Perhaps because of this past (and continuing) attempt to pass off Mexican food as European, many Indigenous peoples also do not view Mexican food, or Mexican people, as Indigenous. Rocky Rodriguez, an Indigenous-rights activist from Denver, Colorado, tells a story of being at an Indigenous gathering in the United States. As she was cooking, she was told she was not preparing Indian food. She was asked why she was cooking Mexican food at an Indigenous gathering. She replied, "The only thing Indigenous that's being cooked here is the Mexican food" (personal communication, November 26, 2006). While she was correct about Mexican food being Indigenous, some argue that all foods can be Indigenized by the mere fact of Indigenous peoples preparing and eating them.[38]

A Visual-Communications View of Tortilla Imagery

In "Visual Semiotics Theory" (2005: 227), Sandra Moriarty defines semiotics "as the study of signs and codes, signs that are used in producing, conveying, and interpreting messages and the codes that govern their use." In the realm of signs, symbols, and imagery, for communication to take place and for meaning to be understood, both the sender and receiver of a message must know the codes. In the case of the tortilla packaging, the imagery is so simple and basic that it is difficult not to understand it. The primary images fall into five basic categories:

1. Maíz by itself or a stalk of corn in a milpa
2. Mexican/Indigenous woman, generally in traditional clothing and braided hair
3. Woman kneading masa on a metate and heating tortillas on a comal
4. Woman kneading masa on a metate and heating tortillas on a comal, with burro, cactus, corn, milpa, mountains, or volcano in background
5. Pre-Columbian Indigenous imagery/designs: pyramids, sun, moon, and maíz

The primary message being delivered is unmistakable: maíz is authentically ancient and Indigenous. It is authentic because the person making the tortillas is an Indigenous woman. Most of the packages use the colors of the Mexican flag, green, white, and red, if not the Mexican flag itself. Semiotic theory can help us to understand the blurring between what is Indigenous and what is Mexican, but it can also help us to understand the limits or borders of what is Indigenous/Mexican. Finally, it allows us to understand why the images and messages are virtually uniform.

A primary feature of semiotics is the distinction between denotation and connotation (Barthes 1967). Analyzing the five primary images, it can be said that they denote, or literally represent, things that people commonly associate with Mexican rural culture. A closer examination reveals that the images connote, or symbolically represent, campesino culture or maíz culture, and more specifically, Indigenous culture.

C. S. Pierce sets up three categories of meaning—"iconic, indexical and symbolic—that are helpful in deconstructing how visuals work and whether they deliver the intended message" (Moriarty and Sayre 2005). In effect, that which is iconic is that which also denotes. The images of the cactus, metate, burro, adobe house, and woman in traditional clothes, taken separately, excluding the maíz itself, could be interpreted through denotation, as something else. The five primary images tend to be found together on tortilla packaging, forming a single picture. The structure of this picture starts from the smallest unit, the maíz, expanding to the woman in traditional clothing, to her kneading the masa, and then the full picture of the woman in front of an adobe house, with the milpa and mountain or volcano in the background. This picture, or variations of it (see, for example, the Esperanza's Tortillas package in figure 10), can be interpreted

Figure 10. Esperanza Tortillas. Courtesy of Patricia Jimenez.

indexically to represent Indigeneity. Yet the symbolic meaning is even deeper: Indigeneity connotes authenticity, the authenticity of maíz culture.

In this respect, using Pierce's (1931) theory of abductive reasoning, a different process of signification can also lead us to infer Indigeneity and authenticity, even when images are changed or added, as long as the primary signifiers remain. The woman can be pre-Columbian Indigenous (from a codex, as in figure 9) or can be from the twenty-first century—but as long as she is taking part in the same process, kneading the masa, making the tortillas by hand, and heating them in a comal, the process of signification remains the same; the tortillas are Indigenous and authentic.

In packaging that utilizes maíz only, since maíz indexes Indigeneity on this continent, no additional image is necessary to represent either Indigeneity or authenticity. But as we see the fuller picture, the images other than maíz become signified by the maíz as Indigenous too. In regard to tortillas, the woman kneading the masa by hand, whether pre-Columbian or contemporary, connotes authenticity. Virtually all the imagery found on tortilla packaging connotes Indigeneity and authenticity by virtue of the connection to maíz, and can thus be interpreted in terms of what John Deely (1990: 24) refers to as Hermetic drift. Moriarty defines this process: "Variously called transactions or commutations by other scholars, the notion of chains [of signification] is similar to how free association works. In this process, a sign that functions as a signified then becomes a signifier that leads to other signifieds" (2005: 233). In the tortilla imagery, each image or sign informs the other signs or images, in a dynamic and never-ending process of meaning making. One can see this process at work especially when attempting to draw distinctions between what is Indigenous and what is rural, campesino, or Mexican in the tortilla packaging. As noted, it is the maíz that Indigenizes all, thereby blurring the distinctions. And once associated with Indigeneity, each sign/symbol is able to Indigenize (or Mexicanize) other signs/symbols.

Only in the case where Spanish imagery is introduced does the Hermetic drift come to a screeching halt. With exceptions, Indigenous and Mexican traits/images are generally not synonymous with Spanish traits/images, primarily because they do not share the same cultural codes.[39] While Mexican consumers appear to make a metaphoric leap regarding Mexican-Indigenous traits/imagery, they do recognize limits: most likely, they see Spanish culture and tortillas as not belonging in the same message—the same picture—partly because the maíz stories are recognizable and ancient.[40] More jarring still are images that come from the fifth category listed above, the hodgepodge of imagery that mixes signs/symbols from different cultures. This mixing is found primarily in packaging from health-food stores that are unfamiliar with Indigenous culture(s) and the codes that communicate Indigenous meaning to consumers. It is possible that such stores, due to their higher prices, do not target Mexican/Indigenous consumers.

In a model created by Barthes (1967), distinguishing between denotation and connotation involves asking two questions: (1) What is it? (2) What does it suggest? These are respectively the denotation and the connotation. Applying this model to the maíz imagery, a third question seems to arise: What is hidden? While Indigeneity is being affirmed through the images, what is also arguably being affirmed is an ancient connection to the earliest maíz cultures of the continent.

Moriarty (2005: 238) equates semiotic analysis with peeling an onion—a process of unlayering to understand meaning. This is what has been done here with the tortilla imagery, particularly in relationship to the deep meaning of maíz. This interpretation suggests a question for further study: whether Indigenous culture, rural culture, and maíz culture are actually one and the same.

While most people associate Indigeneity with rural culture, this was not always the case. In pre-Columbian times, Mesoamerican societies were highly urbanized. In post-Columbian times, Indigenous culture was only allowed to flourish in the countryside, outside of the direct influence of Spanish authorities. Despite this, maíz culture actually permeates all levels of society, which is the basis for the idea of México profundo. Deep Mexico is both maíz culture and Indigenous culture. Bonfil Battalla (1996: 47) argues that colonialism divided space: the cities were for the colonizers, whereas the countryside was for the Indians. This division persists even to this day—allowing Mesoamerican society to be preserved in the country-side. Although conflating Indigeneity with rural culture is limiting, Indige-neity is definitely preserved in the milpa. That may be why rural-themed images only insult those who see in them the "past," rather than continuity.

Conclusion

Food is at the heart of culture, and we are indeed what we eat. When it comes to cultural resilience and resistance, it appears that hundreds of years of attempts to eradicate and demonize Indigenous culture are little match for a cuisine that is minimally seven thousand years old. The resilience of this cuisine and of this culture is partly due to the fact that food itself is a system of communication.

The Elements to Create

María Molina Vai Sevoi

CALPOLLI TEOXICALLI, TLAMANALCO, ANAHUAC
(TUCSON, ARIZONA)

The elements create order to nurture and sustain
in the womb
the spiral
the infinite.
Vibration and rejuvenation emerge
in the womb
the cosmos
the Grand Gourd.
Seeds germinate in darkness
in the womb
in the earth
the Great Mother.
A new generation is born!
May they lift themselves up to Father Sun!
The corn has flourished; the human being has transcended
in the womb
our origin
maíz culture.

Los elementos se ordenan para nutrir y sostener
en el vientre
la espiral
el infinito.
Emerge la vibración de rejuvenecimiento
en el vientre
los cosmos
la gran jícara.
Semillas germinan en la obscuridad
en el vientre
en la tierra
la Gran Madre.
¡Ya nació la Nueva Generación!
¡Que se alcen al Padre Sol!
La planta de maíz brotó; el ser humano transcendió
en el vientre
nuestro origen
cultura de maíz.

Figure 11. Eagle and serpent, Dresden Codex. Depiction courtesy of Cynthia Diaz.

Figure 12. Founding of Tenochtitlan, Mendoza Codex.

Figure 13. Mexican flag, here pictured at a Phoenix protest. Photo by Chris Summitt. Courtesy of the photographer.

The above images are examples of the eagle-and-serpent symbolism of the Aztec/Mexica, which represents the purported thousand-year-old story of a migration from Aztlan to Tenochtitlan/Mexico City. Hidden within that story may be a much older migration narrative related to the Toltecs/Tamoanchanes.

$\mathcal{P}$rimary $\mathcal{P}$rocess and $\mathcal{P}$rincipio

A Return to the Root

They said that when corn is hanging in your kitchen [in Mexico], it's the same as when there's a baby in the house. . . . You can't use any angry language or bad words because the corn can hear you. If it hears all this negativity it won't grow for you the next year.

—KATSI COOK, AWKWASASNE MIDWIFE[1]

Maíz culture manifests itself in and permeates virtually all aspects of Mexican and Central and South American communities in the United States, and that culture is communicated both internally and externally. Here, I examine several Mesoamerican cultural expressions of maíz, including the huehuetlahtolli, *cantos*, and *cantares* of the colonial era, along with murals, poetry, song, theater, the tamalada, ceremony, and danza.[2] This chapter also includes an analysis of the relationship between Mesoamerican written and oral traditions and the practice of cloaking these traditions in Christian morality. The analysis examines the related issue of why Aztec/Mexica imagery and narratives predominate in communities in the United States, often remanding the much older maíz culture and narratives to a secondary role or hiding them beneath the surface. Finally, this chapter explores how elders from Nahua-Maya, Andean, and other maíz-based communities continue to directly influence Chicana/Chicano, Mexican, and Central and South American communities in the United States.

Traditional Methods of Mass Communication in Oral Cultures

That the culture of the peoples of pre-Columbian Mesoamerica exhibited a continuity is now well established. Boone (2000) observed that for several thousand years, up to the Spanish invasion, the peoples of Mesoamerica shared a singular calendrical system, which included the interfacing of a 260-day sacred calendar with a 365-day solar calendar.

It has also been established that with the arrival of Europeans on this continent, this tradition did not simply come to a violent halt. After destroying virtually all Indigenous books and calendars, a number of priests undertook their own project to document that which had been destroyed, resulting in numerous chronicles and post-Columbian codices. Today, mainstream scholars continue to rely on many of these post-Columbian writings—accepting them at face value—while they are justifiably viewed with suspicion by many Mexican/Indigenous scholars. Despite this, there is much useful (concealed) information to be gleaned from them, especially in light of Galarza's (1986, 1992) groundbreaking translation work. For my purposes, the issue is not simply their value but rather whether they constitute part of the cultural heritage of Mexican and Central American communities in the United States. In *Amoxtli San Ce Tojuan* (R. Rodríguez and P. Gonzales 2005), Inés Hernández-Ávila, a Chicana–Nez Perce scholar, responds with an emphatic yes, arguing that they are the rightful heirs to this knowledge. This assertion does not mean accepting these writings at face value but rather simultaneously contesting them and discerning what is hidden in them, then communicating that interpretation/decipherment to the broader community.

Hidden Text and the Huehuetlahtolli

Although hidden text representing Indigenous knowledge can be found in the 1500s–1600s codices and chronicles, most of these books were unavailable to Indigenous peoples during that era, primarily because of censorship (they were not widely published until this past century) and also because mass publication was not common before the twentieth century. However, much of this same knowledge was retained and culturally expressed in the oral traditions, agricultural practices (seeding and cultivation), and seasonal ceremonies of Indigenous peoples. It was also evident in the preparation and consumption of food and medicines,[3] in song, danza, music, *corridos* (ballads), murals, art, *dichos* (sayings), theater, myths, and stories.

Because of the legacies of the Inquisition, much of pre-Columbian spiritual or ceremonial knowledge could not be communicated openly. However, Spanish priests encouraged syncretism; their ability to convert millions of Indigenous peoples depended upon Indigenous converts seeing a connection to this new religion. For this reason, Christian theology was inserted into Indigenous oral and written traditions. This practice is evident in the colonial-era huehuetlahtolli, which contain Indigenous pre-Cuauhtemoc oral traditions, truths and beliefs, filtered through a Christian lens. The huehuetlahtolli are a native method of communication among Nahuatl-speaking peoples, used primarily by the tlamatinis or wise elders to provide guidance and moral instruction, passed down from father to son, mother to daughter, and to legislators, teachers, and others. One compilation of huehuetlahtolli was made by Olmos and another by Sahagún, both in the 1500s. This one is from Sahagún:

> . . . at a time, in a place, which no one can now reckon,
> which no one now can recall,
> by those who sowed the seeds of the ancestral
> grandfathers, of the ancestral grandmothers;
> those who came first, those who arrived first, who came
> sweeping the way . . . were wise men.
> They were called "possessors of the books" . . .
> But the wise men soon departed . . .
> They took with them the learning,
> They took with them all the books of song [and] the flutes.
> (Sullivan 1994: 109)

The huehuetlahtolli purportedly contain the accumulated *Toltecayotl* or knowledge of the Toltecs. During the colonial era, though, as already explained, the huehuetlahtolli were used for the purposes of imparting Christian teachings on rites of passage, marriage, pregnancy, sickness, and death, as well as Christian guidance for warriors. Here are two brief excerpts from Fray de Olmos:

> Instructions from father to son: My blood, my color, I have made you,
> I have shaped you and given you form. Before you, in front of you, I

observe, I hope you are not just precious metals, because that is how you have been raised, because you are sleepy eyed, but you will soon come to know your face. (Silva Galeana 1991: 103)

Instructions from mother to daughter: Now my young daughter, little one, young woman, you have life, you have been born, you have emerged from my womb, you have suckled from my breasts. Because I have raised you, because your father has molded you and made you, he is your lord. I hope you don't suffer on this earth. (91)

While the ancient spirit of the Toltecs may have remained in the hue-huetlahtolli, Fray de Olmos specifically instructed the elders who wrote the guidances "to put down the name of God and his saints in the place of those they identified as pagan gods" (Silva Galeana 1991: 34). As a result, Tloque Nahuaque or the Giver of Life was deemed to be the devil, and Mictlan, the place of the dead, was converted into Hell. This, in effect, is how we know the huehuetlahtolli were filtered.

Silva Galeana believes that the ancient wisdom is apparent despite these kinds of intentional interventions, distortions, and demonizations. He wrote: "In the formulations in the *Huehuetlahtolli*, one can see a cosmovision and worldview of religious rituals, and the prayers themselves as ancient wisdom guided by a divine hand" (1991: 32). While this may be true, it also alerts us to what is at stake, what Indigenous content was subject to Christian distortion—a practice not limited to the huehuetlahtolli. The same form of intervention, and for the same reasons, permeated all aspects of Indigenous communication, which was turned into a tool to demonize Indigenous spirituality and impose Christianity upon the Indigenous masses.

Indigenous oral traditions, which are fortified by codices, ancient stories, and living traditions, provide evidence of consistency and reliability amid change over a wide expanse of time. Before examining these other media of communication, I will contextualize why Aztec imagery became a predominant theme of Chicana/Chicano writers and artists of the 1960s and 1970s, even though most Mexicans are arguably not of Aztec/Mexica origin—though unquestionably from maíz-based cultures.

Principio: A Return to the Root—in Art and Symbols

The idea of maíz culture undergirding Mexican and Mexican American culture can be seen in mural art. During the 1960s and 1970s, Chicana/

Chicano artists prominently utilized pre-Cuauhtemoc imagery such as pyramids, gods, warriors, and maíz. The mere presence of maíz in this art—even if not properly understood, and even when maíz is relegated to the background—serves as a subtle reminder of its ubiquitous presence in the physical and cultural landscape of the Americas. As a cultural root paradigm, maíz continues to be one of the most reproduced icons in Mexican American art.

In conjunction with the 2000 Aztlan exhibit held at the Los Angeles County Museum of Art, co-curator Victor Zamudio-Taylor asserted in "Inventing Tradition, Negotiating Modernism" (2001) that Chicanas/Chicanos invented this tradition of drawing upon pre-Columbian culture and imagery. He is not the only scholar who has suggested that such artists/writers who draw upon these traditions have either invented or reinvented them, particularly when they thereby invoke the concept of Aztlan (Padilla 1989, Klor de Alva 1989, Pérez-Torres 2001, Pérez 1999).[4]

This claim may be partially true, because chances are that most Mexicans are not of Aztec/Mexica heritage. However, the tradition of drawing on the much older maíz imagery is not dependent upon the idea of Aztlan, the purported homeland of the Mexica. The notion of Chicanas/Chicanos identifying with Aztlan may actually correspond better with Benedict Anderson's idea of imagined communities, which holds that peoples do not invent their communities or histories but rather that they imagine or create them (1991: 5–7).

The pre-Cuauhtemoc emphasis of Chicana/Chicano art during the 1960s and 1970s was not invented but rather inspired by the Mexican Revolution of 1910 and its aftermath, in which the Mexican muralist movement attempted to create an Indigenous identity and a liberation narrative. This narrative positioned Mexicans as descendants of Aztecs/Mexica and Mayas, articulating a story of continual resistance against invading Spaniards. It emphasized three hundred years of Spanish oppression and culminated in the Mexican War of Independence of 1810–1821. This war drew from an Indigenous inspiration. From a cultural standpoint, its leaders, many of whom were criollos, during and after independence, rejected all things Spanish and claimed and reclaimed everything that was Indigenous. It was from this cultural and political eruption that the Revolutionaries of 1910 also drew their inspiration.

Turner (1974) couches this turn to pre-Columbian imagery, signs, symbols and Indigenous inspiration during the Mexican War of Independence in the language of Freud, calling it a primary process. Turner wrote that during revolutionary periods "a whole hidden cultural structure, richly clothed in symbols, may be suddenly revealed" (110). Even the criollos, many of whom sided with (and co-opted) the Indigenous revolt of 1810, knew that to create an authentic Independence movement the insurgents or rebels had to go back to, or return to, the root. This they referred to as principio; they determined that the root was the legacy of Cuauhtemoc, the last "defender of the Aztecs" (Florescano 2004).[5] This "going back" was essentially part of a larger centuries-old story of the battle over Mexican identity in relationship to European colonialism and cultural imperialism.

Aside from the actual warfare, pitting Mexican Indigenous forces (alongside Africans, mestizos, and Spanish-born Mexicans) against Spanish-colonial forces, there was an ongoing struggle over who would control Mexico. An implicit question was whose stories, narratives, symbols, images, identity and even foods would prevail?

In triumphing against the foreigners, "New Spain" became Mexico, and the image of the eagle, serpent, and nopal, which symbolized the Aztec/Mexica migration from Aztlan, became the nation's seal, flag, and national narrative.[6] When Independence leader Miguel Hidalgo shouted the *Grito de Independencia* or Call to Independence at dawn on September 16, 1810, underneath his outer shirt he was wearing a shirt decorated with an eagle battling a lion, signifying the battle between Indigenous Mexico and colonial Spain (Florescano 2004: 125). Part of the revolt (primary process) against Spain was a rejection of foreign symbols. In this struggle, Florescano argued in *La Bandera Mexicana* (2004), the symbol of the eagle created unity, origin, heritage, greatness, legitimacy, and prestige—an idea that corresponds to Hobsbawm and Ranger's (1984) belief that new nations reject the present; the older the heritage, the better. The eagle, a Nahua symbol, serves this function. The eagle with nopal becomes a powerful symbol of survival and of the resilience of Indigeneity, as it contradicts the notion of total Christianization and Westernization. If anything, it symbolizes a civilizational struggle (Florescano 2004).

With Mexico's independence and its accompanying idea of principio, the history of Tenochtitlan/Mexico City—which had been the dominant city in the Anahuac Valley—was projected as the history of the entire territory of Mexico, which at that time included the greater U.S. Southwest. This is one explanation as to how Aztec/Mexica history and its imagery became associated with the new nation and with the later Mexican Revolution. It also helps to explain why Chicanas/Chicanos—who went through their own political and cultural eruption in the 1960s and 1970s—inherited these same nationalized stories and symbols. This may help to explain why these stories and symbols often overwhelm the much older story of maíz.

The following sections explore the role of elders and elder knowledge in telling a different story regarding Mexican, Central American, and Chicana/ Chicano culture, one that more closely conforms to the ancient maíz narratives of the continent, as opposed to ones biased by religious zealotry and by romanticized nationalized histories.

Maíz Imagery as Root Imagery and "The Mythology of Maíz"

Florescano (2004) argued that the idea of returning to the root during the War of Independence appears to have been a criollo idea, though perhaps influenced by Indigenous peoples. If it had been an Indigenous idea, it would not necessarily have been about returning to an "Aztec/Mexica" root. Aztec/Mexica culture was not the common denominator for the hundreds of Indigenous nations that called Mexico home. To "return" would have metaphorically meant going back to Tollan/Teotihuacan, where Lords were legitimized, or to Tamoanchan, the birthplace of maíz and of humans and the land of Quetzalcoatl/Kukulkan.

Despite the emphasis on Aztec/Mexica culture during the Chicano Movement, the older maíz story nonetheless managed to remain part of the Chicano narrative, often in the background. For example, the 1970 UCLA *Chicano History* mural is very representative of the early era of the Chicano Movement.[7] In it, brutal scenes of Spanish colonialism and U.S. imperialism are depicted in very much the manner made famous by the murals of the Mexican Revolution. The maíz, as usual, is in the background.

With respect to telling the story of Chicana/Chicano culture through art, two other murals come to mind: the 1978 *We Are Not a Minority* mural in East LA's Estrada Courts by El Congreso de Artistas Cósmicos de las Américas de San Diego (figure 14, plate 6), and José Antonio Burciaga's 1987 *The Mythology and History of Maíz* at Stanford.

We Are Not a Minority, painted by Mario Torero, Rocky, El Lion, and Zade, the members of El Congreso, represents a militancy that was common to Chicana/Chicano mural painting during that era. It also contains a hidden narrative. The mural depicts the popular leftist Argentinean and internationalist leader Che Guevara. His arm is outstretched, with finger extending in the manner of Uncle Sam, delivering a message to the heavily Mexican barrio of East LA. On the surface, it appears to be a message that politically, culturally, and demographically links Chicanas/Chicanos to

Figure 14. *We Are Not a Minority*, East L.A. mural by Mario Torero, Rocky, El Lion, and Zade, 1978. Courtesy of Mario Torero.

the continent. This is a link that was emphasized by one of the strands of the Chicano Movement—a strand that preached solidarity among all the revolutionary movements of Latin America. The idea "We are one, because America is one" is associated with Che and with Cuban patriot José Martí.

A closer inspection of the mural reveals that the word/letter A in is in the form of an ancient pyramid. The pyramid, in Chicana/Chicano art, was usually associated with a different political strand, one that aligned itself not so much with Latin America as with Indigenous America. The pyramid often signals or represents maíz culture.[8] It is the hidden narrative in the mural. The messages, in effect, fuse: Chicanos are not a minority and are Indigenous to this continent. If ever there was a consummate insurgent metaphor in response to the Western master narrative, this is it—Chicanas/Chicanos were not a minority and were going to cease acting like minorities.

Burciaga's 1987 mural emphasizes Indigeneity and is significant because it clearly demonstrates the role of Indigenous elders in influencing

Chicana/Chicano thought and culture. At the behest of Conchero elder Andrés Segura, writer/artist Burciaga went to Mexico to study the origins of maíz. The result was perhaps the symbolic and conscious beginning of a generational shift for Chicanas/Chicanos—from Aztlan as axis mundi to maíz as axis mundi.

Burciaga's mural is divided into three panels. *Mythology of Maíz* depicts the basic story, shared by virtually all Mesoamerican peoples, of how maíz was created through the intervention of the cosmic twins and Quetzalcoatl. *The Introduction of Maíz* shows native peoples introducing maíz to Europeans, a representation that suggests Europeans would have perished without it. The third panel, *Last Supper of Chicano Heroes*, is the history of the Chicano community as told through its heroes and heroines. The backdrop is a milpa. In front of the table, a single stalk of corn is pushing up through the floor.

While maíz appears to be a new axis mundi for Chicanos/Chicanas, it can be argued that the turn toward maíz actually represents an overt return to, or a new understanding of, something familiar. The acceptance of the humble and "heroic" maíz as an origin icon, in preference to a mythical place/city (Aztlan), brings Chicanas/Chicanos a few steps closer to being in line with the ancient maíz narratives of the continent. This shift or return to a maíz axis mundi is significant for many reasons. For one, in the world of symbols, this shift moves Mexicans and Chicanas/Chicanos from being viewed as "people of the sun," or as almost exclusively descendants of Aztecs/Mexica, to being "gente de maíz" or people of corn. In Mexica symbolism, the sun is popularly (though erroneously) associated with war; in Nahua-Maya culture, maíz is associated with birth, creation, and regeneration.[9]

In this shift, one can also see a changed relationship to framing and reframing. The Western master narrative represents a radical reframing of the continent. It also represents a remapping and erasure. The 1960s–1970s Chicana/Chicano Movement was a reaction to alienization; it represented a rejection of both Hispanic and Anglo cultures, including their imposed narratives. The Movement functioned as a belonging narrative; it represented a repositioning and even a rearticulation of who Chicanas/Chicanos are: Aztec, therefore from Aztlan, thus native. It was a reactive reframing. The more recent Chicana/Chicano return to a maíz axis mundi, represented by Burciaga's mural, is not reactive nor a reframing but a conscious effort, guided by Indigenous elders, to realign or reconnect this community not just to the original (or ancient) maíz narratives of the continent but to most of the original peoples of the continent also. And most importantly, this realignment operates in the present, not the past.

Combined, the three murals discussed above deliver the same basic message. The first two reject political oppression; the last rejects Anglo and Hispanic roots in favor of Indigeneity. The two views are not incompatible, and both represent a rejection of the status of Chicanos as aliens. In fact, the UFW flag—with a stylized black eagle in the middle—also belongs in this discussion, as it delivers a similar message; as noted in chapter 3, when turned upside down, it reveals the eagle as a pyramid. The black eagle is always associated with the pre-Columbian. The UFW flag, commonly emblazoned on murals across the United States and associated with labor leaders Cesar and Helen Chavez and Dolores Huerta, appears to be another affirmation of Indigeneity and maíz culture. It can be argued that it functioned as the flag of the Chicano Movement. Two aspects of culture that perhaps affirm Indigeneity and an ancient connection to maíz in an equally profound way are food and medicinal knowledge.

A Dialogue with Maíz

Without question, food is the prototypical expression of maíz culture; it is not simply sustenance but a gift for humanity. In pre-Columbian times, it was the only staple grown in both Northern and Southern Hemispheres and today is an important staple worldwide. Jack Weatherford in *Native Roots* (1991: 113) wrote: "If humans ever invented a miracle food, it must have been corn." Maíz is also highly regarded in the collective memory of Mexico for its role in assisting in the demographic recovery of the Indigenous populations that were devastated by the first hundred years of violent invasion and disease, and the subsequent four hundred years of famine, drought, wars, and revolutions.

Despite corn's incalculable value to the nation historically, at the end of the nineteenth century, in one chapter of Mexico's tortilla discourse, dictator Porfirio Díaz (like the subsequent Revolutionary governments) attempted to wean Mexicans off of tortillas, framing wheat bread, and the cultures that produced it, as inherently superior to maíz (Bulnes 1899). A cursory look at a 2010 Mexican kitchen and diet will reveal that that project failed. Virtually nothing is eaten that does not involve maíz or a tortilla.[10] As Marcos Sandoval wrote in "El Maíz y los Pueblos Indios" ("Maíz and Indigenous Peoples," 2003: 65):

Maíz is a way of being and living that connects us to Mother Earth, with our spiritual forces, and with the living and those that have come before us. Maíz creates a relationship with our ancestors, those who accumulated the knowledge of the maíz in the course of many thousands of years.

Esteva (2003b) concurs, noting that all of Mexico and all Mexicans continue to have a dialogue or relationship with maíz. Much of this dialogue is in the form of myth/stories, nowadays found in archaeological footprints and evident in the everyday life and belief systems of people today. For many, this direct dialogue comes in their daily diet. In 2004, the National Museum of Popular Cultures had more than six hundred registered recipes involving maíz.

This only begins to scratch the surface of maíz's importance. Miguel Vasallo in "Gente de Maíz—Maíz de la Gente" ("People of Corn—Corn of the People," 2004) noted that in the 1990s, more than half of the caloric intake of Mexicans was derived from maíz. He stated that in Mexico, maíz is so prevalent that maíz-based foods are referred to as "Vitamin T: taco, tortilla, tlacoyo, tostada y tamal, our daily maíz, our daily tortilla" (35). This shortest of lists only begins to suggest the number of dishes that use maíz—which is interrelated with beans and squash, alongside chile, cactus, amaranth, and chia in the "Seven Warriors of Nutrition."

Despite access to other foods, a great many kitchens in the United States resemble those in Mexico and other parts of the Americas. The dialogue with maíz is a living relationship, not dependent on ancient knowledge or historias profundas, though they are present nonetheless. In effect, this dialogue is the antithesis of official narratives, which, when disseminated top-down, are often received as static or imposed monologues. The dialogue with maíz is enacted daily, at mealtime; it is creative and is always adapting. This is often when cultural information is communicated, both at a familial level and at a community level.

The Tamalada, Dia de los Muertos, and the Quinceañera

In "Art, Labor, and the Genius of Women: A Short History of Tamales" (2011), Antonia Castañeda writes: "Tamales, the ingenious creation of Indigenous women, originated in Mexico and Central America, possibly as early as 7000 BCE" (15). The making of tamales and the tamalada (tamale party) are a thousands-of-years-old tradition in the Americas. And they have been primarily a women's affair, beyond nations, languages and borders. Castañeda adds: "From the past to the present, the rich and varied history of tamales is embedded in the ancient art, labor, and genius of women" (17).

Anthropologist Vélez-Ibáñez (1996) asserts that the tamalada is the quintessential ceremony for Mexican Americans, primarily because he sees it as the synthesis of all the year's ceremonies compressed into one, albeit as a secular event. It is best equated to a family get-together, except that everyone works.[11] Also, it has not been commercialized in the same way that Día de los Muertos (the Day of the Dead) has, to the point that in many communities it is but the Mexican version of Halloween. The tamalada is a communal affair.

Tamaladas usually occur during the winter season, the traditional time for storytelling, which also coincides with pre-Columbian calendrical cycles (the winter solstice). Most take place between December 24 and January 6, a period that includes Christmas Eve, Christmas Day, New Year's Eve, New Year's Day, and Three Kings Day. In the United States, the holiday season nowadays begins as early as Día de los Muertos at the beginning of November and extends beyond Three Kings Day. Here is a 2006 description from a handout given to customers by the proprietors of the Sacramento Bakery in Madison, Wisconsin:

> On January 6 friends and family gather at the *Rosca de Reyes* party and each person cuts his or her own slice of Rosca. There is much excitement for whoever gets the piece containing the plastic doll (Baby Jesus) becomes the godparent of the baby and is obligated to host a traditional "Tamalada" on February 2nd. . . . A Tamalada is a party where guests are offered Tamales and champurrado—a hot chocolate drink thickened with corn masa.

Unlike the rosca (bread) that is eaten but once a year, tamales are eaten year-round. What distinguishes a tamalada from other events that might involve tamales is the communal preparation of them, the making of the masa, the wrapping, and the cooking. At traditional tamaladas, the whole process is done from scratch. The point of making homemade tamales is to bring families and neighbors together, including relatives from far-off places. In Spanish, this is referred to as *convivencia*. What makes the tamalada unique is that it is the time when news and stories are exchanged, of everything from births to deaths. While some see this as a time simply for *chisme* (gossip), it is actually a time when cultural information is communicated and exchanged, though according to Clark and Tafolla (2011) that is the definition of chisme. While they are irreverent, all recognize the importance of both the event and the information that gets exchanged at this time.

Tamaladas tend to be gendered affairs, with women doing the labor-intensive food preparation, cooking, and interior cleaning, while men buy the ingredients, clean, do the yardwork, and so on; however, in the United States, in recent years the men are also being "invited" to participate in the actual work of the tamalada. Normally, the storytelling is also gendered. When the tamaladas are mixed, stories and information are exchanged freely between men and women. When the genders separate, that is when the chisme begins.

In the cultural sense, for women, the tamalada is when recipes are either exchanged or demonstrated. This happens between mother and daughter or among grandmother/mother, mother/daughter, and daughter/granddaughter. Beyond the sharing of ingredients, the recipe often communicates personal, family, and community history and even national and civilizational history. Many times, the stories are communicated formally as part of the recipe, a place where memory and culture are stored. Pérez San Vicente argued in "Maíz: Nuestra Carne y Sustento" ("Our Flesh and Sustenance," 2000: 17) that a peoples' history can actually be reconstituted on the basis of recipes, particularly maíz recipes. Pérez San Vicente's observation elevates the recipe to a historical document—a cross between the oral and written tradition.

The tamalada, secular in nature, but directly related to ancient maíz culture, can perhaps be considered comparable to Raymond Fogelson's idea of a once-a-year epitomizing event, which is also akin to events that Vine Deloria Jr. (1973) defines as having a profound effect on the "psychic life of a community." It is an event that contributes to the collective memory of peoples (Nabokov 2002: 161).

There is no question that many Mexican Americans and Latinos participate in actual pre-Columbian spiritual ceremonies and rituals, most of which are associated primarily with the Nahua-Maya culture of the peoples of Mesoamerica. In Mexican and Mexican American communities, most of these revolve around danza ceremonies, songs, and rituals, which are related to maíz and associated with the ancient Mesoamerican calendars. More recently, with an influx of Indigenous peoples migrating directly from Indigenous communities, Nahua, Maya, Otomi, Mixtec, Zapotec, and Andean ceremonies and celebrations are now also taking place in the United States. Beyond Mexicans and Central Americans, the influx includes many peoples from Peru, Bolivia, and Ecuador.[12]

While many thousands actually participate in these ceremonies, millions more observe them to some degree when they take place in public parks, plazas, and squares.[13] Additionally, many more participate in the more familiar ceremonies such as the quinceañera, a coming-of-age ceremony held for a young woman on her fifteenth birthday, a celebration that evolved from an Indigenous ritual—Xilonen.

The Xilonen green corn ceremony itself is a coming-of-age ceremony for young women—and it is still held throughout the United States, though not at the scale of the quinceañera. In various conversations with me, Maestra Cobb has indicated that it is she who introduced the Xilonen ceremony in the United States. Similar coming-of-age ceremonies are held by Indigenous peoples throughout the continent, including many within the United States. Women, and young women specifically, are ceremonially associated with maíz, connoting birth, growth, and regeneration.

The quinceañera, while special, has adapted into a commercialized Christian and even secular ceremony. Although many families take part in these expensive celebrations, many are not consciously aware that they are participating in communal rituals or ceremonies that can be traced to pre-Cuauhtemoc traditions.

There are other ceremonies or vestiges of pre-Cuauhtemoc ceremonies that are or continue to be practiced. An example is Día de los Muertos. It is an observance that can range from sacred rituals and ceremonies to parades to, most recently, events resembling Halloween. It is a day to poke fun at death and honor the departed. Many families do this by constructing an altar, often with maíz at the center of it.

Another tradition related to food, described by Sahagún in the *Primeros Memoriales* ([1590] 1997: 71), is a practice that still takes place in many Mexican homes:

> When something was to be eaten, before it was eaten, first a small amount, a tiny piece of food, was cut off and cast before the hearth. When it had been cast there, then they began to eat. No one ate before [the food] had been cast before the hearth.

For some, this is habit; for others, it is ceremony (spirit food), in remembrance of those who are no longer with us.

In many if not most of these ceremonies and celebrations, food continues to play an integral part.

The *Tradición*/Tradition: Hidden Transcripts and Hidden in Plain Sight

> *The circles of feather-crowned concheros dancing in the churchyard of Central Mexico attract the attention of passersby perhaps more than any other religious dance group of the area. The visitor to Mexico is caught by the insistent rhythm, the bright feather headdresses, and the armadillo shell stringed instruments. . . . But Mexican and tourist alike go by, knowing little of the dance itself or the participants.*
>
> —FRANCES GILLMOR[14]

The danza ceremonial tradition is a place where Indigenous knowledge, traditions, and memory are stored and a principal vehicle by which this knowledge continues to be transmitted and communicated, often at a level not apparent to the casual observer. Danza has both a public face—through dances that are generally performed at celebrations and festivals—and a private aspect, in which ceremonies and rituals take place out of the public eye.

Danza is part of a broader movement referred to generally as the *tradición*. It is a tradition that includes dance, ceremony, ritual, story, and intellectual pursuits that all have the primary aim of conserving Indigenous knowledge. However, it has its roots in two very different but related suppressions of Indigenous knowledge: the mass-conversion effort of the Catholic Church in the early 1500s and the *Último Mandato de Cuauhtémoc* or the *Consigna de Anáhuac*, a set of original instructions from Cuauhtemoc, the last leader of the Mexica. In 1521, while leading a heroic defense of Tenochtitlan/Mexico City—but when military defeat seemed certain—he directed his compatriots to "destroy our temples, our places of study, our schools, our ball game fields, and our houses of song" and to instead conceal the knowledge "deep within our hearts" (R. Rodríguez 1997: 11). Henceforth, the parents were to become the teachers, passing on the ancestral knowledge to their children within the home.

Reputedly, it was three elders, Conchero elder Maestro Andrés Segura, Florencio Yescas, and Tlakaelel, who first brought the danza tradition(s) to the United States.[15] While Maestra Cobb, a danzante, started as a student of Yescas, she ranks up there with the three elders for her role in the spreading and teaching of ceremonies in the United States, particularly those associated with women. While each of the three elders brought a different variant, the traditions are generally similar.[16] Much ceremonial knowledge is passed in these circles and much of it is related to and timed to coincide with the ancient ceremonial cycles based on maíz. Anthropologist Martha Stone, who spent a generation inside the Conchero tradition, probed both the public and deeper levels of danza, which she asserted involve deception and double meaning.[17] "An aura of mystery" has always surrounded danza: "Certainly after the conquest it was clothed with secrecy and double meaning" (Stone 1975: 211). Danza might be viewed as a "hidden transcript" whose existence helps to explain how, in a hostile environment, Indigenous traditions and knowledge managed to be preserved over a span of nearly five hundred years since the Spanish "conquest." The traditions and knowledge embedded in danza preceded the European presence in Mexico by thousands of years.

The Conchero danza tradition can be traced to 1537 when a group of "warriors" disguised as dancers were charged with assisting the church in the conversion process. This had come on the heels of the purported apparition of the Virgen de Guadalupe on the hill of Tepeyac where Tonanztin or Mother Earth had been venerated for generations. However, the oral tradition about danza says that it formed also to hide the culture and traditions of the Nahua-Chichimeca peoples, transmitting and communicating them, in a hidden form, via dance, song, and oral traditions. That which was embedded or encoded was ancient knowledge related to origins and migrations and ceremonial and astronomical knowledge.

The tradición was charged with propagating the story of how Guadalupe/Tonantzin appeared so that Indigenous peoples could convert to Catholicism and be saved from all the calamities that had befallen them. Guadalupe appeared where Tonantzin was venerated, and thus began the syncretic model. Many patron saints in Mexico have their Indigenous equivalents in the danza tradition. Similarly, many Indigenous spirits are nowadays referred to by their Christian name, according to Westerners, such as Stone. In this way, the Indigenous spirit and memory is preserved. It is similar to the idea of *Idols Behind Altars* (Brenner 2002) — the idea that peoples hide their preexisting beliefs behind a Christian altar. The Catholic Church also propagated this model; for conversion purposes Quetzalcoatl was actually Saint Thomas (Boturini [1746a] 1990).

On a surface level, danza communicates ancient dance traditions — traditions that are not necessarily understood by onlookers. On a deeper level, danza contains a hidden message, revealing its direct relationship to an ancient cosmology or worldview based on maíz. Many of the danza ceremonies have to do with when to plant, water, and harvest. Some involve the symbiotic relationship between animals, humans, and maíz.[18] Others honor the spiritual forces that make sustenance possible: Quetzalcoatl is honored as the bringer of maíz; Tlaloc is honored as the spirit who brings the rains. To the Maya, Tlaloc is but another manifestation of Quetzalcoatl (Girard 1966). Guadalupe/Tonantzin is honored as the Mother of all things, Mother Earth or the Mother of God. Some of the more prominent ceremonies involve the observation of the winter and summer solstices, the spring and winter equinoxes, the Aztec/Mexica New Year, and one that is specific to maíz and young women, the Xilonen ceremony.

Other major danza ceremonies involve the birth and death of Cuauhtemoc, Easter, and Día de las Ánimas (Día de los Muertos). In the all-night ceremony for the *ánimas* or souls who have passed on, they are not referred to as dead. They are considered still among us, but in spirit form. Many of the ceremonies involve hours of dancing and singing and some last all night. All culminate with communal meals, and, in some cases, are followed by more dancing. Danza also involves other specific commitments, some of which involve pilgrimages and self-sacrifice. Many of the ceremonies take place in private, after public celebrations.

During the 1500s, the church was very uneasy about syncretism and about anything Indigenous that contained a memory of Indigenous traditions. For instance, the church created laws outlawing certain practices related to danza, associating them with idolatry and the devil. This included laws barring Indians from using banners or ancient masks or singing songs of their ancient rites or histories. The laws also designated when and where the dances could take place. There were other repressive laws prohibiting the wearing of *coronas* or headdresses (Stone 1975).

For many Mexicans, Central Americans, and Chicanas/Chicanos who follow Indigenous traditions today, the idea of syncretism is the idea of living the Mandato, of preserving the culture, knowledge, and traditions and continuing to resist. It is dancing in the Zócalo 365 days each year to "knock down the Cathedral" that sits atop the temple of Quetzalcoatl, another example of hidden transcripts: danzantes in Mexico City commonly tell people that they dance so that their vibrations will knock down the Cathedral. This, they say, will force the government to excavate the Temple of Quetzalcoatl, which lies below the Cathedral, built with the stones of the Templo Mayor. The government is reluctant to remove the Cathedral because it is also considered a historic structure. For Indigenous peoples, in effect, the Cathedral represents colonialism itself—a symbol of the spiritual conquest. The widespread practice of erecting churches atop pyramids throughout the continent symbolized conquest and domination (Esteva 2003a).

This idea of preserving the culture can be seen in the *Crónica Mexicáyotl* ([1576] 1998). In it, Tezozomoc admonishes his descendants far into the future to never forget the history of Tenochtitlan—of how "it all began" (3–6). Tezozomoc's words were later echoed in a call by José María Morelos (Afro-mestizo) during the 1810–1821 War of Independence. In it, he invoked the memory of the defenders of Tenochtitlan/Mexico City, including Moctezuma, Cacamatzin, Cuauhtimotzin, Xicotenecatl, and Catzonsi, urging the people to continue their example of resistance against the invading Spaniards (Herrejón 1985: 132).

Danza and the tradición are perhaps the sector of Mexican society most associated with carrying on those calls for cultural resistance. The elder-guided danza, tradición, and ceremonies represent a direct link to ancient knowledge and practices. These traditions involve the same spiritual forces as those recorded in the codices, as those present in today's oral traditions. There is little doubt that ancient knowledge continues to be communicated and transmitted through these ceremonies and rituals. A debate continues, however, about how much of the deep meaning—the historias profundas—should be revealed to the public.

Storytelling, Oral Traditions, Iconic Images, and Language

De-Indigenized Mexicans and Central Americans in the United States are not generally taught Mesoamerican creation stories in public schools. Neither are they taught about their ancient maíz culture, and especially about the traditions found within the huehuetlahtolli. The exceptions are charter and private schools such as Semillas in Los Angeles, which teaches from an Indigenous and maíz-based curriculum.[19]

Whatever culture is taught is usually taught at home, especially that involving pre-Cuauhtemoc knowledge. But among de-Indigenized Mexicans, if in any way this knowledge is taught in the home, it is generally taught as part of the past, not as a part of the family's present-day reality. The reticence about teaching Mesoamerican knowledge is often the result of what Indigenous scholars refer to as historical trauma (Duran and Duran 1995).

The traumatic memory of colonization, coupled with the historic anti-Mexican sentiment in this country, means that many Mexicans experience a double sense of inferiority. As a result, many reject their Indigeneity and do not overtly identify as being part of an Indigenous Mexican maíz-based culture. However, Mexicans in the United States are more apt to accept their Indigeneity than their de-Indigenized compatriots in Mexico, even the "progressive" ones who identify not as Indigenous or mestizo but as part of the "popular" classes.[20] Anthropologist Renato Rosaldo suggests why: "When I've said Mexicans become Indians when they come to the United States, I mean both that they recognize how Indian they are (and even 'remember' Indian grandparents they never speak of in Mexico) and [that] they see that as Mexicans in the United States they are structurally inserted as a minority group comparable to Indians in Mexico. They move *'de mayoría a minoría,'* from majority to minority" (personal communication, December 2, 2005). This dynamic suggests that identity for Mesoamerican peoples, including Chicanas/Chicanos, is situational and contingent. A rise in anti-Mexican sentiment in this country is one situation that has the potential to nudge Mexicans/Mexican Americans and Central Americans toward reidentifying with an Indigenous and/or maíz-based identity. Such reidentification requires learning to reinterpret signs that have long been associated not with Indigeneity but with mestizo or even Hispanic culture. If we examine the role that Nahua-Maya elders have played in influencing Mexican/Chicana/Chicano culture in the United States, perhaps we can say that their role has been to teach the people of maíz how to interpret and decipher the signs, symbols, and imagery that have long been staring at them, often in the mirror.

Maíz, Rain, and the Earth

The religious life of Nahua-Maya peoples permeated everything. With its agricultural roots, the songs, the prayers, the art and poetry—the mass media of the pre-Cuauhtemoc era—all revolved around maíz, rain, the earth, and essentially all the forces that made sustenance possible. Upon contact between Europeans and Indigenous peoples, as part of la Otra Conquista, the Spanish/Christian mass-conversion project, the Spanish priests put down on paper Indigenous "divine hymns" and other prayers. For instance, the primary themes of the twenty sacred songs found in Sahagún's *Primeros Memoriales* ([1590] 1997) are maíz, rain, the earth—their spiritual representations, that is—and warriors. The primary representations of maíz are Centeotl and Chicomecoatl—male and female spirits of maíz. Ruiz de Alarcón ([1629] 1984) defines Centeotl as "the only god, the god without a father." In "El Dios del Maíz en Mesoamérica" (1997), Tomás Pérez Suárez argued that Tlaloc was "the God of Maíz." Mesoamericanist Thelma Sullivan (1994: 171) posits that Tlaloc, often associated with rain, also represented the fertile earth. The following, translated from the

Florentine Codex by Sullivan, shows the importance of and interdependence between the three above spiritual forces:

O' Tlaloc . . . O, Our lord, let it not go on like this,
Let there be fullness and abundance for all!
Or let pestilence seize the people in its grip,
Let the Lord of the region of the dead do his work, take up
his duties. Then perhaps, Chicomecoatl and Centeotl
shall sustain them, shall succor them a little;
perhaps into their mouths she shall put a drop of corn gruel,
a scrap of food, as provisions for their journey.
(Sullivan 1994: 155–56).

Before the arrival of Europeans in Mexico, there were schools that taught poetry and song, associated with writing and the arts. Gruzinski wrote:

Temple schools reserved for sons of the *pipiltin* prepared the future rulers. Within these *calmecac*, wise men — "those called the owners of the book paintings," "the keepers of tradition" — dispensed to the young nobles an education as austere as it was sophisticated, which associated knowledge with modes of speaking and ways of being. Among other things, they learned verses of songs so as to be able to sing what they called divine hymns that were written in characters on painted books. (1993: 9)

After the arrival of Europeans, the function of these schools changed. At the site of the famous Aztec Calmecac or school of higher learning, the College of Santa Cruz de Santiago Tlatelolco was built, becoming an institution that instructed young Indians in the Catholic faith (Olmos [1547] 1992). One can argue that this was ground zero for the great reframing and the great remapping of the Americas — where all the signs, symbols, and images were changed, and a new axis mundi was imposed upon Indigenous peoples. The context of all this was colonization and the destruction of the codices and the overarching Inquisition that feared heresy.[21] The context was survival. In the prologue to his *Historia General de las Cosas de Nueva España* ([1577] 2010), Sahagún posits that to be able to understand an illness, one has to study it. This was the rationale that many of the priests used for writing about pre-Columbian knowledge — to be able to destroy it. However, it is believed that many of the *nahuatlatos* or writers hid Indigenous narratives in them: "Indians preserved the songs in writing, sprinkling them with Christian terms to thwart the censors" (Gruzinski 1993: 57). Despite the Christianization of these songs, several edicts were passed during the colonial era, as early as 1539 and 1546, making it illegal to sing them (Bierhorst 2009: 16).[22]

The practice of concealing Indigenous traditions within poetry, song, and the huehuetlahtolli came with a price. There is no shortage of examples of Indigenous converts being persecuted for holding on to the old ways. Despite this, there must have been a fine line as to what constituted heresy, because much of the cantos and cantares were in fact collected and preserved by or with the assistance of Spanish priests. And in some cases, Indians willingly converted and assisted the priests in the missionization project.

León-Portilla, in the book *Cantos y Crónicas del Antiguo México* (2003b), brought together the flower and song (in xochitl, in cuicatl), the poetry of ancient Mexico, additionally presenting twenty sacred songs from the 1500s. The following is an excerpt from "Canto a Xochipilli" ("Hymn to Xochipilli"):

Oh, I have arrived where the road forks:
Only I am Centeotl.
Where shall I go? Where does the road lead?
The provider of Tlalocan. The gods cry . . .
(102)

In this canto, Centeotl, the spirit of maíz, wonders where his destination is. To Tlalocan—the equivalent of heaven? "The gods cry" is an allusion to rain—the force necessary to make the earth fertile.

When the tlamatinis or wise elders were eliminated, the ability to have such poems properly interpreted was hampered, though not thwarted, because the knowledge also resided in nonverbal media such as dance, song, and art. As far as the Spanish priests were concerned, because Indigenous peoples were under the sway of the devil, any place in their cosmology other than Earth had to be Hell. Thus, they outlawed the ancient songs, on the grounds that they were demonic and "beckoned memories of idolatry" (Bierhorst 2009: 208). For this reason, the role of poetry and of the cantos and cantares took on a far greater importance: the knowledge that had been taught in the Calmecac was also stored there.

When the Chicana/Chicano movement exploded in the 1960s to 1970s, it did not create a unique cultural/artistic expression from nothing. Instead, it turned to Flor y Canto (Flower and Song) and Canto al Pueblo (Song for the People), two national song and poetry festivals that asserted a linkage with the past, particularly with the forms and styles of expression found in the poetry known as in xochitl, in cuicatl. What Chicanas/Chicanos added was the ability to write poetry and songs in three languages (Spanish, English, and Nahuatl), often within the same poem, song, play, or other artwork. Whether it was conscious or not, by taking up the style of in xochitl, in cuicatl, Chicana/Chicano poets arguably took up the seeds of maíz culture, which were waiting to reemerge. Arguably that is also where the seeds of shifting back to maíz as axis mundi were laid, though that shift does not manifest outright until perhaps a generation later.

Theater of the Oppressed and Theater of the Sphere

Theater too was part of Mesoamerica long before the arrival of Europeans. After the first encounter, Spanish priests used theater for the mass conversion of Indigenous peoples. One example that remains with us is the *Pastorela*—the story of the attempt by the devil to keep the shepherds from visiting baby Jesus. Another example is the Christians-versus-the-Moros play—a reenactment of the expulsion of the Moors from Spain.[23] Spanish priests brought both plays to the Americas during the colonial era. Hundreds of years later, theater remains a cultural force in these same communities, albeit with different purposes. In Maní, Yucatán, a yearly reenactment of the 1562 auto de fe takes place to commemorate the Maya books burnt by representatives of the Catholic Church. The play reminds the people that despite Spanish atrocities, the knowledge contained within the books was never lost.

A few thousand miles to the north, theater continues to play an important role in Chicana/Chicano communities, a phenomenon that is tied to the direct influence that various Nahua-Maya elders had in passing on traditional knowledge to these communities in the 1960s and 1970s. During that era, Teatro Campesino was the most influential Chicano theater company, renowned primarily because it grew out of the UFW's grape and lettuce boycotts and because of its emphasis on Indigeneity. Teatro Campesino was unique in its roots and origins, but also in where its actors performed. Rather than perform at great halls, often they would simply roll up in a flatbed truck in the fields and begin their performances. This means of communication was the only one available to deliver Teatro Campesino's messages, as the mass media in the agricultural sectors of the United States were tightly controlled and sympathetic to agribusiness. That's why Teatro Campesino resonated with the workers. That a farm-worker-based theater ensemble would turn to Indigeneity is not coincidental, being that most of the workers themselves were and are Indigenous or Indigenous-based campesinos. In communicating Indigeneity, in one sense, they were but holding up a mirror to the workers in the fields. When Teatro Campesino exploded unto the scene, and then turned to Indigeneity while creating the "Theater of the Sphere," it was criticized by both political and cultural opponents and urban theater groups that considered themselves more leftist and less connected to the land (cofounder Luis Valdez himself had leftist roots). Commenting on the Teatro's work, Broyles-González wrote: "When El Teatro Campesino sought to ground the Theater of the Sphere in Mayan and Aztec mythology it did so with the conviction that those myths constituted an active force within Chicana/o reality. . . . Myth was seen as 'submerged wisdom of life'" (1994: 89–90). The Teatro's inspiration was not abstract; it was not guided by romanticism but by living Indigenous elders. These included principally Martínez Parédez and Conchero Andrés Segura, both of whom had active and ongoing relationships with the Teatro and other sectors of the Chicana/Chicano community nationwide.

The stories that the Teatro accessed were the very same ones that contain the ancient history of humans on this continent and the history of maíz. Many of the *actos* of the theater involved the use of masks and ritual. Perhaps one of the most powerful pieces that was associated with those ancient stories was the Chorti Mayan *Baile de los Gigantes* (*Dance of the Giants*), adapted from Maya scholar Girard's (1962) translation. The theater also included Conchero dances. Many of the members of the Teatro also became part of Xinachtli, a Conchero danza group with several branches throughout the United States, under the direction of Segura.[24]

For Olivia Chumacero, a long-time member of the theater group, the Theater of the Sphere was simply an effort to exchange knowledge and to ground the Teatro's philosophy in ancestral knowledge, acquired through living elders rather than simply from books (personal communication, August 7, 2007). This was true for many other *teatros* and cultural groups throughout the country that also turned to Indigeneity for cultural affirmation.

Conclusion: Embracing the Tortilla

An examination of Mexican culture shows that despite hundreds of years of imposed culture, Indigenous maíz-based culture survives, though syncretized, obviously, and not in its pre-Cuauhtemoc form(s). In part, it appears to have been unintentionally saved by those who sought to destroy it. In an irony of history, akin to the whitewashing of a mural that actually preserves the mural, the tools employed to convert Indigenous peoples en masse are the very same tools that helped to preserve Indigenous culture. The devices used by Spanish priests to reframe the continent were the same ones used by Indigenous peoples to communicate their culture before European contact, and used again afterward to preserve their culture. Nevertheless, many Indigenous peoples lost the ability to read and understand the original Indigenous signs, symbols, and imagery. As a result, many lost connection to their maíz-based stories. This resulted in their de-Indigenization. Yet, in this country, a generation ago, elders from the Nahua-Maya oral tradition began teaching Chicanos/Chicanas and Mexican and Central American peoples how to read those signs again and taught them the stories and the ceremonies. Elder influence, plus the fact that Mexicans continue to be treated as aliens in this country, is what makes them amenable to these messages. More importantly, it is their daily dialogue with maíz that makes them amenable; it is not an invented relationship. It is part of their/our daily lives. That is why even the simple act of embracing the corn tortilla, as Julieta Villegas, the elder at the beginning of this book, suggested, demonstrates that the dialogue with maíz has never truly been severed.

Figure 15. Eagle and condor—symbol of the Americas. Front cover of Maya scholar Domingo Martínez Parédez's 1960 book *Un Continente y Una Cultura*. Photo by the author.

En el Umbral de la Agonía del Maíz Azul

Verónica Castillo Hernández

Aztec Cultures

In this piece I show the history of blue corn and the native corn of the Aztec and Huichol cultures. In the Aztec culture there are myths or legends speaking to the ways in which the people expressed their displeasure at always having to eat the same thing and asked the gods to provide an alternative staple. They offered prayers and gifts to the gods so that they would provide them a staple—called *Tlayölli* or Maíz—that hid behind the mountains. The gods: Tlaloc did not find it, or Tonatiuh, Citlalicue, Ehecatl, Meztli, or Mixcoatl, and in that way the gods passed through without bringing the staple for which the people longed.

However, one of their gods—Quetzalcoatl, better known as the plumed serpent—told them that he was going to bring the staple for which they clamored. The people wondered how he was going to accomplish it if all the others had attempted it and had failed to go through the mountains, and he told them he was going to bring it back. On the way Quetzalcoatl transformed himself into a black ant so that he could go through a small hole and insert himself into the mountain and that was were he found Tlayölli. He took one of the seeds and took it away from the mountain and took it to his people—the Aztecs. When he gave them the seed, Quetzalcoatl told them to plant it, instructing them that when the result emerged they should continue reproducing it, and tend to it and protect it because it was a gift from the gods. That is why the Aztecs and other Indigenous cultures protect our corn from corporations now creating transgenic corn.

Huichol Culture

The Huichol people have other legends or myths; in one they speak about a generous staple that was easy to reproduce, that could be processed with different ways of preparation, and that could be converted to foodstuff. They made great expeditions to find the staple and they could not find it.

They all became disillusioned but a young warrior did not give up. One day he took his bow and arrow and set out on the search. He yearned so much and became so tired that he spied a beautiful tree under which he decided to rest. There he went into a deep sleep, so deep that he did not feel the ants taking his clothes off. Upon waking he came to that realization when the grackles made fun of him for having been left butt naked, just as he came into this world. They did not leave him alone. So upset was the young man that he took his bow and arrow and pointed it directly at the blackbird. Realizing she was in a bad spot, the grackle begged him to spare her life and in exchange she would give him what his people had long sought to obtain. The young man forgave the grackle and followed her.

During the journey the bird transformed into a mature woman. She took him home and before inviting him in said, "For having spared my life I'm going to introduce you to my daughters and you are going to choose one so she can be your wife. Moreover, she will give you the staple, teach you to cultivate it and harvest it and the many ways in which you can prepare it to eat." Upon entering and seeing her daughters, their beauty stunned the young man. Finally, he chose one. The woman told him, "You have chosen the most beautiful and the best of my daughters. You should take care of her and protect her because she is the Blue Corn."

Presently, the blue corn is the most valuable corn among our different Mexican and Mesoamerican cultures. The blue corn is in danger of extinction at the hands of those greedy corporations that have created transgenic corn.

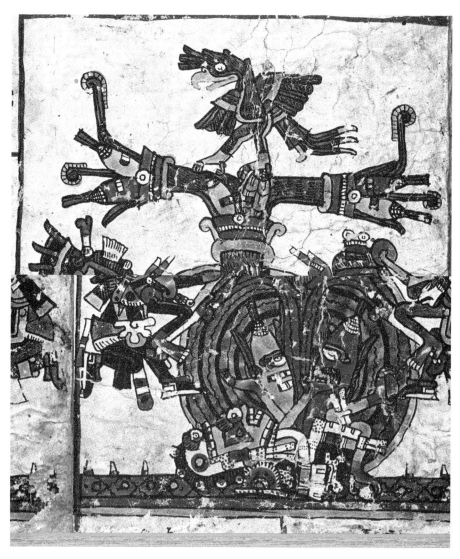

Figure 16. Maíz as axis mundi, Borgia Codex. In this book, the axis mundi or center of the universe for Mesoamerican peoples in the United States shifts from Aztlan to the maíz tree: *non kuahuitl cintli in tlalnepantla*. Courtesy of Foundation for Advancement of Mesoamerican Studies.

CHAPTER SIX

Axis Mundi

From Aztlan to Maíz

What did peoples from maíz-based cultures know about the universe before the arrival of Europeans? If it were possible to give but one answer, it would be that they knew maíz, and they knew its ancient story. Centeotzintli or sacred maíz was not just their sustenance, and the maíz tree was not simply their axis mundi. Corn was also what they were made of, where they came from, what they lived for, and how they counted time. It was how they regulated their lives. This is the seven-thousand-year ceremonial discourse of maíz as a story of the continent that continues to be conveyed through oral and written narratives and often through song, prayer, ceremony and dance. As both Indigenous and de-Indigenized peoples, they/we continue to be the people of maíz.

The previous chapters have examined these narratives and a massive three-hundred-year process referred to as la Otra Conquista. The Other Conquest was an attempt to eradicate that ancient culture and superimpose in its place another axis mundi: the cross of Christ. The maíz and the cross were both sacred, but nonetheless, the Spanish priests began a mass-conversion project and a five-hundred-year war over souls.[1] To their way of thinking, eternal truth and eternal salvation could only be achieved through their teachings. Part of the conversion effort included demonizing Indigenous beliefs and knowledge, and the signs and symbols of this knowledge, and imposing upon the peoples of this continent the Christian cross and a plethora of angels, saints, virgins, and corresponding imagery.

Despite the imposed new axis mundi, even after hundreds of years, my research found that while it was massively disruptive, the effort was not completely successful. Yet we are left to ask: why are the Indigenous images, signs, and symbols difficult to recognize or interpret? Semiotic theory provides one answer: their meaning was changed, inverted, and demonized. Beyond notions of racial and cultural superiority, the signs and symbols were made unrecognizable, framed within the context of good versus evil/ God versus the devil. In the modern era they remain distorted, or rendered harmless as relics of the past, more useful in promoting tourism than for understanding the hidden and suppressed narratives of the continent.

This study used modern communication theories to explain the process of de-Indigenization and alienation. It included reframing theories that are normally applied to moments in time and bits or strips of information. For many Indigenous peoples, five hundred years is also but "a moment in time," particularly considering the age of maíz.

The Spanish friars were not averse to using Indigenous imagery, stories, and symbols for the purpose of imposing their new axis mundi upon the Indigenous world. It appears that Indigenous peoples resorted to the same syncretic methods, with many accepting Christianity, in part because they saw it as compatible with their own spirituality, especially when presented with the brown Guadalupe/Tonantzin. Some embraced Christianity with open arms; others did so for reasons of survival. However, that syncretism was always an uncomfortable dance, as the friars always feared the presence of idols behind altars.

Yet it is not syncretism alone that allowed for the survival of maíz culture; cultural resistance and constant rebellion were also factors. In part, these rebellions against oppression were chapters in the war over imagery, through what Turner (1974) and Florescano (2004) refer to as a primary process and principio respectively. This was a political and cultural eruption, and a desire to return to the root, that surfaced more than once in response to three hundred years of Spanish domination. It surfaced during Mexico's War of Independence and also during the Mexican Revolution. These eruptions brought to the fore long-suppressed Indigenous expressions, including and principally the eagle and serpent icons, along with their hidden maíz narratives, often displayed prominently on seals, flags, and maps.

Primary process and principio also manifested during the 1960s and 1970s Chicano Movement. For this movement, just as for the two mentioned above, resistance meant picking up where Cuauhtemoc, the last defender of the Aztecs, left off.[2] For Mexican Americans, who had long been treated as aliens in lands they believed were formerly theirs, this meant returning to Aztlan and making it their axis mundi, even if many were not actually descendants of Aztecs. Perhaps they were not Aztec, but unquestionably they were inheritors of a much older maíz culture.

Beyond notions of Aztlan or even north-south connections, the most powerful image that has continued to communicate Indigeneity and cultural resilience is the round corn tortilla itself. From axis mundi to sacred sustenance, to human flesh, to its use as the Christian host for the purposes of mass conversion, to a symbol of survival, finally to a symbol of cultural resistance, it is today a most visible, if not the most visible, civilizational marker for Mexican peoples in the United States. A plethora of scholars argue that maíz was the seed whose germination yielded Mesoamerica's cultures and that most of these cultures have the same or similar creation and origin stories.

On this journey, as I traversed various sites of analysis, from maps to maíz to Columbus, to Aztlan and back to maíz, it became clear that the cosmological center for Mexicans and Central Americans in the United States did not shift, that they never lost their maíz culture; what was lost was the ability to recognize its signs, symbols, and stories. However, the advancement in deciphering the signs, symbols, and images of the codices, via the work of Galarza and others, revealing them to be part of a precise language of Nahua-Maya peoples, will soon obviate the need for interpreters. Yet even when they are deciphered, the challenge will be for de-Indigenized peoples to determine whether those signs, that language, and that culture in fact belong to them, or to view them as things of their ancestors or of peoples other than themselves. This struggle over identity offers ample opportunity for further research.

I learned to recognize maíz culture within the everyday lives of de-Indigenized peoples, principally in their diet, but also in their stories, literature, art, murals, song, danza, ceremonies and rituals, medicines, and even on tortilla wrappers. In the end, I had to invert the question: what in Mexican/Chicana/Chicano or Central American culture—what in the Andes—what in Pacha Mama is not maíz-based?

Future research should continue the documentation, including the creation of a maíz map of the continent, charting maíz's genetic/migration path and its civilizational path via maíz stories. Such a map would consist of an analysis of maíz stories, narratives, and symbols. It is also important to examine how maíz-based peoples use corn for purposes of identity formation, how it is used to confer legitimacy, and how the stories also communicate a sense of belonging. Future research should also study the impacts that globalization is having upon the maíz cultures of the continent, and its implications.

While this study has demonstrated the resilience of maíz culture and the maíz narratives of the continent, it has also demonstrated that they continue to inform the lives and the identity of many Mexicans and Central Americans in the United States. Yet this work also shows that without question, after centuries of attempts to eradicate the culture, Indigenous peoples' ability to recognize the stories and interpret the signs, symbols, and imagery of maíz has indeed been altered. Nonetheless, the seeds and the roots of their deep meanings remain, just as maíz culture remains. For many, the maíz tree continues to be the center of the universe: *non kuahuitl cintli in tlalnepantla.*

Contributing to a Creation Story

Over the past few years, I have begun to participate in the creation of (maíz) narratives myself, and also huehuetlahtolli. Truthfully, I believe I was doing this a generation ago, but was detoured by life and later the research process that resulted in my doctorate. That said, I believe it is appropriate to present one of those narratives here: *Quetzalcoatl, the Ants, and the Gift of Maíz.* In a sense, it is ancient yet also contemporary.

While the reader should by now be familiar with the story of how maíz came to the people—as found at the beginning of this book and in the *Leyenda de los Soles*—this story differs in the following way. As I was reviewing talks with elders and the codices about this foundational story, I noticed that it is never explained why the ants were reluctant to share the maíz with Quetzalcoatl. It seemed counterintuitive because we normally associate ants with collectivity, and by extension, sharing. After contemplating the topic—and understanding that stories provide opportunities to teach morals and values—I decided that providing the answer through a "new" story would both give an explanation for the reluctance of the ants and provide a continuance and connection to those ancient stories.

After presenting this story here, rather than explain its significance, I hope the story itself provides the meaning, significance, and current relevance.

Quetzalcoatl, the Ants, and the Gift of Maíz

Not long after humans are created in Tamoanchan, Quetzalcoatl is charged with bringing food to the people. Remembered as the bringer of the arts

Figure 17. The Ants of Quetzalcoatl by Laura V. Rodriguez. Courtesy of the artist.

and civilization to the Americas, this sacred being, while walking along, sees a red ant carrying a kernel of corn on its back. Intrigued, he asks the ant about it, learning that it is food. However, when Quetzalcoatl asks where it comes from, the ant initially refuses to reveal its location.

This cosmic drama actually is part of a much longer story, found in the *Legend of the Suns*, as recorded in 1558 in Codex Chimalpopoca. The *Legend of the Suns* is a creation story involving the birth and death of four previous suns, culminating in the birth of the Fifth Sun. This cosmic drama also involves the creation of human beings by Quilaztli and Quetzalcoatl. After retrieving the sacred bones of humanity from Mictlan, Quetzalcoatl brings them to Tamoanchan. There Quilaztli grinds them up and gives them to Quetzalcoatl, who sprinkles them with his blood, whereupon they come to life. However, in no time, they become weak. At this, Quetzalcoatl sets about his task of finding food for the people.

This and similar stories regarding Quetzalcoatl, the ants, and maíz are a narrative well known to the Nahuatl-Maya Indigenous peoples of Mexico. However, the Codex does not reveal why the red ant initially refused and then why it finally relented and took Quetzalcoatl to Tonalcatepetl or Sustenance Mountain. The missing part of the conversation between Tzicatl, the lead red ant, and Quetzalcoatl is presented here.

Quetzalcoatl: What's that on your back?
Tzicatl: Cintli. It is a kernel of corn. It is our food: Centeotzintli—Sacred Maíz. With it, we grow more maíz and we feed ourselves.
Q: That is what I've been looking for. Can you spare me some?
T: I can give you some. But I won't.
Q: Then at least tell me where it comes from.
T: It comes from a very special place called Tonalcatepetl—the Mountain of Sustenance. There, you find not just the seeds of maíz but also the seeds for all of creation.
Q: Can you take me there?
T: No. Besides, it doesn't look like you need them. You're a giant, but you don't look like a monster. Are you some kind of god or something?
Q: I am none of that. I am just a spirit. Besides, the food is not for me. It's for the newly created humans. They are weak. Without food, they will die.
T: But why not keep looking? Food is plentiful. The earth is rich as are the waters and even the skies.
Q: But you said that the maíz is sacred. That is what human beings need. They are not made well. Right now, they are just bones, blood, and water. They are barely able to move around. With this sacred food, they will grow big and strong and fill out. It will become their muscle. They will be able to walk and spread to all four corners of this good earth.
T: I'm not sure that is such a good idea.
Q: But I told you, if they don't eat, they will die.
T: You mentioned they would grow big and strong. But you didn't mention if they will be intelligent or if they will have a good conscience.

Q: Oh but they will.

T: . . . be big and strong?

Q: Yes, but they will also be intelligent, loving and caring . . . I have also been instructed to teach them the arts of civilization.

T: Will they be as tall as you?

Q: No. They will barely be bigger than monkeys, but with this food you carry on your back, they will stand and walk upright. And they will become as smart as or smarter than the monkeys.

T: If they become big and strong, they will use their muscles more than their brains. We've already lived with that for millions of years and that didn't turn out so good.

Q: But these humans will also have hearts. They will think with their brains and act compassionately with their hearts.

T: But tell me about these humans. What does it mean to be a human being? As you can see, us ants, we are very little. And yet we have survived for many hundreds of millions of years. We have seen many monsters, and many of them just walked all over us. We've seen them dominate this good earth, but we've also seen them become extinct. And yet we remain. How will these humans be any different than the previous monsters?

Q: These humans will not be monsters.

T: Can you know this for sure? These humans that you speak of, once fed, I think they will become arrogant and will try and dominate the planet. They wouldn't be the first to try this either. Besides, as you describe them, they do not seem capable of living intelligently and peacefully for more than just a few thousand years.

Q: That's all they need. By then, they will have figured out how to live, not like the monsters, but perhaps like you. I can see all of you carrying the corn, working together and sharing it amongst yourselves.

T: Working together and sharing it? Yes. But it's more than sharing that is required to partake of this sacred sustenance. If this becomes food for the humans, they will have to take special care of it. They will have to plant the seeds, tend to the fields, and ensure there is enough water. By doing this, they will come to understand the heavens, the celestial calendars. These will teach them when to plant, when to harvest, and when to honor and pay reverence to the maíz. The best part is eating it. It tastes like nothing else on this earth, especially when it is shared among family and neighbors. But that is not the most important part of this sacred food: it can be stored. This is especially beneficial when there is drought, and during harsh winters.

Q: Can't they too be taught this? This is what they need to eat. The act of sharing is what will make them human beings. Spiritual human beings.

T: No. Because as you said, they will have a brain. Eventually, they will devise ways to make more than what they need. They will become greedy. Instead of honoring this sacred sustenance, these humans will devise ways to enrich themselves, this while many of the people around them will starve. They will learn to hoard, rather than share. There will be shortages amid plenty.

Q: But not if you teach me the knowledge and secrets of this sacred maíz.

T: It is not secrets you need. Everything is in the seeds. Everything is on this good earth, in the waters, and in the heavens. Therein is where you will find all the knowledge. With it, they would be able to unlock the mysteries of time and the universe. They would be able to create sacred calendars by observing and recording the movement in the skies.

Q: So then take me to the seeds.

T: You don't understand. What good are the seeds or what good is the knowledge if these humans will come to abuse them? Without wisdom, they are not seeds of life but of exploitation. With the avarice of these humans, I see one day that they too will create the most despicable of abominations: seeds that will bear fruit but once.

Q: But this that you teach me is what I will teach them. Not just that Centeotzintli is their sustenance, but that they themselves are made from maíz—that this is where they come from, that they themselves are sacred beings and this is who they are. I will teach them that they are simple people—*macehuales*, people of maíz—people of this earth. Not something greater than creation, but part of it, along with all the other beings on this earth.

T: But with this greed, will they learn to live peacefully among themselves and more importantly, among the rest of creation? Also, will they know how to take care of her and not abuse her?

Q: Isn't that up to you? If they are not given the opportunity, how will we ever get to know? How can they prove themselves to the world, if they are not given the opportunity?

T: You place the burden on me, but the burden is actually on you. You have to prove that they have both the intelligence and the heart to live wisely and to live peacefully among all of creation. But make no mistake; you we trust. It is the humans that we question.

Q: Then if you trust me, take me to Tonalcatepetl.

At this, the red ant huddles with the other ants in a Tzikatlatokan—a gathering of the ants where they confer amongst themselves. After a brief discussion, the red ant steps forward.

T: I can take you to Tonalcatepetl, on one condition. Tell us what it means to be a human being—what will be their traits and character and what will guide their beliefs?

Q: This too is when I must also have trust. If they eat from this sacred maíz, I trust that they will be able to learn all that you have conveyed to me. I will trust that as they are taught the arts of civilization, they too will come to define for themselves what it means to be human.

T: You actually believe they can be trusted on their own to develop a consciousness of what it means to be good human beings?

Q: If you don't permit me to bring them the seeds, they will never have the opportunity to do so for themselves.

T: You make a good point. We can see why it is you that was chosen to bring food to them . . . and the arts of civilization . . .

Q: But you still hesitate . . .

T: It is because we believe that while they will indeed respect this sacred food, there will come a time in which they will no longer recognize its sacredness. They will forget that this sacred food is not like the others— that it requires special care, that it will not grow by itself, that it needs to be tended to—and that it needs to be protected, not simply eaten and disposed of.

Q: I will teach them in xochitl, in cuicatl. I will record the stories and the knowledge in poetry, song, music, and danza. I will teach them the huehuetlahtolli—the ancient guidances—all this so that they remember to tend to the maíz, protect it, and learn to share it.

T: Actually, it is not them I worry about. It is the future generations who will not understand its sacredness, who will lose the values and understandings that come with the maíz and will no longer bother to honor and protect it. They will forget the huehuetlahtolli.

Q: You may be right. But we cannot just do nothing because a flood, the winds, fire, or an earthquake may ravage the earth. Humans have to be given the opportunity to learn and to teach others the sacredness of these foods and the sacredness of the earth and of life itself. They have to come to understand that they are part of creation itself.

T: Again, you are right. Come with me then. However, there is one problem. Once we get to Tonalcatepetl, there is but one entrance, and it will not be big enough for you to enter through.

Q: As I told you, I am not of human flesh. I am spirit. When I get to that entrance, I will become like you. However, I will instead become a *black* ant.

T: Then what are we waiting for?

From here, Codex Chimalpopoca picks up the story of how Quetzalcoatl enters Tonalcatepetl and retrieves maíz and the other seeds of humanity. The seeds there also include beans, squash, and chia. At first, Quetzalcoatl first tries to take Tonalcatepetl itself back to Tamoanchan—where the humans had been created. But it is too big and too heavy. And so instead, Quetzalcoatl takes the seeds back to the other sacred beings in Tamoanchan, where they are promptly approved as food for the people. This is why maíz is sacred to this day. And this is why many people continue to call themselves "the people of maíz."

As has been seen in this book, all people of corn have stories of maíz or centeotzintli. This is but one of them.

Figure 18. In Lak'ech by Grecia Ramirez. Courtesy of the artist.

Epilogue

Resistance/Creation Culture and
Seven Maíz-Based Values

Since the 1990s, maíz has vaulted into both the national and the international arenas in very dramatic ways, especially now, as manifested in the Zapatista struggle, the controversy over the North American Free Trade Agreement (NAFTA), the immigration crisis, and the highly contentious issue of genetically modified (GM) corn. Equally important, maíz has been at the heart of the controversy over attempts to make illegal the teaching of ethnic studies, in Arizona and nationally. In the case of the Mexican American Studies (MAS) program of the Tucson Unified School District (TUSD), it was the Indigenous-based component that was attacked for being "outside of (Western) civilization." Indeed, it is the maíz-based values — In Lak'ech (You Are My Other Me) and *Panche Be* (To Seek the Root of the Truth) — that were and continue to be at the heart of that struggle.

Sometimes the story of maíz has been front and center, such as in the Zapatista uprising in Chiapas, Mexico, on January 1, 1994. At other times it has been less dramatic, but huge nonetheless; take, for example, the role of maíz in the massive immigration crisis that began literally the day NAFTA went into effect, also on January 1, 1994. The date of the uprising was no coincidence; the Zapatistas rose up precisely on that date to warn the world that their maíz-based culture would be decimated if NAFTA were implemented. The twenty-year history of this inhumane agreement has given their warning the status of a prophecy. And that is only the beginning of the story.

The abuse of maíz — driven by the corporate profit motive — has been implicated in the obesity crisis that has exploded in the last generation in

170

the United States. High-fructose corn syrup, made from maíz, as a replacement for cane sugar, is present in a great many processed food products and beverages. It is also suspected in the nation's diabetes and heart-disease crisis, especially among Indigenous peoples, including the U.S. Mexican/Chicano population.

All of these important developments have given rise, in the United States, though particularly in Arizona, to what I term a *resistance/creation culture*, or in Nahuatl *tlalnamikilliztli chikahualitzli uan yankuik*. At the heart of this resistance/creation culture, which has been under heavy assault by xenophobes, is maíz.

When the Zapatistas rose up, they warned that if cheap U.S.-subsidized GM corn were imported en masse to Mexico, it would destroy their maíz-based way of life. The Mexican government, rather than permanently protect the maíz, instead overturned the bedrock article 27 of the Constitution, which protected communal or *ejido* lands, a fundamental achievement of the Mexican Revolution. This action paved the way for the human crisis that would unfold; just as the Zapatistas predicted, U.S.-subsidized GM corn went south and the people went north, with tragic consequences, as many thousands of people have died trying to cross the Mexico-U.S. border since NAFTA.[1] Today, several million Indigenous people from the corn-growing regions of southern Mexico—unable to compete or subsist on their traditional lands—have migrated north.

The Zapatista revolt that has lasted a generation is historic, the greatest social movement in Mexico since the Mexican Revolution of 1910. While the student movement of 1968 was also a powerful epoch in Mexico's history, this revolt is not only larger but has forced Mexico to deal with live Indigenous peoples, not simply with historical myths and folklore. This ongoing revolt can be viewed as a maíz rebellion, guided by the precept "Never again a world without us." Indeed, this revolt is historic primarily because it is about voice, about not ever being silenced again. Also unique to it is that Indigenous women are not marginalized, as evidenced by the Women's Revolutionary Law, which insists upon the equality of women.[2] Another historic aspect of this revolt is that it is not confined to Chiapas. While there have been continual Indigenous revolts during the past five hundred years, the modern Zapatista revolt has had an influence on other Indigenous movements throughout Mexico and the continent and worldwide. At the heart of these movements are a rejection of colonialism (in all of its forms) and a refusal to be subsumed under other popular/leftist struggles.

The problem with NAFTA is its massive displacement of millions of people, many of whom now find themselves living in the United States.

Peoples Indigenous to this continent have not found solace or welcoming arms in the nation that caused their displacement. They have been dehumanized and branded as (illegal) aliens in the United States, part of that ugly Eurocentric narrative called "the immigration crisis," in which xenophobic politicians portray these migrants as peoples less than human, with the objective of forced (Indian) removal.

That narrative has for a generation been contested by Mexicans/Chicanos and Central and South American peoples living in the United States, who have often asserted their Indigeneity.[3] It has likewise been contested by Indigenous movements representing many of the peoples that have been forced to flee north. They are not accepting the narrative that says they are alien. Some elements within these movements have stepped forward with the declaration that "we cannot be foreigners on our own continent," as first proclaimed in 2007.[4] While that idea has been around for many years, unquestionably the declaration is part of a contemporary Indigenous narrative, born in 1992 in reaction to the imposed celebration of five hundred years of colonialism known as the Columbus Quincentennial. In these movements, maíz has always played a central role. There is recognition by many Indigenous peoples that maíz unites the continent, a fact that reflects the reality of millions of Indigenous and Indigenous-based peoples throughout the continent, a millennia-old reality. Maíz is who we are.

Without question, Chicanos/Chicanas have played integral roles in these movements, including involvement with the International Indigenous Treaty Council, long before 1992, but also in reaction to the Quincentennial, beginning with a historic gathering in 1990 in Quito, Ecuador. It was at these and subsequent gatherings that Indigenous peoples decided that they would no longer be subsumed under the banner of the "popular" movements.[5]

From that was birthed an Indigenous movement to unite the continent as foretold in the Prophecy of the Eagle and the Condor. The eagle represents North America and the condor represents South America. This prophecy is shared by peoples across the continent. Aside from continuing gatherings, one of its greatest symbolic manifestations has been the Peace and Dignity Journeys. These are runs, primarily by Indigenous peoples, that start at the tip of North America and the tip of South America and end up in the center of the continent. They take place every four years. The first one was in 1992 and ended in Teotihuacan; the one in 2012, dedicated to water, concluded at a ceremonial site in Uaxactun, Guatemala. Chicanos/Chicanas have been integral members of the Peace and Dignity Journeys since their inception.

The issue of GM corn requires its own separate treatment. Many peoples have come to see this particular issue as the issue of our times. GM foods have the potential to negatively impact all of humanity, all of life. Because they have only been in existence for twenty years, conclusive findings on their health impact are not yet available; scientists believe that only long-term studies would be able to detect the damage to the human body. However, among Indigenous peoples, opposition to GM foods includes but goes beyond concerns about health. Genetic modification is also seen as a cultural and spiritual assault on the peoples and cultures of this continent. For this reason, there is a huge battle to protect the original seeds and to reject genetically altered foods. People throughout the world, including on this continent, believe the old adage: we are what we eat. The prospect of eating GM foods is repulsive for many, particularly foods grown from "terminator seeds" and seeds that rely heavily on the use of chemicals. In the first place, commercial corn is considered not sacred by many Indigenous peoples; the selling of foods is viewed as taking away from their sacredness (Esteva 2003b). Enter GM foods, and the thought is beyond sacrilegious. Because food is a multi-trillion-dollar industry, those corporations involved in GM foods have a vested interest in fighting labeling foods to indicate that they have been genetically altered. At a time when most peoples are no longer connected to the land, their only power with respect to GM foods appears to be as informed consumers. Yet even the right to reject GM foods is nullified when consumers have no other choices. Precisely because of the possibility of severe and long-term damage to our bodies, this is perceived as a struggle for the ages, potentially terminating our world "as we know it."

NAFTA, the immigration crisis, diseases, and GM foods affect us materially, yet arguably also affect the spirit. However, there is another critical struggle that affects both the mind and the spirit: the struggle over ethnic studies in Arizona, and not just in Arizona but nationwide. This struggle has become perhaps the greatest symbol of the civilizational clash evoked in this book.

Upon arriving at the University of Arizona in 2007, I soon became aware that Tucson was embroiled in a struggle of epic proportions. The year before, Arizona superintendent of schools Tom Horne had begun a campaign to declare ethnic studies illegal and, specifically, to terminate TUSD's highly successful MAS program.[6] His contention was that the program was un-American and that Arizona children should be exposed to Greco-Roman culture, the foundation for Western civilization, not the culture being taught in MAS.[7] Indeed, the philosophy of the MAS curriculum is founded, not upon Columbus, or the Pilgrims' East-to-West narrative, but rather upon the continent's seven-thousand-year-old maíz culture. Elements of this Maya-Nahua culture are reflected in the Maya concepts of In Lak'ech and Panche Be and the Mexica/Aztec concepts of the Four *Tezcatlipocas.*[8]

After two unsuccessful attempts, a bill (HB 2281) was passed by the legislature and signed by Governor Jan Brewer in May 2010 that made it illegal to teach ethnic studies in the state's K–12 schools. However, Horne's actual political target was Tucson's MAS program. In January 2012, after protracted struggles in the courtroom, in the street, in the state capital, and at TUSD headquarters, the school board, on the basis of HB 2281, terminated MAS.[9] Within days, its teachers were ordered to remove all of their books, artwork, posters, and other classroom materials.[10] This included ordering one teacher, Norma Gonzalez, to stop teaching the maíz-based Aztec Calendar. A few days later, MAS teachers were served a memo with nine directives, titled "Guiding Principles for MAS Teachers." The first directive states, "Assignments cannot direct students to apply MAS perspectives."

The bill, written by Horne with the specific purpose of outlawing MAS, in effect charges that MAS: (1) promotes the overthrow of the United States government, (2) promotes resentment toward a race or class of people, (3) is designed primarily for pupils of a particular ethnic group, and (4) advocates ethnic solidarity instead of the treatment of pupils as individuals.

In Horne's ten-page supporting document, signed on December 30, 2010 (when the bill went into effect), he asserted that two books utilized by MAS-TUSD, *Occupied America* by Rodolfo Acuña (1999) and *Pedagogy of the Oppressed* by Paulo Freire (1970), were anti-American. While that was par for the course, he also cited lyrics from Aztlan Underground and Victor E. of El Vuh, because both invoke the concept of Aztlan.

At the core of the dispute is Horne's insistence that MAS-TUSD does not emphasize Greco-Roman culture. Actually, he is correct. As noted, the philosophical foundation for MAS is derived from maíz culture, which unlike Greco-Roman culture is Indigenous to this continent.

Since 2006, students and community have been waging an unprecedented struggle to save MAS, including filing a lawsuit in 2010 against the state challenging the constitutionality of the law. Throughout this struggle, students, teachers, and supporters have shown that they do not simply believe in the right to MAS; they actively defend that right. During 2006–2013 there were countless protests, including the takeover of the state government building in Tucson the day after the governor signed HB 2281. Fifteen MAS supporters were arrested.[11] On April 26, 2011, nine students dramatically chained themselves to the TUSD board's chairs while hundreds of MAS supporters occupied the boardroom. In taking this action, the student group UNIDOS invoked the 2007 UN Declaration on the Rights of Indigenous Peoples, which protects the right to education. On May 3, 2011, seven women MAS supporters were arrested for reading out loud during the school board meeting, while perhaps a thousand supporters converged inside and outside TUSD headquarters, this amid a massive police presence.

In 2012, MAS was dismantled. In March 2013, in *Acosta v. Huppenthal*, Judge A. Wallace Tashima of the U.S. Court of Appeals for the Ninth Circuit upheld three of the four provisions of HB 2281, though striking down as unconstitutional the provision banning classes tailored to students of a particular group. That ruling is under appeal.

Unbeknownst to many, the MAS curriculum, which is supposedly incompatible with Western civilization, in fact revolves around the maíz-based concepts of In Lak'ech and Panche Be.

Seven Maíz-Based Concepts

The political battles, the protests, marches, and rallies: that is the resistance part of resistance/creation. The creation aspect of it I see in our runs, and in the philosophical core that undergirds MAS.

When the second attempt was made to outlaw ethnic studies in 2009, as a community we ran through the desert from Tucson to Phoenix in 115-degree heat. Since then, many runs have taken place not just in defense of ethnic studies, but also to bring awareness to issues such as obesity, diabetes, heart disease, cancer, alcoholism, and domestic and sexual violence. Calpolli Teoxicalli, a Nahua Indigenous-based group of families in Tucson, brought us together with these runs, in an effort to not only spiritually cleanse our communities but also strengthen ourselves. This was something done not against others but for ourselves.[12]

The concepts of In Lak'ech and Panche Be, taught in the TUSD-MAS classrooms, are what we as a community fought for and what has guided us in the MAS struggle. Both form the basis of what it means to be human. In that sense, these concepts do not necessarily resemble what the world recognizes as Western civilization or American culture. Or better stated, this core is not traced to Greco-Roman culture. The following is a synopsis of these concepts, primarily derived—gifted, actually—from the works of Maya scholar Domingo Martínez Parédez.

In Lak'ech translates to *Tu Eres Mi Otro Yo* or You Are My Other Self. It teaches students to see themselves in each other. Thus, it would be difficult to truly hate others because to do so would be to hate oneself. This concept is closely related to the Golden Rule found in virtually every religion. This rule has many variations, including the Christian creed: "Do unto others as you would have done unto you."[13] In Lak'ech actually differs slightly from the Golden Rule in that it is not exclusively about human relations but about relations with all living beings, including the earth and the universe itself.

Panche Be is *Buscar la Raíz de la Verdad* or To Seek the Root of the Truth (or To Find the Truth in the Root[s]). This concept is not simply about the search for the truth, or even about teaching students to be critical thinkers, but about the pursuit of peace, dignity, and justice.

As I close this book, I would like to leave the reader with five additional maíz-based concepts that I teach in my classes at the University of Arizona, for a total of seven. They are *Hunab Ku, Men, K'ochil, Et P'iz,* and *Yaxche-Baalche.* They come primarily from the work of Martínez Parédez, but also from many of the elders mentioned throughout this book (see also appendix 1). As presented here, perhaps they are unrecognizable to the Maya, yet this is how we have interpreted them in Arizona, not just in our battles to save a program but in our efforts to become better human beings.

Hunab Ku: the name the Maya gave to the equivalent of the Supreme Being or the Grand Architect of the Universe or "The Great Mystery" (Martínez Parédez 1970). This is a simple acknowledgment that all peoples everywhere in the history of humanity have given a name to how they perceive and understand (the function of) the universe, and that, contrary to the teachings that were brought by European colonizers five hundred years ago, no one understanding is superior to any other understanding.

Men has three components: *creer, crear y hacer*—to imagine or believe, to create, and to do or carry out. Translated: to imagine and believe in the creation of our own reality. Men is a power within our psyche, part of our will (Martínez Parédez 1970: 68–69). It is the idea that if we believe we will lose, we will, and conversely, we win if we believe we will win. We construct our own reality and follow up.

K'ochil: education with a true sense of responsibility (Martínez Parédez 1977: 17). From this came the idea that the objective was not simply to save ethnic studies but to spread it nationwide, and that this was not an option but a responsibility. One is born with and dies with this responsibility. Nothing or no one can shirk it. We cannot forget that our conscience is just and prudent. From this, the expression: "By the ruler with which we measure, we too will be measured."

Et P'iz: The law of compensation and responsibility or cause and effect. It is also the idea that whatever good or bad people experience depends on how they conduct themselves. No one escapes this law. Each person is responsible for what they think, say, and do. This is one of the most important ethics. It is applicable in life, but also in political battles.

Yaxche-Baalche: The tree is the human being, the human being is the tree. It is a philosophy; without vegetation, there are no humans and no life. It is an ecological concept: "The Maya thinker thinks first of the tree or *yaxche*, and then the animal with the expression *baalche*, because without vegetation there would be no animals. That's how they determined that: the death of the last tree signifies the death of the last human being" (Martínez Parédez 1977: 141). The tree is the ultimate symbol of life and of creation. It represents vegetation; if vegetation is destroyed, humans cannot exist. Yaxche-Baalche is the concept of ecological balance and interdependency lasting seven generations.

Philosophically, it would be difficult to argue with the teaching of In Lak'ech. This is what children in Tucson's MAS program recited:

Tú eres mi otro yo.	*You are my other me.*
Si te hago daño a ti,	*If I do harm to you,*
me hago daño a mí mismo.	*I do harm to myself.*
Si te amo y respeto,	*If I love and respect you,*
me amo y respeto yo.	*I love and respect myself.*

In effect, the battle over MAS has been falsely projected by the state as a battle between Western civilization and Mexican or maíz culture, a continuation of a battle that, in effect, began in 1492. It is not a true civilizational war. It is only depicted as such by those with hegemonic agendas, which have manifested in a dramatic way in Arizona, but which have since spread to Texas and nationwide. The pursuit of my research was based on the idea that maíz-based peoples cannot be illegal anywhere, particularly on this continent.

The backdrop to this dynamic has been Arizona, a state that has for years been passing anti-immigrant, anti-Mexican, and anti-Indigenous racial-profiling bills. The vitriol has been so extreme that the red-brown peoples of the state feel under siege. The sense is that if the state could deport every brown person, it would. But because it can't, the fallback strategy is a throwback Americanization program that calls for the forced assimilation of the brown peoples that remain. All this translates to an attack on the body, the mind, and the spirit.[14] Or as Yaqui scholar Vivian G. Lopez terms it, it is an attack on our "spirit of being"—an attack not simply on the individual, but on all those related to us.[15]

In the battle over the curriculum, the attempt to ban ethnic studies represents an attempt at forced assimilation; specifically, it is an attempt to de-Indigenize Mexicans and Central and South Americans living in the United States. The state of Arizona, via HB 2281, recognizes the right of American Indians to learn their history and culture—purportedly a federal right, though there is no actual federal mandate requiring the teaching of American Indian studies. The legislation does not extend that same recognition to Mexican Americans. In part, this is due to the belief that Mexicans/Chicanas/Chicanos are not Indigenous, that their history begins but in 1848, or at the very earliest, 1519. Even the discipline of Chicano studies generally adheres to that timeline; this book rejects that timeline and its associated historiography. It asserts that the identity of Mexicans and Central Americans—peoples of the Americas in general—is defined, not by war or conquest, but by our living maíz culture, which includes stories, memory, and daily sustenance. Maíz continues to be an integral part of our daily lives. The state insists upon erasure and the people say no. More than de-Indigenizing them, the state has created a very hostile climate that breeds dehumanizing and racially motivated laws and attitudes.

For the state, the solution is simple: continued demonization and dehumanization permits mass deportations and forced assimilation. Therein lie the seeds of what Horne refers to as a civilizational clash or war. Indeed, from his end, eliminating the teaching of non-Western cultures would bring about bliss and harmony for Arizona and U.S. schools. From the point of view of the defenders of the MAS program and the discipline of Mexican American studies, it amounts to cultural genocide, and is unacceptable. The ability to teach a people's history and culture is a principle that is protected by every international human-rights treaty, declaration, and convention relevant to the topic.[16] The right of peoples to their culture, history, identity, language, and education—their CHILE—is protected for a very good reason: in the history of humanity, large nations and governments have always swallowed up smaller nations or peoples and have attempted to forcibly assimilate them. Such is the case in the United States, particularly in Arizona. As far as the state is concerned, maíz culture is permissible in the home and in restaurants, just not in the schools, and also not in public. Look for this conflict to be exported nationwide.[17] Look for action not just in U.S. courts but also in international courts. In the end, look not toward the courts as the final arbiter but toward the people themselves. Maíz culture will survive if the people see a need for it to survive, if they see it as relevant to their daily lives. The students and the Arizona community—and their supporters nationwide—have answered that question, sometimes with their feet, but always with their spirits.

My parting thoughts here actually came in the final days of preparing this book, relative to the concept of civilizational war, a needless war that has been imposed upon this continent. After I was meditating on this work one day, a revelation came to me: many of us have been trying to win this war, and yet, as human beings, I don't think winning civilizational wars is what we actually want. What we want is to end these contrived wars—on the basis of mutual respect—not win them. That is embedded in the precept of In Lak'ech, and I believe it is the true message of our heroic maíz. In that respect, think of this work not as part of a war but rather as a song, a story, a prayer, a dance . . . a cosmic drama.

> They came for our spirits, but they did not know where to look. (*La Otra Conquista*, Carrasco 1999)

Ohoyo Osh Chisba

Alicia Seyler, Choctaw, farm advocate

Of all the southeastern tribes, it is said that the Choctaw were the most successful and productive agriculturalists. They were often raided by other tribes for their vast stores of corn, beans, squash, and other crops. They amassed stores of over forty different varieties of corn each season. It was the "Unknown Woman," or Ohoyo Osh Chisba, that first gave corn to the Choctaw. Ohoyo Osh Chisba was a sacred entity, the beautiful daughter of the Choctaw Lord himself. To the Choctaw, corn was a woman — a life giver — and all Choctaw women were the givers of life, responsible for planting the corn, beans, and squash that sustained Choctaw communities. Because Choctaw women had responsibility for planting, tending, and harvesting corn, it is Choctaw women that mediated among the worlds — creating powerful allegiances among fertility, health, family, culture, life, death, and spirituality. The Choctaw people loved the corn and nurtured it:

One day, two hunters set out to feed their families and their community. But having been unsuccessful in the chase, they found themselves at the bend of the Alabama River with no kill and nothing to satisfy their own hunger except a black hawk, which they had shot with an arrow. They cooked the hawk and sat down to partake of their modest meal when their attention was taken by the low but distinct and melancholy tones of the dove, but produced by something that they did not know. At different intervals it broke the deep silence of the early night; it became more frequent and distinct as the night wore on.

Throughout the night, they searched up and down the river to find the noise, but could find nothing except the sandy shores glittering in the moonlight. Happening to look behind them in the direction opposite the moon they saw a woman of wonderful beauty standing upon a mound. She had suddenly appeared out of the moonlit forest. She was loosely clad in snow-white garments, and bore a wreath of fragrant flowers. She asked the hunters to approach. At once they approached the spot where she stood and offered their assistance to her, in any way they could be of service. She replied she was very hungry. One of the hunters offered her the roasted hawk to feast upon. She accepted it with grateful thanks; but after eating a small portion of it, she handed the remainder back to them, replying that she would remember their kindness when she returned to the home of her father, Shilup Chitoh Osh—the Great Spirit of the Choctaw. She then told them that when the next midsummer moon should come they must meet her at the mound upon which she was then standing. She disappeared saying nothing more.

The two hunters returned to their camp for the night and early next morning sought their homes, but kept the strange incident to themselves. When the next midsummer moon arrived, the hunters stood at the mound of Ohoyo Osh Chisba, but she was nowhere to be seen. Then remembering that she told them they must come to the very spot where she was then standing, they at once ascended the mound and found it covered with a plant they had never before seen. The plant yielded wonderful and strange food, which was ever afterwards cultivated by the Choctaw, and named by them *tunchi* (corn).

Corn grew out of the very ground that Ohoyo Osh Chisba had stood upon and linked the Choctaw's three spiritual worlds. Its roots reached deep into the ground, the place of the Below World, where death, fertility, and powerful spirits resided. Its stalk rose toward the Above World, the home of Aba, the Great One Above, and the place of the most powerful—the sun. Corn provided sustenance for the People of this world. Its roots and stalks tied all of the worlds together and because the plant crossed the boundaries of the three worlds, it was considered powerful and sacred. It remains the sacred and staple crop of the Choctaw community today.

Figure 19. *Maíz Tree* by Verónica Castillo Hernández. Courtesy of the artist.

The Children of La Llorona

I would like my last thoughts in this book to be in the form of a story. The story of La Llorona or The Weeping Woman is one of the cultural root paradigms of Mexican peoples. But the following story is not so much about her as about her children: in effect, the subjects of this book.

A woman wails through the ancient streets of Mexico City/Tenochtitlan: "Where are my children—where might they be?"

Who is she and where are her children, people ask, looking at this brown woman as though she has lost her mind.

Lost her mind? Maybe, but what is not in doubt is that she has definitely lost her children. She knows not where they are.

She is the woman who bore the children of a conquistador turned aristocrat, who purportedly loved her. He said he did.

"I love you, my India. Till the end of time."

She wails every night because one day, when his European bride-to-be stepped off a ship from across the great ocean, he banished the native woman and their children from the city. In those days, Europeans did not consider native peoples equal . . . or human. Not truly human. In those days. In these days . . .

"Get out of here! Don't ever enter or even look at this city again," he admonished her and the children.

Devastated, the native woman drowns her children in a nearby river. Since then, she has wailed through the streets looking for them.

There are other and older variations of this story, but this is the most widely known version. Some say it is but European lies, an effort to dishonor and cast a stain upon La Llorona, an effort to blame an Indian woman for the death of her children. It is also an effort to portray her children as illegitimate children, as fatherless children.

Even to this day, many peoples from the villages and pueblos that have existed long before Europeans came to the Americas say the story is incorrect. That it was twisted. That La Llorona never actually drowned her children: that they were swept away by a raging river as she bathed them. All the versions agree that no bodies were ever recovered.

That's why she wails. Not because she drowned her children or because they never received a proper burial, but because they may still be alive, somewhere, downstream or upstream.

"Where are my children—where might they be?"

Today, if one goes outside the ancient city of Tenochtitlan/Mexico City in any direction, people of the surrounding villages and towns report an occasional sighting and say that her screams can still be heard in the wind. Certainly her story has not been forgotten. For many centuries, in the European accounts, she has been seen as an evil or deranged woman. Children are warned: "*Si no te portas bien, se te va a aparecer La Llorona!*" "If you don't behave, La Llorona will come and take you away!" But today, no one in the nearby villages sees her that way. Quite the contrary.

They recount that it was she and she alone who cared for her children, before and after she was abandoned, and that the conquistador cared about nothing, except slandering her and the children.

"They are all lies," the villagers say. "She was a good woman. It is she who took care of her children. It is he who betrayed them. It is he who abandoned them and who banished them from the city."

There are many stories and even legends about her, but there are also stories about the children. Most of these have been lost to history. Or they have never quite made it to the printed page. Only the wind retains the children's memory and remembers their story.

It is said that the children actually survived and left many tracks as they went from village to village, looking for their mother. These same stories are heard throughout the continent, especially near rivers or other bodies of water, even in what is today the United States or El Norte.

This story, some say, was first told during the years of war and famine, a time when the conquistadores were laying waste to the countryside and were busy exterminating the continent's original peoples. It was a time of depopulation. It was a time of unprecedented forced migrations—peoples turned into refugees, fleeing from the merciless violence. It was a time of widows and a time of orphans. It was a time of suffering and a time of wailing. It was a time of disease and a time of suffering.

During these years, the children of La Llorona were taken in and raised mostly by Indigenous mothers and grandmothers. Originally, they knew not who these brown children were, yet later they began to hear the stories—the lies—spread by those who bore swords. The mothers and grandmothers had their own children to raise during these difficult times, but collectively, they took these lost children in, cared for them as best they could, sometimes giving them care and sustenance when there was nothing to give, even when their own children and grandchildren went without.

When these children grew up, they too heard the many conflicting stories. One story is that the children weren't actually sired by the conquistador. That the actual father was killed by the conquistador.

"Due to jealousy, the conquistador killed the actual father."

Many villagers affirm that the actual father never abandoned his own children, that he was separated from them by the sword, so that the conquistador could steal their beautiful mother.

That's what everyone agrees about: that she was beautiful. That she was beautiful before she lost her husband . . . and her children. That she was beautiful, until she lost her mind.

"It is true," they say. "She was the most beautiful woman from Tenochtitlan—the most beautiful woman in the entire valley of Anahuac."

For many years, her children lived but were rejected by all, treated as if they'd been contaminated simply because they were born. The Europeans had spread rumors that she was but a woman of the streets and that her children were illegitimate mongrels. They wanted nothing of these brown ones.

In many of the villages too, the children were rejected because they were seen as bastard children, the product of rape. But the native mothers and grandmothers who took them in knew not the word *illegitimate* or *mongrel* or the concept of bastard children. They accepted them as family.

"Some of you bear the marks and even the color of the conquistadores, but in most of you, we can see your mother. We can also see the mark of your Indigenous fathers. But to us, all of you, without distinction, are the children of the Creator. And we recognize you as our children."

The mothers and grandmothers raised the children of La Llorona to love their mother and to love themselves. Yet over the years, her children also began to believe the stories told about them, as they had forgotten who their mother actually was. The more they heard the false stories, the more they despised her. Eventually, they rejected the mothers and grandmothers that raised them, rejected their teachings, rejected themselves, and often, turned ferociously against their other relatives. Despite this, the mothers and grandmothers accepted them, especially when they would not accept themselves.

"Even though you may forget who raised you, even though you may one day come to hate us, the love of a mother is unconditional and eternal."

It is said that nowadays, it is not La Llorona who is looking for her children, but her children who are looking for her.

"Where is our Mother—where might she be?" they ask.

In later years, there were many other lost children like them—despised and rejected by all.

Because it continues to be a time of famine and often a time of drought, many of these children continue to move on, often never being able to settle in but one place.

It is said that today one can see them braving mountains and deserts and even crossing rivers, still looking for their mother and a place to call home. Many never quite make it, their bodies often claimed by the hostile desert, mountains, and treacherous rivers.

It is said that if they ever find their mother, no matter how long they've denied her and denied themselves, if they honor her and come to her in a good way, she will always embrace them and they will always have a home.

This is the story of the children of La Llorona.

"Where are my children? Where might they be?"
"Where is our Mother? Where might she be?"
"Where do we belong? Where is our home?"

Conclusion

A story—this story—is another way to explain or describe the angst of de-Indigenized peoples. But it also points to resiliency: seemingly rejected by all, these peoples find their own linkage to the maíz culture of this continent and create their own stories, stories that speak to their needs and their reality. And what they generally also find, and the point of this story, is that even when they reject their own grandmothers, their grandmothers will always welcome them back.

*Nahua-Maya Expressions**

huejkatlan Mexico	México profundo, deep Mexico
Hunab Ku	the only giver of movement and measurement (Maya)
In lak'ech.	You are my other self. (Maya)
Inin tlalnamikiliztli hualeua itech nin yolotzin.	These principles come from the heart.
in tlili, in tlapilli	the red and the black: writing
in xochitl, in cuicatl	flower and song: poetry
kenin itech tikitaske kenika tik zaloske nin tlalnamikitliztli kanin to koltsiuaan	a guide to learning from the knowledge and wisdom of our ancestors
kilnamikiliztli masehualli	Indigenous memory
neltilitzli	the root and foundations of all things (same as Maya *panche be*)
Non kuahuitl cintli in tlalnepantla.	The maíz tree is the center of the universe.

---

* In Nahuatl if not otherwise specified. Most of the Nahuatl expressions come from Indigenous educator Paula Domingo Olivares of Cuentepec, Morelos, Mexico. The Maya expressions come from Domingo Martínez Parédez's works.

okichike ka centeotzintli	made from sacred maíz
panche be	to seek the root of the Truth (Maya)
In tlanexia, in tonatiuh.	May your sun shine brightly.
Tojuan titehuaxkalo panin semanhuak (Pacha Mama).	We are Indigenous to this continent.
San ce tojuan. Ti masehualme, okichike ka centeotzintli.	We are one. We are macehual, made from sacred maíz.
Amika amo tlapuale.	No human being is illegal.
Nin Tonantzin non Centeotl.	Our Sacred Maíz is our Mother.
Ri loq'oläj Ixim ja ri' Qate'.	Our Sacred Maíz is our Mother. (Kaqchikel)
tlalnamikilliztli chikahualitzli uan yankuik	resistance/creation culture

Abbreviated Bibliocartography

The information contained in these maps can be interpreted either as a continuation of a millennial Indigenous tradition of communicating stories/ narratives of origins and migrations through maps, or else as a syncretism between Indigenous/Western stories and narratives. The importance of the information is not so much that it is accurate, or may be, but that it actually appears on historical maps of the 1500s–1800s. The listing here reflects the general order in which my research traced the maps—from 1847 back to the 1500s.

*

John Disturnell, 1847. *Mapa de los estados unidos de Méjico, según lo organizado y definido por las varias actas del Congreso de dicha república: y construído por las mejores autoridades.* New York: J. Disturnell. Although not officially commissioned by the U.S. government, Disturnell's map was used to determine the boundary between the United States and Mexico as part of the Treaty of Guadalupe Hidalgo, which ended the 1846–1848 U.S. war against Mexico. The war resulted in Mexico ceding half of its northern territory to the United States. The map, with its prewar boundaries, notes three sites in what is today the U.S. Southwest that form part of a southerly migration route. The first of these sites is the Antigua Residencia de los Aztecas (Ancient Dwelling of the Aztecs), located at what appears to be the present-day confluence of the Colorado and Green Rivers in Utah. The second migration point is present-day Casa Grande near Tucson, Arizona, while the third point is Casas Grandes or Paquime in the state of Chihuahua.

Alexander von Humboldt, 1804. *A map of New Spain from 16° to 38° North latitude: reduced from the large map drawn from astronomical observations at Mexico in the year 1804.* This map depicts four points of the purported Aztec/Mexica migration: the same three points that appear on Disturnell's 1847 map, plus a more northern point that appears to be the Great Salt Lake, annotated as follows: "perhaps the Teguayo lake, from the borders of which according to some Historians, the Azteques removed to the river Gila." The note for the migration point that Disturnell recorded as the Ancient Dwelling of the Aztecs on this map reads, "First abode of the Aztecs. Came from Aztlan in 1160. Tradition uncertain." Many of the codices put the date at 1064 (see chapter 3 for discussion). Notes for the other two migration points read as follows: "Ruins of Casas Grandes. Second abode of the Azteques from whence they passed by Tarahumara to Hueicolhuacan Culiacán" and "Casas Grandes: Third abode of the Azteques."

José Antonio de Alzate y Ramírez, 1768. *Nuevo Mapa Geográfico de la América Septentrional.* This precursor to the 1804 Humboldt map contains the same four migration points, beginning with the Great Salt Lake, labeled *Teguyo* (Teguayo): "The Mexican Indians are said to have departed from the shores of this lake to found their empire" (Desde los contornos de esta laguna, dicen haber salidos los Indios Mexicanos a fundar su imperio).

Francisco Álvarez Barreiro, 1728. *Plano, corografico é hidrográphico, de las provincias de el Nuevo México, Sonora, Ostimuri, Sinaloa, Culiacán, Nueba Vizcaya Najarit, nuevo reino de León, Nueva estremadura á Coaguila, y la del nuevo reyno de Philipinas, provincia de los Tejas.* Reproduced in *Mapping the West: America's Westward Movement, 1524–1890* (Cohen 2002), this is the earliest map containing direct references to the four migration points depicted in the Humboldt and Alzate maps. The northernmost point (the Great Salt Lake) reads: "Teguayo Lake or Blue Lake, from which the Mexican Indians left with their Prince to found Mexico" (Laguna de Teguayo o Ostero Azul donde salieron los Indios Mexicanos con su Príncipe para poblar a México); "their Prince" no doubt refers to Huitzilopochtli. The other three points also correspond: "first Great House of the Mexican Indians" (1a. Manción de los Indios Mexicanos), "second great house that the Mexican Indians built" (2a. manción que hicieron los Indios Mexicanos), "third Great House of the Mexican Indians" (3a. Mansion de los Indios Mexicanos).

Bernardo de Miera y Pacheco, 1778. *Plano geográphico, de la tierra descubierta, nuevamente, á los Rumbos Norte, Noroeste y Oeste, del Nuevo México.* This map contains a citation that may refer to the same location John Disturnell noted as Antigua Residencia de los Aztecas on his 1847 map: "There is evidence here of large ruins of ancient Indian populations" (Aqui se manifiestan las ruinas de grandes Poblaciones de Yndios antiguos). However, it appears in a different region, east of the confluence of the Colorado and Nabajoa Rivers and past the Animas River. This seems to correspond to the location given the 1845 map by Pedro García Conde. It may be present-day Mesa Verde, Colorado, or Aztec, New Mexico.

Pedro García Conde, 1845. *Carta geográfica general de la República Mexicana.* There are many maps that, like Disturnell's, depict the ancient Mexican Indian migration route. However, on this map, what appears to correspond to the Antigua Residencia de los Aztecas simply reads "Great ruins of the Aztecs" (Grandes ruinas de los Aztecas). It may correspond to present-day Mesa Verde, Colorado, or Aztec, New Mexico, as opposed to the confluence of the Colorado and Green Rivers. A second location directly south of that notation, and still within the U.S. Southwest, reads "Ruins of the Aztecs" (Ruinas de los Aztecas). This may correspond to Casa Grande in Arizona.

The *Aztlanahuac* *Interviews*

Most of the interviews summarized here were video-recorded and utilized for
the origins/migrations documentary *Amoxtli San Ce Tojuan—We Are One*
(R. Rodríguez and P. Gonzales 2005); if an interview does not appear in that
documentary, a different source is specified. The interviews were conducted
jointly by Patrisia Gonzales and me, and have been donated to the library
at the University of Arizona. Because I have a permanent relationship with
these elders and knowledge keepers, many of them were subsequently "interviewed" several times, continuing up to this day on the topic of this book.

Carlos Aceves, Texas. Speaks of the significance of the region of El Paso,
a corridor where maíz passed from Mexico into the United States. The
site of Hueco Tanks contains petroglyph evidence of those contacts and
migrations, including that of Tlaloc. Anthropologist Kate Sutherland traced
Tlaloc and Quetzalcoatl to this site.

Tupac Enrique Acosta, Arizona. This Indigenous-rights activist has been
present at virtually all Indigenous gatherings throughout the continent,
representing Chicanos/Chicanas. He speaks not only of the Disturnell map
but also of the dreams that Chicanos received from the Hopi. Also explains
that treaties are signed with maíz.

Alurista (Alberto Urrea). Recognized as the author of "El Plan Espiritual
de Aztlan" (1970), this poet is highly regarded as the person responsible for

---

* Indicates those who are now deceased.

equating the idea of Aztlan with the U.S. Southwest and the lands Mexico lost to the United States during the Mexican American War of 1846–1848.

Don Felipe Alvarado Peralta,* Amatlán, Morelos, Mexico. Although blind in his last years, Peralta "read" me the story of the ants who lead Quetzalcoatl to Tonalcatepetl or Sustenance Mountain, where he locates the seeds of maíz.

Don Aurelio Cazarez, Amatlán, Morelos, Mexico. This Nahuatl-speaking elder told me of the ten-thousand-year history of maíz, taking me to Cinteopa, the Temple of Maíz. It was he, along with several other elders, who told me to "follow the maíz" to find my roots.

David Castro, Los Angeles. He was asked to organize an Indigenous symposium in the early 1980s at Hopi in northern Arizona to discuss the Treaty of Guadalupe Hidalgo, for the purposes of taking up the Treaty at the United Nations. At that time, the 1847 Disturnell map was revealed.

Rarámuri elder **Olivia Chumacero**. She explained the direct relationship and direct influence that Maya scholar Martínez Parédez and Maestro Segura had with Chicanas/Chicanos and Teatro Campesino in the 1960s and 1970s (2007 interview).

Maestra Angelbertha Cobb, of Puebla, Mexico. This is the elder who pointed me towards the works of Maya scholar Domingo Martínez Parédez, who argues for the linkage of the entire continent. Also, her narrative of being able to speak with Hopi elders in her own language, Nahuatl, points to north-south connections. Her narrative is elaborated in chapter 3.

Doña Enriqueta Contreras, Puebla, Mexico. This elder speaks of the need to treat all peoples as full human beings, regardless of position in life (R. Rodríguez and P. Gonzales 2002).

Tata Cuaxtle Félix Evodio, Mexico. This Nahuatl educator at Semillas del Pueblo in Los Angeles identifies Aztlan, the home of the Aztecs-Mexica, as a place of ants.

Vivian Delgado, Colorado. The author of *You're Not Indian, You're Mexican* (2007), she posits that colonization is what prevents people from recognizing Mexicans as Indigenous peoples (R. Rodríguez and P. Gonzales 2002, 2005).

Nahuatl educator **Paula Domingo Olivares**, Mexico. This young educator is both my teacher and a knowledge keeper, as she possesses the oral traditions of her ancient Nahuatl-speaking Tlahuica community of Cuentepec, Morelos. Through continuous collaboration, we gave name to the concept of centeotzintli, the maíz narratives of the continent, and also the title of this book (R. Rodríguez and P. Gonzales 2004, 2005).

Jack Forbes.* This highly respected American Indian scholar is the author of *Aztecas del Norte* (1973), in which he recognized Mexican peoples as Anishinaabe or Indigenous. Less known is that ten years earlier, as part of the Native American Movement based in southern California, he wrote "The Southwest Heritage of Aztlan" (1961–1962). This movement and this document regarded Chicanos as Indigenous.

Jose Garza, Texas. This danzante led a reenactment of a migration in 2000, from Mexico City/Tenochtitlan to Wall Lake, New Mexico, passing through the Gila Cliff Dwellings in New Mexico, the site of seven caves.

Helga Garza, Texas. Coordinated the 2000 reenactment of the Aztec/Mexica migration from Tenochtitlan to Wall Lake. At a water ceremony, she explains that, in the end, all peoples will be fighting over contaminated water.

Olga Gonzalez, Colorado. She describes the Otomi birth ceremony held for her daughter in the United States. The Otomi believe that if one has even one drop of Otomi blood, one is Otomi.

Frank Gutierrez,* East Los Angeles. It was this elder, educator, and counselor who first passed on to me the Disturnell map. He had received it from a Hopi elder, Thomas Banyacya, in the 1970s. It showed the Antigua Residencia de los Aztecas in the U.S. Four Corners region. Gutierrez asserted that this was proof that Mexicans were not alien to this country. Ongoing collaboration.

Alfredo Figueroa, Blythe, California. This elder, since 1957, has searched for Aztlan, asserting that it is in the vicinity of the mouth of the Colorado River. He is the author of *Ancient Footprints of the Colorado River: La Cuna de Aztlan* (2002).

Gustavo Gutierrez,* Arizona. This is a Chicano-Opatah elder who was present at the first International Encounter of Indigenous peoples in Ecuador in 1990. From this summit were born the Peace and Dignity Journeys, set in motion by the Prophecy of the Unity of the Eagle and Condor. Gutierrez headed the Peace and Dignity runs. He passed away during the 2012 Journeys as a result of falling off a horse in northern Arizona.

Corbin Harney,* Western Shoshone. This elder explained that Western maps are like photographs; they frame or capture a moment in time, tying peoples to lands that they may simply be passing through. The Shoshone, he said, used to roam the entire continent (2001 interview: in R. Rodríguez and P. Gonzales 2004).

LaDonna Harris, New Mexico. Speaks of Uto-Nahuatl peoples in the United States being aware of their mutual connections, and of annual meetings that affirm these connections.

Inés Hernández-Ávila, California. This Nez Perce–Chicana scholar reminds us that most Chicanas/Chicanos are not of Aztec/Mexica ancestry, per se, yet argues that the Mesoamerican codices are indeed part of Chicana/Chicano culture (R. Rodríguez and P. Gonzales 2002, 2005).

Lauro Tarire Hinojostra, Peru. This elder says that the oral traditions of his people affirm that the peoples of South America traded for maíz from peoples from North America, primarily via the oceans. This included relations with the Huichol of Mexico.

Dolores Huerta, California. This cofounder of the United Farm Workers union says that the vast majority of farm workers are not simply connected to the land but are in fact Indigenous peoples from Mexico and Central America.

Claudia Huizar, El Salvador. While Salvadoran society generally discounts the existence of Indigenous peoples, she affirms that her family is Pipil. The Pipil are Nahuatl-speaking peoples connected to the Uto-Azteca language family group (2004 interview: in R. Rodríguez and P. Gonzales 2004).

Ted Jojola, University of New Mexico. This American Indian scholar speaks of a trade route going from central New Mexico southeast to the Colorado River, then down what is now the Mexican coast, reaching all the way into South America.

Luis Leal.* After studying the topic of Aztlan as part of his academic studies, he came to the United States looking for Aztlan in 1927. Believes Aztlan is a spiritual concept.

Sylvia Ledesma, Kalpulli Izcalli, Albuquerque, New Mexico. Recalls the 1992 pilgrimage made by Xinachtli, led by Maestro Andrés Segura. This pilgrimage to Tenochtitlan/Mexico City, a reenactment of the 1100s-era Mexica migration, began in Aztec, New Mexico (R. Rodríguez and P. Gonzales 2002, 2005).

Mariano Leyva,* Mexico. At the site of Xochicalco, this cofounder of Nahuatl University reminds us that the peoples of Mesoamerica relied on mathematical, scientific, and astronomical knowledge for the creation of their calendars (R. Rodríguez and P. Gonzales 2002, R. Rodríguez 2004).

David Lujan, Tonantzin Land Institute, Albuquerque, New Mexico. He informed me that when the Disturnell map was revealed at an Indigenous gathering a generation ago, he was present as a translator. He also noted that a Hopi elder (now deceased) told them that there were other documents "at the bottom of a pile in an important building" (R. Rodríguez and P. Gonzales 2002, 2005).

Enrique Maestas, Texas. Speaks of the affirmation of Chicano Indigenous identity. Also stresses the Nde/Apache roots of many Mexicans/Chicanas/Chicanos.

Lucila Maestas, Texas. Of Aztec background, she learned that much of the Hopi language is similar to the Aztec/Mexica language of Nahuatl. She learned of this because her son's name is Cuauhtli (eagle). The Hopi name for eagle is similar.

Nora Chapa Mendoza, Michigan. Tells a story about her niece, who grows up unaware (ashamed) that she is Mexican/Indigenous until one day she sees a Mexican across the room, only to find that she is looking at a mirror. A fitting metaphor for this entire work.

Sara Mendoza, Mexico and Los Angeles. She reminds us that relations between north and south were not simply in the realm of trade, but also involved continuous admixture between peoples. Ongoing collaboration.

Arturo Meza Gutiérrez, Mexico City. This elder posits that the Aztlan–Tenochtitlan story is a Western concoction, intended to match up with Biblical stories. He posits that the Mexica, rather than looking for a promised land, migrated on the basis of astronomical-mathematical guidance.

Jose Montoya,* California. This elder of the Chicano Movement says that American Indian activists heavily influenced Chicanos during the 1960s and 1970s. It was not until later, through contact with Nahua-Maya elders, that Chicanos learned that they had similar Indigenous traditions, such as the *temezcal* (purification ceremony) (R. Rodríguez and P. Gonzales 2002, 2005).

Lorena Montoya, California. From El Salvador, she speaks of danzantes being peoples from throughout the Americas, not just of Mexican ancestry.

Julia Nava, South Texas. Speaks of her Apache roots and of relations with Uto-Nahuatl peoples (2004 interview: in R. Rodríguez and P. Gonzales 2004).

Ramón Nenadich, Universidad de Puerto Rico. Speaks of the Taino and Arawak peoples and their connections with other peoples of the Americas and the Caribbean. This includes contact and trade with peoples referred to as the Ticumua of Florida.

Cecilio Orozco*, California. This educator deduced that Utah was the site of Nahuatl—the Four Rivers. He spent a generation studying the region of central Utah and the Green River for evidence of Nahuatl culture.

Apache elder **Grandma Emma Ortega**, San Antonio, Texas. A storyteller, she speaks of the importance of stories, of how they pass on not just oral traditions but values as well, and about our relationship with animals, our oldest teachers (R. Rodríguez and P. Gonzales 2002).

Celia Perez, Michigan. This elder speaks of the work of Tlakaelel and the Four Arrows migration of more than a thousand years ago. She also speaks of ceremonies in which Indigenous peoples of Canada recall stories of contact with Mexica peoples.

Martha Ramírez, Mexico. This cofounder of Nahuatl University speaks of the role of and importance of maíz to the peoples of Mesoamerica, particularly the role of the red ants and Quetzalcoatl in bringing maíz to the people (R. Rodríguez 2004).

Rocky Rodriguez. Tells a story of being recognized by Indigenous peoples of Canada as being related to the people of Quetzalcoatl (R. Rodríguez and P. Gonzales 2004, 2005).

Sonya Rosario. This filmmaker speaks of collaborating with Paiute peoples in Idaho who assert a relationship with all Uto-Nahuatl peoples (2004 interview: in R. Rodríguez and P. Gonzales 2004).

Guillermo Rosette, Taos, New Mexico. This danzante speaks of maíz being traded from Mexico into the United States and up the Mississippi River.

Maestro Andrés Segura,[*] Mexico City/Tenochtitlan. He led a reenactment in 1992 of the eleventh-century Mexica migration from Aztec, New Mexico, to Mexico City. In part, it was his guidance and his research on ancient north-south connections that ensured that I did not abandon my map research. He also affirmed that the pre-Cuauhtemoc, maíz-based songs associated with the dance ceremonies are where Indigenous knowledge and history is stored (1997 interview: in R. Rodríguez and P. Gonzales 2004).

Professor Armando Solórzano, University of Utah. Upon moving to Utah, he met with the chief of the Utes and was told, "Welcome to Aztec Country." The Utes are a Uto-Aztecan-speaking people.

Robert Upham. This researcher asserts that there is a relationship between the game of lacrosse and the great ball-court game of the Nahuatl-Maya peoples. Both are in turn related to agriculture, he argues.

Nahuatl educator **Julieta Villegas**, Santa Catarina, Morelos, Mexico. This elder, cited in the prologue, is the one who reassured Mexican American teachers at Nahuatl University that despite being disconnected from their (Indigenous) language, culture, and ways, they were still Indigenous. "If you ever doubt it, eat a tortilla" (2003 interview: in R. Rodríguez and P. Gonzales 2004).

Laurie Weakie, New Mexico. Speaks of cultural connections, interchange, and trade between the north and the south, documented in various ways including through petroglyph evidence.

Notes

Prologue

1. Nahuatl is an Indigenous language, often associated with the Aztec/Mexica. It is part of the large Uto-Aztecan language family, spoken by many peoples from Canada to Central America. In some parts of Mexico, it is also known as Mexicano or Macehual. Spelling and pronunciation often vary because it is an oral language.

2. Leyva was cofounder of Mexico's Teatro Mascarones and of Nahuatl University.

3. The figure and story of Quetzalcoatl are complex, but the original Quetzalcoatl is considered the bringer of knowledge and civilization to this continent.

4. The story of the ants is contained in the *Legend of the Suns* (or *Leyenda de los Soles*)—a pre-Cuauhtemoc creation story of the Nahua peoples of Mexico, recorded in the Codex Chimalpopoca ([1558] 1945).

5. *Tamuanchan* is the spelling in Maya, whereas it is *Tamoanchan* in Nahuatl.

6. While there is no "one" actual story of the continent of the Americas, the maíz stories, combined, help to explain its birth and the civilizational impulse that spread throughout it several thousand years ago, radically altering it.

7. Here a blind Don Felipe was "reading" a Spanish-language publication he had authored, *Ce Acatl Topiltzin Quetzalcoatl* (Alvarado Peralta 1992).

8. In other versions, it is said that Tonalcatepetl also contained beans, squash, and chia; some oral versions say all of humanity's seeds were there.

9. Patrisia Gonzales originally interviewed Don Felipe on this topic in 1992 (I was present) for her book *The Mud People* (2003: 202–6).

10. Per renowned Maya scholar Domingo Martínez Parédez (1960), Quetzalcoatl is known by various names throughout the continent, including *Kukulkan* among the Yucatec Maya, *Gucumatz* among the Maya Quiché of Guatemala, *Itzam* among the Huastecs, *Tohil* among the Zapotecs, and *Arara* among the Quechua of the Andes.

11. It is uncertain what the original idea behind Quetzalcoatl was. However, in Teotihuacan, in Mexico, Quetzalcoatl was identified with creation. There, the valley was flooded annually to the point where the waters reached up to the image of Quetzalcoatl in the "temple of Quetzalcoatl." At those times, the feathered serpent appeared to be emerging from creation's primordial waters (Florescano 2006: 19).

12. A complex concept, *Indigeneity* refers in this context to people who are rooted to this continent, from before the arrival of Columbus. Definitions vary in each country and range from narrow to broader interpretations, without any consensus. In the United States, Indigeneity is generally restricted to American Indians or peoples with a tribal affiliation, though the U.S. Census Bureau has recently accommodated Indigenous peoples from Mexico, Central America, and South America.

13. *De-Indigenization* describes peoples who are not tribal and who are not consciously connected to a traditional pueblo or Indigenous nation, language, or culture. In the present context, it applies mostly to peoples from Mexico and Central America (but also South America and the Caribbean) who today live in the United States. While different peoples, they generally have experienced colonialism (usually Spanish colonialism) and, nowadays, often share with each other the "enemy-other" position in this country, especially in relation to immigration debates.

14. Historical maps, because of many inaccuracies, cannot by themselves be considered proof of anything.

15. Most peoples of Mexican and Central American origin continue to have this daily relationship with maíz.

16. The importance of maíz, especially for peoples who depend on tortillas for their daily sustenance, has been magnified since the advent of the North American Free Trade Agreement in 1994. Since it was enacted, millions of campesinos/Indigenous peoples throughout Mexico have had to uproot themselves because their *milpas* or cornfields cannot compete with cheap, U.S.-subsidized (and genetically modified) corn.

17. For more on the research protocols, see the introduction. These protocols also resulted in the creation of the concept of collective copyright for the documentary mentioned earlier, *Amoxtli San Ce Tojuan* (R. Rodríguez and P. Gonzales 2005). All those that contributed to it—those who shared stories or edited, or did the interviews— share in it. It also includes the equally important concept of collective responsibility.

18. Former Boise State scholar Vivian G. Lopez uses the term *AmerIndigenous* for the Indigenous peoples of the Americas. Arnoldo Vento uses the term *Amerigenous*. Other scholars utilize *Amerindian*. Members of Tonatierra in Phoenix, a leading Indigenous voice for Chicanos, have long used the Nahuatl term: *Nican Tlaca*.

19. One of my related research projects is the creation of a maíz map of the Americas, tracing both the genetic route of maíz and its accompanying stories.

20. Despite his Alzheimer's, my father could easily access childhood memories.

21. Aside from words that are connected to food and geography, I may have learned my first Nahuatl words from my mother as she told me the Mexica migration story when I was a child: *tihui, tihui* ("forward, forward"). That is what a hummingbird purportedly sang to guide the Mexica on their journey south.

22. Cuauhtemoc was the last *tlahtoani* or speaker of the Mexica peoples and is an enduring Indigenous symbol of resistance throughout the Americas. He was killed in 1524. The use of *pre-Cuauhtemoc* and *post-Cuauhtemoc* is itself an act of resistance used by Mexican Indigenous peoples in place of *pre-Columbian* and *post-Columbian*. In this book, they are used interchangeably, particularly when referring to the entire continent.

Introduction

1. In *Educadores del Mundo* (1969), Ignacio Magaloni Duarte notes that the *Popol Vuh* was written down by Diego Reynoso in the sixteenth century, lost for nearly two centuries, then found and translated in Guatemala by Fray Francisco Ximénez in 1700. In this work, I have examined five translations and interpretations of the *Popol Vuh*: Girard 1966, Martínez Parédez 1968, Tedlock 1996, Goetz and Morley 2003, and Montejo 2004. The epigraph is taken from Goetz and Morley's translation.

2. As I begin this book with the *Popol Vuh*, it is important to note Victor Montejo's words in "Heart of Heaven" (2004: 60): "Obviously the achievements of the ancient Maya are exceptional. But if we focus our attention solely on the ancient Maya, we miss something equally important, the knowledge and creativity of the contemporary Maya." Likewise, if we ignore the recent history of genocide in Guatemala and the contemporary human-rights struggles of Indigenous peoples throughout Mexico and the rest of the Americas, including the United States, we will miss the greater context of this maíz story.

3. Not all Indigenous cultures on this continent are maíz-based and many retain even older stories and ways of looking at the world.

4. Turtle Island was also known as *Cemanahuak* by Nahuatl-speaking peoples. It means the land between the waters, thus the Americas. *Abya-yala*, a word from the Cuna peoples of Panama, and *Pacha Mama*, which means Mother Earth in Quechua (Runasimi), a language of the Andes, are similarly used. Turtle Island imagery is often associated with American Indians. The turtle is also central to the Maya: Hun-Nal-Ye, the spirit of maíz, was reborn from a cracked turtle shell and can be found in Orion (Montejo 2004).

5. In the context of my work, *the continent* refers to the Americas—including the Caribbean. Maíz had spread throughout the Caribbean long before the arrival of Europeans. *Maíz* itself is a Taino word that the Spanish imported into what is today Mexico.

6. The Spanish priests included, at different times during the era of colonization, Franciscans, Dominicans, Augustinians, and Jesuits .

7. Boaventura de Sousa Santos, in "Beyond Abyssal Thinking" (2007), speaks of a similar five-hundred-year process called "epistemicide," though the idea of the Other Conquest is focused more on Indigenous spirituality than Indigenous knowledge.

8. Regarding the notion that Cortés was greeted as Quetzalcoatl: all primary research indicates this never occurred, though it appears he may have been greeted as Quetzalcoatl's representative (Toscano 1953, Blaut 1993, D. Carrasco 1999). Cortés ([1500s] 1990) wrote that only Moctezuma believed that he was a representative of Quetzalcoatl. However, the continual massacres convinced even Moctezuma that the invaders had nothing in common with the peace-loving Quetzalcoatl (*Anales de Tlatelolco* [1528] 1948). Despite this, the "Cortés as Quetzalcoatl" myth lives on in much academic scholarship (Restall 2003).

9. Mendieta ([1595–1596] 1997: 37) wrote: "In the native language a temple to Satan was called *teocalli*, a word composed of *teotl* (god) and *calli* (house), its meaning therefore being house of god."

10. Mestizos were/are not, as is commonly assumed, a fifty-fifty Spanish-Indigenous mixture. The European admixture has always been small in Mexico and Central America.

11. De-Indigenization occurred in part due to religious indoctrination and a violent uprooting from the land.

12. Dussel in *The Invention of the Americas* (1995) argues that the church and the conquistadores created this concept as a way to signify everything that "civilized Europeans" were not. By inventing the Americas, they thus were entitled to conquer and convert "the savages."

13. Martínez Parédez (1960) argued that, per his Yucatec Maya oral tradition, the originators of Mesoamerican culture were the Tamuanchanes, predecessors of the Olmecs, the Maya, the Teotihuacanos, and later the Aztecs/Mexica. The Tamuan-chanes/Toltecs, whose primary language was Maya, were purportedly learned peoples and possessors of all the arts of civilization.

14. Decolonization is an ongoing process because the vestiges of Spanish colonialism are with us to this day, especially among de-Indigenized peoples.

15. The people that the Spaniards encountered in Tenochtitlan were Mexica, but historians mislabeled them Aztec because they purportedly came from Aztlan.

16. Many peoples that live by the Aztec calendar refer to it as the *Tonalmachiotl.*

17. Much Chicana feminist scholarship points to 1519 as the birth of Chicanas/os, whereas others see it as the beginning of resistance. My work emphasizes the birth of maíz as the symbolic birth of Chicanas/os, who are also "gente de maíz."

18. Mesoamerican calendars were created in relation to maíz. For instance, according to the Codex Vindobonensis Mexicanus I, the 260-day Tonalpohualli divinatory almanac—with twenty-day months—was created from twenty grains of maíz.

19. Elder epistemology is both a method for gathering knowledge and elder knowledge itself. As developed by scholar Rosemary Christensen (2002), there are four basic tenets: respect, reciprocity, relationship, and responsibility. I have added *regeneración*, resistance, and resilience. It is through this method that the historiography of Chicanas/os is pushed back by thousands of years to the birth of maíz.

20. The motivation for creating these (evolving) principles is having observed various kinds of abuse that take place under the guise of research, particularly affecting Indigenous communities and other communities of color. Most abuses by scholars fall under the categories of misrepresenting themselves or their research and claiming ownership of knowledge that is not theirs. Western scholars have a long tradition of entering Indigenous communities worldwide and (1) interpreting or misinterpreting the cultures of the peoples they study and (2) demeaning those cultures and beliefs. This is often done by using the West as the standard and comparing all cultures and peoples to that standard.

21. While Western academicians have traditionally viewed nonwritten traditions as unreliable, American Indian scholars have demonstrated the reliability of oral traditions (Cajete 2005, Fixico 2003, L. Smith 1999, Deloria 1973). In my work, codices and other Indigenous forms of memorialization further support oral narratives and traditions. Yet European sources, rather than being outright rejected, are

instead examined to understand their function and relationship to the continent's maíz narratives.

22. An argument can be made that Chicanos/Chicanas have been plotting out their story for at least a generation.

23. Fernando Tzib, a Belizian instructor of Yucatec Maya at the University of Madison at Wisconsin, theorizes regarding the authenticity of Maya stories: "Whether they [others] find them believable or not, it does not matter. They work for us" (personal communication, April 9, 2005). The stories work, he added, because they contain knowledge and traditions that are passed down to the young, who remember what they need to remember.

24. The word *Mexican* derives from the word *Mexica*, though in modern usage they are not synonymous. The Mexica are the people popularly known as Aztecs—so named by Spanish chroniclers in the 1600s because of the belief that they had come from Aztlan.

25. A fuller discussion on Aztlan can be found in chapter 3.

26. During the Spanish-colonial era in the Americas, the authorities placed all peoples into a racial-caste system. Those who were not categorized as "pure" were considered *castas* or mixed-race peoples. While there were many subcategories, the system was not so much a racial system of categorization as an apartheid-type system that determined who had human rights. In this system, only "pure-blooded" white people born in Spain were entitled to full rights. Nicolás León, in *Las Castas del México Colonial o Nueva España* (1924), documented fifty-five racial categories. However, he wrote that in effect there were but two: Spanish/white and all others, "gente de color" or people of color (8).

27. Amoxtlis represented mathematical, astronomical, calendrical, and ceremonial knowledge. Amoxtlis were different from European books because they were made from the bark of the *amatl* tree and read from back to front and folded in the form of an accordion.

28. Díaz Balsera refers to this as "epistemic violence" (2005), with specific reference to the use of fear in theater plays to convert native peoples.

29. The reducciones were a conversion project that resulted from Las Casas winning the debate (on paper) over whether Indigenous peoples had souls.

30. In the 1500s, Las Casas, Fernando Ixtlilxochitl, Diego Durán, and Fray Motolinía all believed that Quetzalcoatl was Saint Thomas. The eighteenth-century historian Lorenzo Boturini ([1746a] 1990) was also a proponent of this idea.

31. Traditionally, in the public realm, Western stories/narratives are regarded as truths but Indigenous stories are not. As Michel-Rolph Trouillot points out in *Silencing the Past* (1995), this is part of a colonial mind-set, which also affects the peoples of Africa and Asia.

32. Robert Entman and Andrew Rojecki, in *The Black Image in the White Mind* (2000: 93), say this about stereotypes: "Thinking stereotypically is not only an easy habit to fall into, it is a normal way of thinking; in essence, stereotypes are schemas, short-cut mechanisms for processing what would otherwise be an overload of information."

33. Songs and dance were actually rituals, as opposed to "poetry" (Bierhorst 2009: 45).

34. The story that Maestra Angelbertha Cobb shares in chapter 3 is a good example of this practice of withholding information from Western academics.

35. Librado Silva Galeana of the Semanario de Cultura Náhuatl en la Universidad Nacional is a native Nahuatl speaker.

36. Regarding colonial censorship, Arnulfo Trejo wrote: "To assure that people in the colonized New World remained subservient to their European rulers, laws were passed and enforced to prevent the unauthorized publication and distribution of printed books. Only books approved by the King through the Council of the Indies were permitted and these were mostly of a religious nature" (1980: 173).

37. Elizabeth Hill Boone, in *Stories in Red and Black* (2000: 31), informs us that the pictorial or iconic form of writing "is actually a more modern form of communication system because it is designed to be understood by people of different languages."

38. The concept of acknowledging rather than validating elder knowledge comes from Dr. Vivian G. Lopez, formerly at Boise State.

39. My research with Patrisia Gonzales resulted in the Aztlanahuac interviews (R. Rodríguez and P. Gonzales 2004), plus several documentaries including *Going Back to Where We Came From* (R. Rodríguez and P. Gonzales 2002), "Teo Cintli" (R. Rodríguez 2004), and *Amoxtli San Ce Tojuan* (R. Rodríguez and P. Gonzales 2005). All treat the subject of origins and migrations. The first documentary focused on map research whereas the latter two focused on the centrality of maíz to Indigenous peoples of the Americas. The interviews have been donated to the University of Arizona Library.

40. Urbanization is not necessarily what de-Indigenizes people. In pre-Columbian times, Mesoamerican societies were highly urbanized. Bonfil Batalla (1996) argued that colonialism divided space: the cities were for the colonizers, whereas the countryside was for the Indians (though subservient Indigenous peoples were permitted to live in segregated urban barrios). This created a division that persists to this day, and that has allowed Mesoamerican culture to be preserved in the countryside.

Chapter 1

1. This saying is taken from *Hopi: Songs of the Fourth World* (Ferrero et al. 2008).

2. The belief that Indigenous peoples were illiterate is what delayed by centuries the translation of Mesoamerican codices, and why the early friars resorted to images for religious instruction.

3. The peoples of Teotihuacan also wrote. No books have survived from that ancient city, but evidence of writing does exist on the buildings and pottery.

4. If the revolt had been led by Indigenous peoples, it would not necessarily have focused on a return to the Aztecs. Mexico was home to hundreds of peoples, not just Aztecs.

5. The late Steve Casanova, an Indigenous Coahuiltecan/Chicano scholar, always insisted that many Indigenous peoples, particularly from the Texas region, were people of mesquite, not maíz.

6. Where the Aztec/Mexica were concerned, the Spanish priests recognized Ypalnemoani (that for which we live), also known as Tloque Nahuaque, as the equivalent of the Christian God. Among the Maya, Hunab Ku was the equivalent concept: the only giver of movement and measurement (*el único dador del movimiento y la medida*). Among the Quechua of the Andes, the equivalent was Arara (Martínez Parédez 1963: 36–37).

7. The debate over whether Indians had souls took place in Valladolid, Spain, in 1550–1551, pitting primarily Las Casas against Juan Ginés de Sepúlveda.

8. Gómez-Quiñones (2012) argues that Las Casas was pro-church, rather than pro-Indian.

9. While Poma was pro-conversion, he was highly critical of the Spanish greed: "Even worse are those of this generation, the Spaniards, the *corregidores* [magistrates], priests, *encomenderos*. With the greed of gold and silver, they are going to hell" (Adorno 2000: 125).

10. I did not intend to examine a centuries-long process; it was the research process that led me there. Communication theories generally deal with much shorter periods or events.

11. While I analyze la Otra Conquista as a reframing project, this three-hundred-year project can also be viewed as a preliminary communications study of demonization, which is helpful in understanding how it continues to work into the twenty-first century.

12. Similarly, a news article (Johnson 2013) reveals that very few dark-skinned Mexicans grace Mexican magazines.

13. Jerónimo de Mendieta painted everything on lienzos: articles of faith, the seven sacraments, the Ten Commandments. Also painted were scenes of the European arrival in the Americas. While the paintings were converted to text (Mendieta [1595–1596] 1997) as well, imagery was the preferred mode of instruction.

14. Rebellions were so numerous during the colonial era that only a few can be cited to illustrate their often pan-Indigenous character: the Mixton War led by Tenamaztle in the mid-1500s in the central part of Mexico (León-Portilla 2005), the Pueblo Revolt led by Po'pay in 1680 in the U.S. Southwest (Sando and Agoyo 2005), and the struggle of Túpac Amaru in the 1700s in South America (Adorno 2000).

15. In *Images at War* (2001), Gruzinski argues that this tendency to see devils everywhere was a reflection of the beliefs of the priests, not that of Indigenous peoples. For example, Sahagún was commissioned in 1558 not to do ethnographic work but to contribute to the mass conversion of Indigenous peoples.

16. Viviana Díaz Balsera notes in *The Pyramid Under the Cross* (2005: 63) that in conducting these conversion projects, the friars had to convince the Indigenous populations that their conversion was voluntary.

17. Klaus Jensen defines semiosis "not as a system, but as a continuous process of signification that orients human cognition and action" (1995: 11).

18. Syncretism is the combination of different systems of philosophies, religions, or worldviews.

19. Artist Alma López (2011), theorizing on the image of Guadalupe, believes it may have been conjured up, not by the church, but by Indigenous peoples, as a means of survival.

The traditional Guadalupe narrative is arguably the quintessential frame in Mexico's continuing war over images. In *Destierro de Sombras* (1986), Edmundo O'Gorman argues that the archbishop of Mexico, Montúfar, commissioned an Indian artist named Marcos (Cipac de Aquino) to paint the image of Guadalupe and Juan Diego Cuauhtlatoatzin in 1556. One hundred years later, the story was put in writing in *Imagen de la Virgen Madre de Dios de Guadalupe* (1648), by Miguel Sánchez, and in Nahuatl, *Nican Mopua* (1649), by Luis Lasso de la Vega. The later works omitted mention of Marcos or Archbishop Montúfar. Contemporaneous with Montúfar, Sahagún argued vehemently against this form of syncretism, what Gruzinski (2001) terms "a cult of substitution." Díaz Balsera (2005) argues that there is actually no evidence of successful mass conversions.

20. Jeanette Favrot Peterson (2005) cites an interview with José Sol Rosales, who conducted a microscopic analysis of the image in 1982 and concluded that it was a result of human craft. However, his findings were suppressed by the church until 2002, after the canonization of Juan Diego.

21. Because of the repressive environment surrounding la Otra Conquista, Indigenous peoples also turned to the oral traditions, because they left no trace . . ."unless the ears acquired by the friars took it upon themselves to inform against what was going on" (Gruzinski 1993: 17). "Ears" alludes to young, Christianized spies.

22. López Austin comments on Mesoamerica: "What we call Mesoamerica was a historical reality. It was a sequence, spanning 1000 years, of strongly linked societies" (1993: 12)—though he notes that connections actually began with the domestication of maíz between 6000 and 5000 BC.

23. A recent book (Esteva and Marielle 2003) and exhibit in Mexico City proclaimed *Sin Maíz No Hay País* (*Without Corn, There Is No Nation*). The idea affirms the centrality of maíz to Mexico.

24. Martínez Parédez acknowledges the oral nature of the tradition for much of the knowledge he advances, which, he argues, makes little sense to Westerners.

25. Galarza spent forty-five years working to decipher the Aztec/Mexica codices, and also to craft scientific and disciplined rules for this decipherment, before making his conclusions public. He argued that Aztec/Mexica writing was not simply complex and precise, but that it was multilayered writing, which included color codes. It could be understood phonetically, but also with imagery, as there was no separation between text and "illustration" (Galarza 1992).

26. Chicana scholars have been writing about women, foodways, and the kitchen for a generation.

27. Broyles-González's anthology *Re-Emerging Native Women of the Americas* (2001b) is an example of the ascendancy of Indigenous scholarship among U.S. Chicana/Xicana and Latina scholars. The contributors include Antonia Castañeda, Elizabeth Martínez, Cherríe Moraga, Alma Villanueva, Teresa Córdova, Amalia Mesa-Bains, Lorna Dee Cervantes, María Herrera-Sobek, Margaret Montoya, and Elizabeth Salas. Inés Hernández-Ávila, Gloria Anzaldúa, Inés Talamantez, Lara Medina, and Irene Lara have also been instrumental in the ascendancy of Indigenous scholarship within Chicana/Chicano studies. This attests to the fluidity of identity.

28. José de Acosta was the first European to suggest the Bering Strait land-bridge theory: "The first inhabitants of the West Indies came by land, and so by consequence that the first continent of the Indies joins with that of Asia" ([1604] 1970: 455). Scientific research has pushed back this migration scenario to possibly forty thousand years. In *The Settlement of the American Continents* (Barton et al. 2004), a series of scientific essays posit—through the use of genetic evidence—that native peoples of the Americas essentially migrated from Asia, either by land or water. Contrarily, many leading American Indian scholars continue to scoff at these theories. Vine Deloria Jr. led this rejection in *God Is Red* (1973) and continued it in the dialogue in *Evolution, Creationism, and Other Modern Myths* (2002). In *The American Discovery of Europe* (2007), Forbes argued that peoples from the Americas may have migrated in the opposite direction, along with the horse, to Asia.

29. Maestas (2003) is one of the few scholars who has acknowledged and examined the Nde/Apache (Athabascan) roots of many Mexicans and Chicanos/Chicanas. The area known as Apachería covered what is today the U.S. Southwest and Mexico's northwest, in effect, the same territory that Chicanos have claimed to be Aztlan. Throughout history, Mexicans and Apaches have mixed willingly or unwillingly. Rudolfo Anaya (1989) acknowledges the native admixture of Chicanas/Chicanos with Pueblo, Apache, and Diné peoples of the Southwest.

30. Due to historical segregation, the Mexican American population does not have a centuries-long tradition of university-trained scholars. Most of its intellectuals from the nineteenth century and early twentieth century were journalists. Prior to 1970, the few Mexican American intellectuals that existed were generally not writing about Aztlan.

31. Acuña was more widely known for advancing a notion of a unified history than an Aztlan origin. Additionally, his concept of "occupied America" was considered part of the internal-colonialism model—a political theory that asserted that as a result of the war against Mexico in 1846–1848, Chicanos became colonial subjects within an imperial nation.

32. This coincided with the advent of postmodern scholarship that rejected the notion of a singular, unitary, and male-centered voice in history with no accommodation for the voice of "the other" (Gutiérrez 2000, Valdés and Rochín 2000).

33. Through the work of Aguirre Beltrán, *La Población Negra de México, 1519–1810: Estudio Etno-histórico* (1946), many scholars nowadays do not neglect the "third root" of Mexico, the African. Aguirre Beltrán's research indicates that there were more Africans in Mexico during the three-hundred-year colonial era than Europeans.

34. Vasconcelos's idea of the cosmic race consisted of viewing Mexico as being composed of all the peoples of the world. The idea of a mestizo Mexico was seen as a unifying project, at the expense of living Indigenous peoples.

35. The nationalism that Pérez-Torres refers to is the same one that Chabram-Dernersesian addresses. The nationalism of the post-Revolutionary period tended to romanticize the heritage of Pre-Columbian Mexico, at the expense of living Indigenous peoples.

36. While Corky Gonzales's "Yo Soy Joaquín," one of the Chicano Movement's seminal poems, was considered Revolutionary nationalist, a careful analysis could lead one to conclude that Gonzales too viewed Chicanas/Chicanos as having multiple and fluid identities. In later life, he viewed Chicanas/Chicanos as Indigenous peoples. In *Brown-Eyed Children of the Sun* (2005) George Mariscal also posits that, though indeed male-centered, Chicano nationalism has been misconstrued as a narrow ideology; he argues that it was more humanism than ethnic nationalism, identifying with worldwide revolutionary struggles.

37. *Anishinaabe* is an Algonquian word referring to an ancient cultural confederation of the Ojibwe, Odawa, and Potawatomi, sometimes used to describe all Indigenous peoples.

38. It has been argued that while Chicano scholars mark 1848 as the beginning of Chicano history, Chicana feminist scholars mark 1519, the beginning of mestizaje in Mexico, as the actual point of origin. The early Chicano scholars also stressed Aztec-Maya roots whereas the feminist scholars stressed mixture. Dennis Valdés (2000) notes that Antonia Castañeda first staked out the claim of a colonial origin for Chicano history in 1990, while Martha Menchaca did so in 1994. Regardless of who is advancing this claim, the result is to conflate the concept of Chicana/Chicano with the concept of mestizo/mestiza. Menchaca (2000: 185) has actually argued that people of Mexican descent in the United States are essentially Indigenous and questions the usefulness and historicity of the category of Chicano/Chicana. Additionally, her book *Recovering History, Constructing Race* (2001), specifically tries to determine when Mexicans stopped being Indian. While her answer is complex, she concludes that however they have been classified legally, dark Mexicans have historically been treated as inferior to light Mexicans and whites in general.

39. Whereas most Chicana/Chicano scholars acknowledge an Indigenous heritage, there was generally no discussion early on of when Mexicans/Chicanos ceased being Indigenous. Most of the early scholars did not satisfactorily explain when this break occurred.

40. In the United States, approximately two-thirds of those categorized as Latinos are of Mexican heritage. Approximately three-fourths are Mexican or Central American. Many are Indigenous, though most are de-Indigenized.

41. The term *Hispanic* is a highly problematic term that has crept into the U.S. body politic. The U.S. Census Bureau and the media first began using it to refer to peoples from Spain and Latin America in 1970. In my work, it rarely, if ever, refers to Mexican and Central American peoples and never refers to Indigenous peoples because the term obliterates their Indigeneity. As Gómez-Quiñones notes in *Indigenous Quotient* (2012), all terms related to the peoples that are the subject of this book are highly loaded.

42. The priests saw themselves as engaged in an actual celestial war on earth, which provided a moral justification for the colonial efforts of the church and crown. The priests saw their world as godly, orderly, and coherent, and the world of Indigenous peoples as chaotic, incoherent, and demonic. In that sense, the counternarrative they created to carry on their evangelization project continues to this day, adapted to an Anglo world.

43. In 1493 the Pope issued bulls that divided Indigenous lands among European powers (Spain and Portugal). In short order, also issued were *Requerimientos*, which were legal declarations that informed native peoples (in Spanish) that they had the option to accept the church and crown, or else be subjected to war (Las Casas [1500s] 1985).

44. Mass-communication theory is primarily the work of twentieth- and twenty-first-century scholars. As such, much of it is relatively difficult to apply to narratives and frames with origins in the 1500s. However, most of Lakoff's work on framing, along with Santa Ana's (2002) and L. Smith's (1999), is applicable for my work.

45. This in part explains why my work begins with maíz narratives, as opposed to Spanish or European narratives, which arrived here post-1492, or efforts at resistance to them, including those that became prominent in the 1960s–1970s.

46. This centering was also practiced by other peoples of color during the 1960s–1970s. It led to counternarratives, resistance narratives, and narratives unto themselves. I consciously bring to the center Mexican/Indigenous scholars that are relevant to my work and often marginalized by academe.

47. It appears that those Indigenous peoples who chose syncretism, along with other forms of resistance, used high-level frames as a vehicle with which to maintain their culture.

48. Nabokov (2002: 161) equates Deloria's "psychic life of a community" to Raymond Fogelson's "once a year epitomizing event"—an event that contributes to peoples' collective memory .

49. Approximately two hundred historical maps that I located as part of my research allude to the original homeland of the Aztecs/Mexica or of other Mexican Indigenous peoples, while also tracking migrations southward into Mexico.

50. There have always been nonscholars who have addressed these issues, but predictably, their writings are not generally given legitimacy by the academy.

51. Whereas various elders pointed me towards maíz in my search for origins and migrations, it was elder Maestra Angelbertha Cobb that pointed me to the work of Martínez Parédez.

52. The historia más profunda of the bird and serpent will be discussed in further detail in chapter 4.

53. Given three hundred years of colonization and the mass-conversion project of the Catholic Church, a complete erasure would not be surprising.

54. Many within the U.S.-Mexican and Mexican American communities participate in spiritual ceremonies associated with "Aztec danza." This research does not examine in depth their ceremonies, most of which continue to be timed to the ancient maíz-based calendars. Because danza is ceremonial dancing, my own ethics do not permit me to write about its specifics. I do touch on the topic generally and briefly in chapter 5. A colleague, a *danzante* from San Jose, California, does write about ceremonial dancing in her dissertation, "Danza Mexica: Indigenous Identity, Spirituality, Activism, and Performance" (Luna 2011).

55. De la Peña does not share Bonfil Batalla's belief in mestizos as de-Indigenized Indigenous peoples. What is problematic about his analysis is that he has placed himself in the position of determining who is and who is not authentically Indian.

Chapter 2

1. In Tucson, Calpolli Teoxicalli—a family of Indigenous families—lives by a ceremonial calendar, the same calendar that has been observed for thousands of years on this very continent. Many other *calpollis* or *kalpullis* in Mexico and the United States also adhere to ceremonial calendars.

2. Gruzinski (2001), Mignolo (2006), and Florescano (2006) write extensively on the use of syncretism for purposes of mass conversion.

3. Despite the acknowledgment that maíz was created by human engineering, Oneida scholar Cornelius (1999) points out that, historically, scientists have tended to discount the Indigenous role in maíz's development, attributing it to accident or prayer. This attitude, she added, is common to all books in which Indigenous contributions to corn (several thousand years' worth) are dispensed with in but several pages.

4. For this narrative, it does not matter what the precise age of maíz is; scientists continue to debate this, though most appear to have settled on seven thousand years. In regard to the diversity of Indigenous peoples, Jane and Kenneth Hill posit that it "has been overemphasized by Occidentals in order to keep Indians separated from one another and diminish their capacity for resistance" (1986: 49).

5. In *A Forest of Kings* (1990: 38), Schele and Freidel posit that the Olmec in 1200 BC "were the people who forged the template of world view and governance that the Maya would inherit a thousand years later when they began to build their own cities."

6. Over the years, many of these mounds have been razed, particularly those in the United States. According to Boturini (1746b: 113), pyramids were an attempt to replicate the tower of Babel, a story that was memorialized in Indigenous peoples' ancient *cantares*.

7. Martínez Parédez (1960) provides a coherent narrative about the origin of Mesoamerican peoples: The Tamoanchanes came from across the oceans, settled, and created many of the civilizations throughout the continent. This, he tells us, comports with the teachings of his Maya ancestors, and it also comports with a similar narrative found in book 10 of Sahagún's *General History of the Things of New Spain* (Florentine Codex [1577] 1961: 190): After the ancient descendants of the Mexica arrived from across the ocean and disembarked at the Panutla River, the people looked for Tamoanchan, then later scattered in all directions. Some went toward Guatemala, some went north. Those that went north eventually returned south, reuniting with the peoples they originally came across with. These accounts are purported to be from Indigenous sources.

8. The intent of these book-burning campaigns was not simply to wipe out "paganism"; they were accompanied by hangings and violent repression perpetrated against the peoples themselves (Landa [1566] 1938: 102–3).

9. While the division of the world into Old (Eurasia and Africa) and New (the Americas) is inaccurate, the paradigm nonetheless appears, for research purposes, to serve a legitimate function: the cultures of the Americas do exhibit a uniqueness that is explainable as a result of their relative isolation from the other continents. They developed without the use of firearms, the wheel as transportation, the horse, heavy farm animals, or heavy metals, and without the European narrative of history.

Despite this seeming lack of direct influence from Eurasia or Africa, there is plenty of evidence that suggests either contact or trade (Morison 1971, Melgarejo 1992). One example of possible contact is the Olmec heads of La Venta, Mexico. With striking African features, they minimally suggest contact. Another example is the many "wheeled toys" featuring horses on wheels that have been found throughout the Americas. They appear to be of Asian origin (Marschall 1979).

10. Richard Stockton MacNeish places the age of agriculture in Mexico at twelve thousand years (cited in García Cook 1997). Countering a widely held misconception, another ingrained frame, J. M. Blaut argued in *The Colonizer's Model of the World* (1993) that European advantages, outside of warfare, were minor. He wrote that modern historians have telescoped history, believing in some form of technological determinism: "Europe's progress was not pre-colonial . . . but as a result of colonialism instead" (109).

11. Up until recently, it was thought that corn had made its way to Bat Cave, New Mexico, some six thousand years ago, and spread eastward from there (Forbes 1973, Waldman 2000). However, recent studies indicate the corn found there is but some 3,120 years old (Meltzer 1999). A Tucson site, reportedly the oldest cornfield in the United States, is dated to 4,200 years ago (Nabhan 2012–2013: 70–71).

12. The botanical name for the predecessor of maíz is *teosinte*, from the Nahuatl name *teocinte* (Weatherford 1991).

13. The connection to maíz culture is greater for those peoples who continue to cultivate, harvest, store, and cook maíz and practice the associated pre-Columbian ceremonies.

14. In *America on Paper* (1989) Lynn Glaser acknowledges the brutality and genocide of the conquest and even the clerical greed for gold, but then plays down the violence against Indigenous peoples by ascribing reports of it to a propaganda battle between competing Europeans.

15. A study of 1,170 Indigenous cultures worldwide shows that the Americas (which includes the Aztec culture) were far less violent than the rest of the world. This evidence, drawn from history, archaeology, and anthropology, speaks clearly: "The New World prior to Columbus was a far less violent place than the Old World" (DeMeo 2005).

16. Arnoldo Vento in *Mestizo* (1998) traces the manner and methods used by Inquisitors to distort the writings of the early priests. He also documents the complaints of priests and native scholars who articulate how their words are being distorted by the censors and who also note that what is being published about the Americas does not correspond to the reality of the continent.

17. In *Dances of Anahuac* (1964), Gertrude Prokosch Kurath stated that "idolatry and ritual human sacrifice form the 'Black Legend' of the Aztecs" (12). The Romans, she argued, shed more blood simply for entertainment purposes than the Aztecs did. The Spanish priests, for their part, regularly took part in massacres or torture (12–15). Aztec human sacrifice has historically been used as a justification for European conquest. In *City of Sacrifice* (1999), Harvard Mesoamericanist Davíd Carrasco argues that all peoples throughout history have sacrificed, and that compared to the Americas, peoples of Europe were much more brutal. In *Al Otro Lado*

de las Sombras (*On the Other Side of the Shadows*, 1993) Mexica elder Arturo Meza Gutiérrez argues that none of the cultures in the Americas practiced human sacrifice in the manner described by Spanish priests. Much was actually punishment as opposed to sacrifice. In *El Universo de Quetzalcóatl* (*The Universe of Quetzalcoatl*, 1962), Laurette Séjourné noted that in pre-Aztec days, human sacrifice was expressly prohibited, purportedly by Quetzalcoatl. The Aztec emperor Itzcaotl in 1428 is said to have destroyed archives containing tenth-century references to this prohibition.

18. In *Silencing the Past* (1995), Trouillot makes a similar point regarding why Western historians erased or silenced Haiti's liberation by slaves: because it did not make sense to them.

19. An argument can be made that Spaniards were not trying to Europeanize Indigenous peoples, but Christianize them.

20. The supposition, even to this day, is that (superstitious) Europeans had something to save Indigenous peoples with.

21. Martínez Parédez argues that because non-Indigenous peoples have been unable to understand Indigenous thought and culture, they have not shaken off their perceptions of who Indigenous peoples are. These perceptions, created in the 1500s, include the idea that Indigenous peoples are "beasts, cannibals, imbeciles and savages, unable to think" and but "one step removed from animals—waiting 'to be saved' by Hispanos" (1968: 11).

22. While the (nine-thousand-year-old) Kennewick Man debate is useful for those who advance the theory that Caucasians have been on this continent for many thousands of years, it does not fit into this religio-vision either.

23. In "Five Hundred Years of Injustice: The Legacy of Fifteenth Century Religious Prejudice" (1992), Steven Newcomb argued that this divine mandate is related to the "doctrine of discovery" and two papal bulls, one from 1452 and the 1493 *Inter Caetera*, which "gave" European powers the "right" to divide up and conquer the non-Christian world.

24. Mignolo defines the master narrative in this manner: "During the period 1500 to 2000, one local history, that of Western civilization, built itself as the point of arrival and owner of human history. Ownership was expressed by building a system of knowledge as if it were the sum and guardian of all knowledges, past and present" (2012: x).

25. "Counterstories" also contest the master narrative. Delgado and Stefanic in *The Latino/a Condition* (1998: 259) make a forceful argument regarding the power of stories: "Stories, parables, chronicles, and narratives are powerful means for destroying mindset—the bundle of presuppositions, received wisdoms, and shared understandings against a background of which legal and political discourse takes place."

26. Under reframing, the solution would be not to grant the centrality of the master narrative and instead simply view it as another, competing narrative.

27. In "Death by English" (1998), Juan Perea argues that the Spanish language is racialized in the United States; those who speak it are discriminated against and ostracized.

28. Three recent examples are the 2013 PBS series *Latino Americans*, the National American Latino Museum, and the National Park Service's essay collection *American Latinos and The Making of the United States: A Theme Study*. All three begin in the fifteenth and sixteenth centuries, erasing Indigenous foundations.

Chapter 3

1. The portion of the Disturnell map was given to me by elder and educator Frank Gutierrez (see figures 6 and 7 and plate 5). He had received it from Hopi elder Thomas Banyacya at a gathering of Indigenous-rights activists and elders in the early 1980s, gathered to examine the Treaty of Guadalupe Hidalgo. A short time later, Conchero elder Andrés Segura passed the Boturini Codex to me, which documented the Mexica migration journey. Thereafter, I was informed by two Indigenous-rights activists, David Lujan and Tupac Enrique Acosta, both of whom had been present at the same gathering, that Banyacya, now deceased, had informed those present that there were older documents and maps at the bottom of a pile in an important building (R. Rodríguez and P. Gonzales 2004).

2. James Scott, in *Domination and the Arts of Resistance: Hidden Transcripts* (1990), argues that subordinated groups often communicate in a language unfamiliar, and oftentimes unintelligible, to dominant society. The Disturnell map can be seen to function as a hidden transcript, affirming that Chicanas/Chicanos were not aliens to the Southwest and countering the U.S. master narrative of history.

3. On early European maps of the Americas, such as the 1562 Gutiérrez map, wild beasts and native peoples alike are placed in the oceans and non-European lands, connoting the need to tame these faraway and uncivilized places.

4. Menchaca examined court and legislative records from 1848 to 1947, revealing that the skin color of Mexicans strongly influenced their treatment: "During the nineteenth century, Mexican-origin individuals who were predominantly of Indian descent were subject to heightened racial discrimination" (1998: 393).

5. It was during the 1950s that the term *Mexican* and the derisive term *wetback*—which comes from swimming north across the Rio Grande—became synonymous with illegal aliens.

6. The anti-immigrant hysteria has been most extreme in the state of Arizona.

7. Just as Benedict Anderson (1991) wrote of imagined communities, the observation can be made that the United States is arguably the quintessential imagined nation-state where Indigenous peoples are aliens in their own lands. Arguably, all nation-states are imagined.

8. These anti-Mexican attitudes have manifested on television, and to an even greater extent on the silver screen. Mexicans, since the advent of these industries, have generally been projected as bandits and easy señoritas. They have also, like American Indians, been shown as fodder for cowboys and the U.S. military (Wilson and Gutiérrez 1995).

9. Lakoff wrote: "When you hear a word, its frame (or collection of frames) is activated in your brain" (2004: xv). The frame today is "illegal aliens." But as he reminded us: "It is not just language. The ideas are primary—and the language carries those ideas, evokes those ideas." What is activated is the frame or metaphor of the nation as family. Evoked is the idea that "these aliens" are not part of the American family (4–5).

10. Arizona's anti-immigrant SB 1070, signed in 2010, has spawned copycat or even more stringent anti-immigrant legislation nationwide.

11. Billig has noted that it is rare for Western scholars, when examining social realities, to look at the larger sociopolitical context—the nationalism and imperialism of European powers, and now globalization and U.S. hegemony. He wrote that societies cannot or should not be viewed as self-contained units "to be studied in isolation" (1995: 53). He further suggested that in the past, not crossing disciplines prevented Western scholars from seeing that larger context.

12. In "El Plan Espiritual de Aztlan" (1970), Alurista referred to the Southwest as "the land of our forefathers." The poet, who became one of the principal figures of the Chicano Movement, injected Indigeneity into Chicano culture and literature.

13. Zapata had been killed less than fifty years before when Cesar Chavez convened Mexican farm workers in Delano, California, to join Filipinos in the first grape strike of what became the UFW. "Posters of Emiliano Zapata filled the hall when César Chávez addressed the farm workers at the strike meeting on September 16, 1965" (Bebout 2011: 86).

14. Aztlan detractors viewed Aztlan as nationalistic, patriarchal, and homophobic. The right wing, on the other hand, continues to hype Aztlan as an actual movement to retake the U.S. Southwest (Bebout 2011).

15. Perceived by many Chicana/Chicano scholars as being ahead of her time, Anzaldúa's *Borderlands/La Frontera: The New Mestiza* (1987) is associated with the concept of borderlands as a third space, drawing on her Indigenous-mestiza roots.

16. The U.S. Census Bureau reported in 2010 that of more than fifty million Hispanics/Latinos in the United States, approximately 75 percent are of Mexican or Central American origin.

17. Another reason for its disuse is that it is associated with narrow and intolerant views, namely mysogyny and homophobia.

18. Since the late 1970s, many Chicanos/Chicanas who have worked and collaborated with native peoples of the U.S. Southwest have come to know that they consider the conceptualization of Aztlan as a Chicano homeland to be a (colonialist) imposition upon native lands. As a result, many Chicanos/Chicanas no longer emphasize Aztlan as a literal future homeland and instead emphasize relations with the continent as a whole and, most importantly, with the other original peoples of the continent.

19. Galarza and Libura (2000: 19), based on an analysis of the *Tira de la Peregrinación* (the Boturini Codex), give AD 1116 as the likely date of the Mexica departure.

20. The Seven Cities were associated with the legend of Cíbola, traced to AD 750. In *Lost Treasures on the Old Spanish Trail* (1992: 1), George Thompson recounts how a bishop of Lisbon traveled into an unknown Western ocean and reached a land—the Seven Cities of Cíbola—that was very rich in gold. This idea has been conflated throughout history with Moctezuma's gold. It was reputedly never recovered (by Europeans) and stories abound that it remains hidden, perhaps ensconced somewhere in the original homeland of the Aztecs in the north (Thompson 1992, Boren and Boren 1998: 103).

21. After the sack of Tenochtitlan, Hernán Cortés, convinced that there were more riches to be found, went searching for Hueitlapalan (Huehuetlapallan), associated with the ancient Toltecs. Armed with Aztec/Indigenous codices he had been given by

Moctezuma, he was convinced that the legendary place of origin of the Aztecs, the Seven Caves, had to be the Seven Cities of Gold (Boone 1998). He traveled up the West Coast and into the Gulf of California, to the mouth of the Colorado River. His search ended in failure. Francisco Coronado in 1542 took an inland route. While he did locate what Cabeza de Vaca reported (Seven Cities of Gold, minus the treasures), he too returned home disgraced.

22. The Aztlan-migration story as told by the Indigenous writers cited above was gleaned from "native informants." Subsequent chroniclers of that era most likely gleaned it from each other.

23. Historically, there has been confusion over Toltec identity. Florescano, in *Memoria Indígena* (1999), identifies the Toltecs with ancient Tollan/Teotihuacan. Other historians have identified them with the later (tenth-century) city of Tula. Florescano argues that those from Tula simply took the prestigious name, but that the original ones, the ones that brought and spread civilization to the rest of the continent, are the ones associated with the Tollan/Teotihuacan of at least two thousand years ago.

24. Most early Spanish chronicler priests were convinced that all native people of the Americas were descendants of Adam and Eve. Based on that belief, they debated how they came to the Western Hemisphere. There was no shortage of theories, including that they were part of the Lost Tribes of Israel (Durán [1581] 1967). During that era, everything had to be explained by the Bible. However, stories regarding traversing oceans often connote Atlantis (Buelna 1887).

25. The attestation of these place-names may simply mean that Indigenous peoples wanted to keep remembering their places of origin and replicated the names in new places; mapmakers then recorded these sites.

26. The relationship between Tamoanchan and Aztlan is explored in the section on hidden narratives later in this chapter.

27. The Disturnell map takes on added weight because it was attached to the Treaty of Guadalupe Hidalgo, the treaty that ended the 1846–1848 U.S. war against Mexico and that was used to take half of Mexico's territory.

28. The migration stories on these maps clearly indicate that the "memory" of an ancient Mexican Indigenous presence in what is today the United States was alive, at least among mapmakers, prior to the twentieth century.

29. "In the Maya language," Martínez Parédez explained, "the etymological meaning of Tamoanchan is as follows. *Ta* means place. *Moan* means bird and *chan* means serpent. When they went looking for Tamoanchan, they were looking for the place of the bird and serpent" (1960: 52).

30. Alurista, who had never seen any of the maps in question, noted his belief that *Tolm* or *Tolman* was most likely a distorted spelling for *Tollan*, the legendary city also associated with the Toltecs (Aztlanahuac interview, 2004: in R. Rodríguez and P. Gonzales 2004).

31. I am unable to definitively ascertain if the Toltec/Tamoanchan migration story concurs with the longer version of the Aztlan-migration story as recorded by Sahagún (Florentine Codex [1577] 1961: 190). When Conchero elder Segura passed the Boturini Codex to me, he stated that the *Tira de la Peregrinación* is missing some pages and alluded to the idea that Aztlan represents crossing an ocean, rather than a

lake, thereby possibly connecting the stories recounted by Martínez Parédez, Girard, and Sahagún.

32. The three documentaries produced as a result of the Aztlanahuac interviews revolve around the same basic idea: migrations, belonging, and maíz as that which unites the continent. In "Teo Cintli: Story of the Continent" (R. Rodríguez 2004), David Castro, pointing to the *penca* or cactus leaf, noted: "These are our papers." (The other two documentaries are R. Rodríguez and P. Gonzales 2002, 2005.)

33. According to linguist Jane Hill of the University of Arizona, Maestra Cobb could not have carried on full conversations with the Hopi elders because the Hopi and Nahuatl languages separated some 4,000–4,500 years ago (personal communication, August 20, 2007).

34. It is possible that much information shared with the early colonial chroniclers by Indigenous peoples was misinformation, for the purpose of protecting (sacred) knowledge. It could also simply be the case that many of the "informants" were not tlamatinis, the learned elders trained to read the codices.

35. In regard to notions of what constitutes writing, the study of the quipu among the Inca is revealing that it was not simply an abacus or an accounting system, but that it was also a repository of memory and history. The quipu (or *khipu*) is a color-coded knot system that has been compared to a modern computer for its complexity (Mignolo 2006). The Spaniards ordered the quipus burned, as they saw them as "idolatrous objects" (Mann 2005). Gartner argues that "they also served as maps" (1998: 290).

On this topic, most often overlooked is that ancient Mexicans (pre-Aztec/Mexica) had an equivalent system called the *nepohualtzintzin*. This is its entry in the Siméon Nahuatl dictionary: "Strings of different colors that when knotted, similar to the quipu from Peru, recalled major events; this custom seems not to have been part of ancient Mexico, except in its most remote history" (Siméon 2004). A speculation can be made that the Iroquoian tradition of wampum belts may be related—at least in concept.

Saramamalla

1. En la lengua kichwa de herencia inca de los Andes, *runa* significa "ser humano," que lamentablemente ha sido alterado y despojado de su real significado hasta denigrarlo en su valor, categorizándolo como algo inservible, carente de valor, no fino, rudo, rústico. Sin embargo gracias a ese alimento sagrado con el cual los runas de este continente nos hemos alimentado, hay sabias profesías de los ancestros andinos que decían volveremos y seremos millones como los granos de maíz, y ahora esta palabra *runa* constituye nuestra voz de nuestra existencia y permanencia. Ahora tenemos orgullo de ser runa de Abya-yala, pero con el sentido original como siempre ha sido.

2. In the Kichwa language of the Andes, *runa* means "human being," which unfortunately has been altered and stripped of its real meaning and even denigrated, so that it has come to mean something useless, lacking in value, not fine, rude, rustic. On the other hand thanks to the sacred sustenance with which we runas of this continent have fed ourselves, there are wise prophecies of our Andean ancestors that used to say that we will return by the millions, like the kernels of maíz, and for that now this *runa*

word constitutes the voice of our existence and permanence. Now we are very proud to be runa of the Abya-yala, but with the real meaning as it has always been.

Chapter 4

1. *Huazontli* or amaranth bread was also a primary staple for Mesoamerican peoples. However, because it was associated with Huitzilopochtli, who was the devil incarnate to the Spaniards, it suffered the opposite fate as maíz; the church banned it for 350 years (Rojas Rabiela and Sanders 1985). In *Indian Givers* (1988: 76), Jack Weatherford wrote that the church "forbade the cultivation, sale or consumption of amaranth under penalty of death."

2. It is believed that beans were the first crop domesticated in Mexico, nine thousand years ago (Long-Solís 1998).

3. In *The Invasion of America* (1976: 86), Francis Jennings noted that the Hurons traded maíz with Indigenous peoples from northern Canada.

4. The mano, held in the hand, is the implement that smashes the corn on the metate, the grinding stone. The metate normally has two legs in the back and a shorter one on the front. The *molcajete* (the Mexican blender) is similar, but is shaped like a bowl (Abarca 2006: 72).

5. A line in the 1500s-era Testerian Codices (Galarza and Monod-Becquelin 1992: 48), from the Our Father prayer in Nahuatl, translates as: "and from this day forward, you give us our daily tortilla, which we will use for our daily sustenance."

6. The continuity frame is also evidence of a different temporality, in the sense of standpoint theory (Harding 1987).

7. In response to Edward Said's polemic on Orientalist essentialism, in the 1980s, the academy accepted that "no longer could unity or continuity be assumed when studying peoples and cultures. This created a quandary for scholars" (Klor de Alva 1997: 59).

8. In northern Mexico and in the United States, the flour tortilla, which is not Indigenous to the Americas, has been thoroughly Mexicanized or "Indigenized," as it nowadays accompanies a great deal of the Mexican food or cuisine in these regions.

9. The idea of cultural root paradigms is attributed to Turner (1974). In regards to the "calendar," many Mexicans are unaware of the historical narrative contained within it, instead seeing it only as a piece of Aztec artwork.

10. Mestizaje forms another of Mexico's cultural root paradigms. This is symbolized by the image of the conquistador Cortés with La Malinche, his translator and mother of his first son. *La Llorona* (the Crying Woman) is another of these paradigms. Her story—one version of it—is also the story of mestizaje, of an Indian woman weeping through the streets because she drowned her children as a result of their Spanish father abandoning them.

11. In U.S. popular culture, white bread is a metaphor for WASP culture, and in WASP culture, the tortilla (in fact, Mexican food generally) is often denigrated.

12. Coincidentally, tortilla art is also a medium. Tortillas as canvases first became popular in the 1970s, exhibited primarily in barrio museums.

13. Salsa, which is often eaten with corn tortilla chips, now outsells ketchup in the United States. The tomato, the core ingredient of both salsa and ketchup, is indigenous to the Americas. Ketchup is often associated and eaten with French fries; the potato is also native to this continent. The popularity of salsa points to two things: (1) the explosive demographic growth of peoples from the south now living in the United States, and (2) the Indigenization of the U.S. diet/cuisine.

14. The association of Mexicans with animals may be a legacy of Spaniards associating corn with animals or pigs. As Guadalupe Pérez San Vicente (2000) notes, corn was initially imported to Europe as animal feed, and it remained such for many years. Similar attitudes and practices prevailed in the United States. In fact, most corn harvested here today is fed to animals, including genetically modified corn.

15. Maíz has not generally been associated negatively with Indigenous peoples of the north or marketed in the mass media that way. This perhaps may be rooted in the British/American idea of the noble savage.

16. Negative associations include referring to the U.S.–Mexico border as the "Tortilla Curtain." On a personal note, as a reporter in 1986, I witnessed the following at UCLA: as an Indigenous elder, Ernie Longwalker Peters, was giving a prayer in support of Mexican/Chicano students who were protesting racism, a truckload of fraternity and sorority members drove by shouting obscenities and throwing corn tortillas at them.

17. This colonial practice of ranking crops is found in other contexts as well. In *Black Rice: The African Origins of Rice Cultivation in the Americas* (2001: 166), Judith Carney describes how Europeans have tended to view African foods as weeds or more fit for animals than humans.

18. Amaranth is a popular cereal at health stores, as is spirulina. Cactus is generally touted as an antidote for diabetes. Huitlacoche, also known as corn smut, is nowadays found mostly in upscale restaurants. These foods are also sold in *mercados* or markets as filler for quesadillas.

19. The Maya recognize Paxil, Guatemala, as the site of the origin of maíz (Girard 1966).

20. While the birth of maíz and the beginning of the calendar count do not appear to coincide, an explanation may be that the calendar marks when maíz became part of the culture as opposed to when it was created.

21. Lowrider cars and highly decorated taco trucks in the United States and buses in Mexico are excellent examples of mobile cultural spaces.

22. My Tortilla Mapping Project grew out of a University of Wisconsin seminar. Since then, I continue to collect these wrappers wherever I go, and I have not noticed much variation that would alter what I initially found.

23. E-mail message from company representative, May 29, 2007.

24. Aside from maíz and tobacco products, Indian imagery has also been a favorite for American sports teams' logos and mascots. This has generated a backlash, with groups calling on teams to cease utilizing such imagery (Harjo 2005).

25. This imagery will be analyzed later in this chapter utilizing a semiotic interpretation.

26. I have not detected a relationship between the packaging imagery and the consumer's decision to buy a particular brand of tortillas. In a study regarding the effect

of a sixty-second ad by Macintosh, it was determined that two hundred thousand Macintosh computers were sold overnight (Moriarty and Sayre 2005). With tortillas, one could not gauge a similar cause and effect because of the lack of TV advertising.

27. The tortilla is the equivalent of an edible spoon or plate. Corn tortillas form the basis of tacos, enchiladas, taquitos, flautas, quesadillas, tostadas, and chips, the primary popular Mexican dishes.

28. A bomb threat received at the Indigenous Semillas school in Los Angeles in 2006 contained obscenities laden with references to burnt tortillas and burnt chile, affirming that bigots negatively associate Mexicans with Indigenous foods.

29. Acapulco Tortilleria in East Los Angeles has, as its logo, "Centiocihuatl: female Aztec spirit of mature corn" (Centiocihuatl: diosa azteca del maíz maduro). They now carry the story of corn, which I wrote for them, on their wrappers in Nahuatl, Spanish, and English.

30. In *Indian Givers* (1988), Jack Weatherford estimates that the Americas have provided 60 percent of the world's foods and 25 percent of its medicines.

31. While the imagery associated with tortilla packaging may constitute continuity, it can also be construed as locating Mexicans in the past (Moriarty and Rohe 2005: 122).

32. Pérez San Vicente also notes that it is female hands that continue to create tortillas (2000: 17).

33. Even Frito Lay, maker of Frito's corn chips, appears to have learned this in the previous generation; it had been subject to a national boycott because of its use of a Mexican bandit to sell its chips.

34. Images on tortilla wrappers include warriors or gods. Several Mexican companies depict Aztec warriors or Aztec calendars. Some use deer dancers, pyramids, or volcanoes, associated with ancient Mexico, whereas others utilize symbols associated with Indigeneity, including the sun and the moon. A Chicago company uses the image of the volcano Popocatepetl, which is virtually a cultural root paradigm unto itself, because its imagery is associated with an ancient Indigenous legend involving another volcano, Iztaccihuatl—a woman who dies and lies down and becomes a mountain. The warrior mourns her and also joins her, lying down beside her. La Banderita tortillas substitute the eagle and serpent of the Mexican flag for the image of maíz. The name and imagery of the nationally distributed Mission Tortillas reflects an ignorance about missions. They were oppressive institutions where Indigenous peoples were forced to convert to Christianity and provide cheap labor. Nowadays, they are considered quaint tourist destinations. Finally, some non-Mexican companies create generic "gods."

35. A parrot is depicted on several of the packages, including Fiesta Corn Tortillas from Houston, and a rooster appears on El Gallito Rice, distributed by a Laredo, Texas, firm. The rooster and cockfighting are the central feature of many celebrations, including one of Mexico's most famous fairs, the Feria de San Marcos in Aguascalientes.

36. In health-store products, Aztec, Maya, and Inca images are often confused and combined, along with petroglyphs. Pre-Columbian imagery and petroglyphs constitute actual communication where memory is stored and can still be read (Boone and Mignolo 1994, Mignolo 2006). However, some companies simply project anything

Indigenous. Frontera chips from Chicago (Whole Harvest Foods) and Que Pasa tortilla chips from Canada are examples of hodgepodge imagery that appears "slapped together." Mexican companies that sell tortillas will often do the same thing, but not in quite the same offensive manner, often combining pre-Columbian Indigenous imagery with incongruous colonial-style buildings.

37. Tucson's El Minuto restaurant utilizes the Mexican sleeping against a cactus as part of its logo. Interestingly, the restaurant gives away a calendar that reproduces the entire Boturini Codex, depicting the Mexica migration story, with a complete explanation of it. One tortilla package, from Manny's Soft Tacos, based in Wisconsin, depicts a Mexican sleeping against a cart rather than a cactus.

38. Also being cooked was frybread, made with wheat and deep-fried, which indeed is Indigenous food, though post-Columbian. What this means is that Indigenous peoples, like all other peoples, adapt and adopt that which is useful and desirable, especially in times of hardship.

39. On the other hand, things Spanish—in fact, things European, African, or Asian—can be Indigenized and Mexicanized. The *china poblana* (Chinese woman) is an example of something non-Indigenous being incorporated into the Mexican/Indigenous culture.

40. The idea that things Spanish are not Mexican is part of a Saussurean or structuralist formulation. Things Mexican are Indigenous, but not Spanish (Moriarty 2005: 230).

Chapter 5

1. Quoted in *Iroquois Corn in a Culture-Based Curriculum* (Cornelius 1999: 258).

2. The huehuetlahtolli, as explained in previous chapters, were a moral form of instruction and guidances using Nahua thought and philosophy.

Cantos were poems. Cantares were religious songs.

The tamalada is an event when family and friends gather to make tamales and can last overnight and even two–three days. Vélez-Ibéñez (1996) calls it the quintessential secular ceremony for Chicanas/Chicanos.

Danza does not necessarily refer to dance in general but instead generally to ceremonial dances connected to Nahua-Chichimeca culture. They are also referred to as Aztec/Mexica dance.

3. *Red Medicine* (P. Gonzales 2012) and *Women and Knowledge in Mesoamerica* (Martinez-Cruz 2011) argue that use of pre-Columbian medicines survives to this day.

4. The idea of peoples and nations inventing their traditions comes from Eric Hobsbawm and Terence Ranger (1984). They argue that peoples who are struggling for legitimacy, particularly when creating new nations, often reject the present and claim a remote antiquity (14).

5. For many Indigenous peoples throughout Mexico, "Montezuma" (Moctezuma II) is the last defender of the Aztecs. This includes the Pueblo people in New Mexico, in whose communities, from the 1600s through the twentieth century, "sacred

fires were kept burning against the day when he would return as the native people's deliverer from Spanish oppression" (Bierhorst 2009: 69).

6. After Mexican Independence and the Mexican Revolution, the oral tradition was ascendant. Later, when professional historians took control of writing history, utilizing Western methodologies, they began to rely on Western documents and texts. Florescano in *National Narratives in Mexico* (2006: 368) wrote: "The myths, rituals, and traditions transmitted by collective memory were classified as legends or were defined as testimonies without scientific support."

7. The mural, painted by Ed Carrillo, Saul Solache, Sergio Hernandez, and Ramses Noriega, has been in storage in a UCLA warehouse since 1991.

8. Prior to maíz, there were no cities. Cities, and specifically pyramids to the sun, the moon, and the morning star (Quetzalcoatl)—all connected to maíz—are part of a complex pre-Columbian cosmology (Florescano 2006).

9. While admittedly not all Mexicans and Chicanas/Chicanos are people of maíz, at least this is a more inclusive idea than that of everyone having Aztec roots. Many people of maíz do have roots from peoples of the north, including Apache, Navajo, and Pueblo (Maestas 2003). Also, being part of maíz culture does not involve allegiance to a nation, or to nationalisms of any kind, or to any border.

10. For Mexicans, maíz is akin to rice in African American culture. It is not simply present at every meal as sustenance, it is also a knowledge system, a technology, linked to cultural identity and an entire cultural system. Postharvest, the technology is a women's knowledge system (Carney 2001: 167).

11. For a detailed explanation of the tamalada, read *Tamales, Comadres, and the Meaning of Civilization* (Clark and Tafolla 2011). Beyond a primer on tamales and the tamalada, it is full of tamale wisdom, humor, and even theology.

12. Recent migration into the United States includes peoples who have migrated en masse from Indigenous communities and regions—peoples who maintain not just individual but, importantly, collective Indigenous identities. Perhaps that is what differentiates de-Indigenized peoples: individual versus collective identities.

13. Over the past generation, many Chicanas/Chicanos have also been participating in northern ceremonies (for example, Lakota and Diné ceremonies).

14. From Gillmor's foreword to *At the Sign of Midnight* (Stone 1975).

15. The *concha* is the armadillo shell that serves as the back of a stringed instrument used during danza and song ceremonies. It is what defines the danzantes named Concheros.

16. My research ethics prevent me from writing about the specifics or inner workings of these traditions and the variances among the different groups, primarily because I have had an association with various groups since long before I became a researcher.

17. The major studies on the Concheros have included "The Conchero Dancers of Mexico" (Mansfield 1953) and Stone's *At the Sign of Midnight* (1975). An example of deep or double meaning is that in some cases, Christian images are superimposed upon Indigenous images, the names of which are not made public. In other cases, things are present during ceremonies that are not revealed to the public.

18. Don Aurelio of Amatlán, Morelos, told me that the people protect their corn crops from animals by growing an extra row just for them (personal communication, August 11, 2005).

19. The Semillas curriculum includes the Nahuatl language and Indigenous mathematics, astronomy, history, and culture. When students graduate, they literally know more than many Chicano/Chicana-studies professors regarding Mexican Indigenous cultures.

20. During the massive 1992 protest against the Columbus Quincentennial in Mexico, Indigenous peoples were joined by the "popular" classes. Even at that point, many de-Indigenized Mexicans were reticent about identifying as mestizos or as Indigenous peoples.

21. Carlos Ometochtzin—grandson of Nezahualcoyotl (famed Mexica poet) and son of Nezahualpilli—was burned at the stake for keeping codices, and more unforgivably, for not believing in the centrality of the Catholic faith (Gruzinski 1993: 15–16).

22. Mendieta ([1595–1596] 1997) cautions regarding the people and their songs: "It is much to be advised that they not be allowed to perform the ancient songs, because all of these are filled with memories of idolatry, or be allowed to perform them with diabolical or suspicious insignias which represent the same" (translation cited in Bierhorst 2009: 210).

23. I first saw this play when my aunt, who was mayor of Tepalcingo, Morelos, a town purportedly four thousand years old, took me to an Indigenous festival in nearby Huazulco.

24. Martha Ramirez noted that the Mascarones, a theater group from Mexico, of which she was a member, performed *Chilam Balaam de Chumayel*, a play regarding the Maya creation of the universe (personal communication, December 21, 2007).

Chapter 6

1. Theologian Jeanette Rodriguez wrote: "It is impossible to date the end of the conquest, because the psychological process is ongoing and changes with every new contact" (1994: 2).

2. The death of Cuauhtemoc continues to stir passion among Indigenous/Mexican peoples because he was tortured and then hung from a tree. Before Hernán Cortés hanged him and two other Indigenous leaders, the three were baptized, thus "saved" (*Crónica Mexicáyotl* [1576] 1998).

Epilogue

1. See, for example, the Arizona Recovered Human Remains Project (Coalición de Derechos Humanos 2013).

2. The Women's Revolutionary Law was revealed to the world on January 1, 1994, at the beginning of the Zapatista uprising. It has ten edicts (Ortiz 2001).

3. Tonatierra has represented the voices of Indigenous Chicanos at national and international Indigenous gatherings for a generation. La Red Xicana has fulfilled a similar role for women since 1997.

4. By Tonatierra, at the closing plenary of the third Continental Summit of Abyayala in Iximche, Guatemala.

5. Interview with Tupac Enrique Acosta, March 13, 2013.

6. Though the MAS struggle is ongoing, with constant developments, a good summation can be found in R. Rodríguez 2012b.

7. While invoking Greco-Roman culture is one of Superintendent Horne's staples, one of his most memorable references to it came in a speech before the arch-conservative Heritage Foundation (Horne 2007).

8. For a more in-depth view of the Maya-Nahua curriculum within MAS, read R. Rodríguez and N. Gonzalez 2012.

9. Though HB 2281 was signed by the governor, supporters of the MAS program do not recognize it as a law (Arizona Revised Statutes §§15-111 and 15-112) because it is both unconstitutional and in violation of virtually every international human-rights treaty and convention that safeguards Indigenous and other peoples' right to education, history, culture, language, and identity.

10. Five books and one video by me were part of the MAS curriculum. The weekly syndicated Column of the Americas (Universal Press Syndicate), cowritten by Patrisia Gonzales and me, was also an integral part of the curriculum.

11. Most of those arrested were students, ranging from middle-school students to university students, plus two University of Arizona faculty, including myself.

12. The concept of *running epistemology* was birthed through these runs (R. Rodríguez 2012a).

13. Based on Horne's public statements, an argument can be made that he and his supporters object to the teaching of In Lak'ech not because of its content but because it does not emanate from the Judeo-Christian or Greco-Roman traditions of the West.

14. This is similar to what Andrea Smith describes: "This colonial system is based on 4 pillars: taking the land; use of force; killing of culture; and control of mind, body, and spirit" (2005: 189). She argues that in attempts to eradicate Indigenous cultures, women are always primary targets. I contend that this is particularly true of attempts to eradicate maíz culture.

15. Dr. Lopez first described this in public at the symposium Tlakatl: What It Means to Be Human symposium, November 19, 2013, University of Arizona.

16. The nine treaties and conventions are listed in R. Rodríguez 2012b.

17. In February 2013, a New Mexico state senator suggesting banning the MAS books from New Mexico schools. In March 2013, two bills were also proposed in the Texas state legislature to disallow Mexican American and African American as core classes in Texas university classrooms. Instead, a mass movement in support of MAS resulted in the Texas Education Agency issuing Proclamation 2016, which calls for new ethnic-studies textbooks and, in effect, encourages the teaching of ethnic studies statewide.

References

Codices and other Indigenous texts are cited by name. Often, either the authors are unknown or non-Indigenous authors have been credited with works that are clearly Indigenous. Most codices utilized for this book are from the 1500s–1600s era, though most were not published until the nineteenth or twentieth centuries. The knowledge, in most cases, is pre-Columbian in nature, though there is clear evidence of European influence. The colonial-era chronicles by various named authors likewise incorporate Indigenous knowledge.

Abarca, Meredith E. 2006. *Voices in the Kitchen: Views of Food and the World from Working-Class Mexican and Mexican American Women*. College Station, TX: Texas A & M University Press.

Acosta, José de. (1604) 1970. *The Natural and Moral History of the Indies*. Vol. 2, *The Moral History*. Trans. Edward Grimston. Ed. Clements R. Markham. Reprint, New York: Burt Franklin.

Acuña, Rodolfo. 1971. *A Mexican American Chronicle*. New York: American Book Company.

———. 1999. *Occupied America*. 4th edition. Upper Saddle River, NJ: Pearson Education.

Adorno, Rolena. 2000. *Guaman Poma: Writing and Resistance in Colonial Peru*. Austin, TX: University of Texas Press.

Aguirre Beltrán, Gonzalo. 1946. *La Población Negra de México, 1519–1810: Estudio Etno-histórico*. Mexico City: Fuente Cultural.

———. 1958. *Cuijla: Esbozo Etnográfico de un Pueblo Negro*. Mexico City: Fondo de Cultura Económica, Sección de Obras de Antropología.

Aldama, Arturo J. 2001. *Disrupting Savagism: Intersecting Chicana/o, Mexican Immigrant, and Native American Struggles for Self-Representation*. Durham, NC: Duke University Press.

Alurista (Alberto Urrea). 1970. "El Plan Espiritual de Aztlan." *Aztlan: Chicano Journal of the Social Sciences and the Arts* 1: 1.

Alvarado Peralta, Felipe. 1992. *Ce-Acatl Topiltzin Quetzalcoatl*. Mexico City: Juan Anzaldo Meneses.

Anales de los Cakchiqueles. (1571) 1972. Francisco Hernández Arana Xajilá and Francisco Díaz Gebuta Quej. Ed. Manuel Galich. Trans. Adrián Recinos. Havana: Casa de las Americas.

Anales de Tlatelolco. (1528) 1948. *Unos Anales Históricos de la Nación Mexicana y Códice de Tlatelolco.* Ed. Heinrich Berlin. Mexico City: Porrúa.

Anaya, Rudolfo. 1989. "Aztlán: A Homeland Without Borders." In Anaya and Lomelí 1989: 230–41.

———, and Francisco Lomelí, eds. 1989. *Aztlán: Essays on the Chicano Homeland.* Albuquerque, NM: Academia/El Norte.

Anderson, Benedict. 1991. *Imagined Communities: Reflections on the Origin and Spread of Nationalism.* London: Verso Books.

Anzaldúa, Gloria. 1987. *Borderlands/La Frontera: The New Mestiza.* San Francisco: Aunt Lute Books.

Asturias, Miguel Ángel. (1949) 1988. *Men of Maize.* New York: Verso Books.

Aubin Codex. (1576) 1963. *Historia de la Nación Mexicana: Reproducción a Todo Color del Códice de 1576.* Ed. and trans. Charles E. Dibble. Madrid: Ediciones José Porrúa Turanzas.—1980. *Códice Aubin: Manuscrito Azteca de la Biblioteca Real de Berlin; Anales en Mexicano y Geroglíficos Desde la Salida de las Tribus de Aztlán Hasta la Muerte de Cuauhtémoc.* Trans. Bernardino de Jesús Quiroz. Mexico City: Editorial Innovación.

Balderrama, Francisco E., and Raymond Rodríguez. 1995. *A Decade of Betrayal: Mexican Repatriation in the 1930s.* Albuquerque, NM: University of New Mexico Press.

Baldiano Codex. (1552) 2002. Martín de la Cruz. Mexico City: Instituto Nacional de Antropología e Historia.

Barreiro, José, ed. 1989. *Indian Corn of the Americas: Gift to the World.* Published as *Northeast Indian Quarterly* 6.

Barthes, Roland. 1967. *Elements of Semiology.* New York: Noonday Press.

Barton, C. Michael, Geoffrey A. Clark, David R. Yesner, and Georges A. Pearson. 2004. *The Settlement of the American Continents: A Multidisciplinary Approach to Human Biogeography.* Tucson, AZ: University of Arizona Press.

Bebout, Lee. 2011. *Mythohistorical Interventions: The Chicano Movement and Its Legacies.* Minneapolis, MN: University of Minnesota Press.

Berger, Thomas R. 1991. *A Long and Terrible Shadow: White Values, Native Rights in the Americas, 1492–1992.* Vancouver, BC, Canada: Douglas & McIntyre.

Bierhorst, John. 2009. *Ballads of the Lords of New Spain.* Austin, TX: University of Texas Press.

Billig, Michael. 1995. *Banal Nationalism.* London: Sage.

Blaut, James Morris. 1993. *The Colonizer's Model of the World: Geographical Diffusionism and Eurocentric History.* New York: Guilford Press.

Bonfil Batalla, Guillermo. 1996. *México Profundo: Reclaiming a Civilization.* Trans. Philip Adams Dennis. Austin, TX: University of Texas Press.

Boone, Elizabeth Hill. 1998. "Maps of Territory, History, and Community in Aztec Mexico." In *Cartographic Encounters: Perspectives on Native American Mapmaking and Map Use,* ed. G. Malcolm Lewis: 113–33. Chicago: University of Chicago Press.

———. 2000. *Stories in Red and Black: Pictorial Histories of the Aztec and Mixtec.* Austin, TX: University of Texas Press.

———. 2005. "In Tlamatinime: The Wise Men and Women of Aztec Mexico." In *Painted Books and Indigenous Knowledge in Mesoamerica: Manuscript Studies in Honor of Mary Elizabeth Smith*, ed. Elizabeth Hill Boone: 9–25. New Orleans, LA: Middle American Research Institute.

———, and Walter D. Mignolo. 1994. *Writing Without Words: Alternative Literacies in Mesoamerica and the Andes.* Durham, NC: Duke University Press.

Boren, Kerry Ross, and Lisa Lee Boren. 1998. *The Gold of Carre-Shinob.* Springville, UT: Bonneville Books.

Borgia Codex. (Pre-Columbian) 1993. *A Full-Color Restoration of the Ancient Mexican Manuscript.* Ed. G. Diaz and A. Rogers. New York: Dover.

Boturini Benaducci, Lorenzo. (1746a) 1990. *Historia General de la América Septentrional.* Ed. Manuel Ballesteros Gaibrois. Mexico City: Instituto de Investigaciones Históricas, Universidad Nacional Autónoma de México.

———. 1746b. *Idea de una Nueva Historia General de la América Septentrional.* Madrid: En la Imprenta de Juan de Zúñiga.

Boturini Codex. (1530–1541) 2000. *La Tira de la Peregrinación.* Ed. Joaquín Galarza and Krystyna Libura. Mexico City: Ediciones Tecolote.

Brah, Avtar. 1996. *Cartographies of Diaspora: Contesting Identities.* New York: Psychology Press.

Brenner, Anita. 2002. *Idols Behind Altars.* Mineola, NY: Dover.

Broda, Johanna. 2000. "Calendrics and Ritual Landscape at Teotihuacan: Themes of Continuity in Mesoamerican 'Cosmovision.'" In *Mesoamerica's Classic Heritage: From Teotihuacan to the Aztecs*, ed. Davíd Carrasco, Lindsay Jones, and Scott Sessions: 397–432. Boulder, CO: University Press of Colorado.

Broyles-González, Yolanda. 1994. *El Teatro Campesino: Theater in the Chicano Movement.* Austin, TX: University of Texas Press.

———. 2001a. "Colonizing the Colonizer: The Popular Indianization of Catholicism." In Broyles-González 2001b: 650–65.

———, ed. 2001b. *Re-emerging Native Women of the Americas.* Dubuque, IA: Kendall/Hunt.

Buelna, Eustaquio. 1887. *Peregrinación de los Aztecas y Nombres Geográficos Indígenas de Sinaloa.* Mexico City: Tipografía Literaria de Filomena Mata.

Buisseret, David. 1998. "Meso-American and Spanish Cartography: An Unusual Example of Syncretic Development." In *The Mapping of the Entradas into the Greater Southwest*, ed. Dennis Reinhartz and Gerald Saxon: 30–55. Norman, OK: University of Oklahoma Press.

Bulnes, Francisco. 1899. *El Porvenir de las Naciones Hispanoamericanas ante las Conquistas Recientes de Europa y los Estados Unidos.* Mexico City: M. Nava.

Cajete, Gregory. 2000. *Native Science: Natural Laws of Interdependence.* Santa Fe, NM: Clear Light.

———. 2005. *Spirit of the Game: An Indigenous Wellspring.* Skyland, NC: Kivaki Press.

Carey, J. W. 1992. *Communication as Culture: Essays on Media and Society.* Media and Popular Culture 1. New York: Routledge.

Carney, Judith Ann. 2001. *Black Rice: The African Origins of Rice Cultivation in the Americas*. Cambridge, MA: Harvard University Press.

Carrasco, Davíd. 1990. *Religions of Mesoamerica: Cosmovision and Ceremonial Centers*. Long Grove, IL: Waveland Press.

———. 1999. *City of Sacrifice: The Aztec Empire and the Role of Violence in Civilization*. Boston: Beacon Press.

———. 2000. *Quetzalcoatl and the Irony of Empire*. Chicago: University of Chicago Press.

———, Lindsay Jones, and Scott Sessions. 2000. "Reimagining the Classic Heritage in Mesoamerica." In *Mesoamerica's Classic Heritage: From Teotihuacan to the Aztecs*, ed. Davíd Carrasco, Lindsay Jones, and Scott Sessions: 1–20. Boulder, CO: University Press of Colorado.

Carrasco, Salvador. 1999. *La Otra Conquista*. Carrasco and Domingo Films Production.

Castañeda, Antonia. 2011. "Art, Labor, and the Genius of Women: A Short History of Tamales." In Clark and Tafolla 2011: 15–17.

Chabram-Dernersesian, Angie. 2006. "I Throw Punches for My Race." In *The Chicana/o Cultural Studies Reader*, ed. Angie Chabram-Dernersesian: 165–82. New York: Routledge.

Chavero, Alfredo. 1884. *Mexico a Través de los Siglos*, vol. 1, *Historia Antigua de la Conquista*. Mexico City: Editorial Cumbre.

Chávez, John. 1989. "Aztlán, Cibola, and Frontier New Spain." In Anaya and Lomelí 1989: 49–71.

Cheng, Vincent John. 2004. *Inauthentic: The Anxiety over Culture and Identity*. New Brunswick, NJ: Rutgers University Press.

Christensen, Rosemary. 2002. "Cultural Context and Evaluation: A Balance of Form and Function." Paper delivered to the National Science Foundation, Arlington, VA, April 25.

———. 2004. "Teaching Within the Circle." In *Identifying Race and Transforming Whiteness in the Classroom*, ed. Virginia Lea and Judy Hefland: 171–91. New York: Peter Lang.

Clark, Ellen Riojas, and Carmen Tafolla. 2011. *Tamales, Comadres, and the Meaning of Civilization: Secrets, Recipes, History, Anecdotes, and a Lot of Fun*. San Antonio, TX: Wings Press.

Clavigero, Francesco Saverio. (1826) 1964. *Historia Antigua de México*. Mexico City: Editorial Porrúa.

Coalición de Derechos Humanos. 2013. Arizona Recovered Human Remains Project. Accessed March 18. http://derechoshumanosaz.net/projects/arizona-recovered-bodies-project.

Codex Anónimo Mexicano. (1500s) 2005. Ed. R. H. and B. Glass-Coffin. Logan, UT: University of Utah Press.

Codex Borbonicus. (Pre-Columbian) 1979. Francisco del Paso y Troncoso. *Descripción, Historia y Exposición del Códice Borbónico*. Ed. E. T. Hamy. Mexico City: Siglo Veintiuno.

Codex Chimalpahin. (1621) 1997. Domingo de San Antón Muñón Chimalpahin Quauhtlehuanitzin. *Society and Politics in Mexico Tenochtitlan, Tlatelolco, Texcoco, Culhuacan, and Other Nahua Altepetl in Central Mexico.* Ed. and trans. A. J. O. Anderson and S. Schroeder. 2 vols. Norman, OK: University of Oklahoma Press.

Codex Chimalpopoca. (1558) 1945. *Anales de Cuauhtitlán y Leyenda de los Soles.* Trans. Primo Feliciano Velázquez. Mexico City: Imprenta Universitaria.

Codex Cospi. (Pre-Columbian) 1994. Ed. F. Anders, L. Maarten Jansen, and L. G. Reyes. Mexico City: Fondo de Cultura Económica. (Part of Borgia Group.)

Codex Vindobonensis Mexicanus I. (Pre-Columbian) 2007. *La Creación del Mundo.* Ed. Manuel A. Hermann Lejarazu and Krystyna Libura Krystyna. Mexico City: Ediciones Tecolote.

Codex Zouche-Nuttall. (1300s) 1992. *Crónica Mixteca: El Rey 8 Venado, Garra de Jaguar, y la Dinastía de Teozacualco-Zaachila: Libro Explicativo del Llamado Códice Zouche-Nuttall.* Ed. Ferdinand Anders, Maarten Jansen, and Gabina Aurora Pérez Jiménez. Mexico City: Fondo de Cultura Económica.

Cohen, Paul E. 2002. *Mapping the West: America's Westward Movement, 1524–1890.* New York: Rizzoli International.

Coleman, Cynthia-Lou. 1996. "A War of Words: How News Frames Define Legitimacy in a Native Conflict." In *Dressing in Feathers: The Construction of the Indian in American Popular Culture,* ed. S. Elizabeth Bird: 181–93. Boulder, CO: Westview Press.

Colitt, Raymond. 2007. "Brazil's Indians Offended by Pope Comments." *Reuters,* May 14. http://www.reuters.com/article/2007/05/14/us-pope-brazil-indians-idUSN 1428799220070514.

Contreras, Sheila Marie. 2008. *Blood Lines: Myth, Indigenism, and Chicana/o Literature.* Austin, TX: University of Texas Press.

Cooper Alarcón, Daniel. 1997. *The Aztec Palimpsest: Mexico in the Modern Imagination.* Tucson, AZ: University of Arizona Press.

Cornelius, Carol. 1999. *Iroquois Corn in a Culture-Based Curriculum: A Framework for Respectfully Teaching About Cultures.* Albany, NY: SUNY Press.

Cortés, Hernán. (1500s) 1990. *Como Conquisté a los Aztecas.* With Armando Ayala Anguiano. Mexico City: Editorial Diana.

Craib, Raymond B. 2004. *Cartographic Mexico: A History of State Fixations and Fugitive Landscapes.* Durham, NC: Duke University Press.

Crónica Mexicáyotl. (1576) 1998. Fernando Alvarado Tezozomoc. Trans. Adrián León. Mexico City: Universidad Nacional Autónoma de México.

Cutler, Charles L. 1994. *O Brave New Words! Native American Loanwords in Current English.* Norman, OK: University of Oklahoma Press.

Davalos, Karen Mary. 2001. *Exhibiting Mestizaje: Mexican (American) Museums in the Diaspora.* Albuquerque, NM: University of New Mexico Press.

Deely, John N. 1990. *Basics of Semiotics.* Bloomington, IN: Indiana University Press.

de la Peña, Francisco. 2002. *Los Hijos del Sexto Sol: Un Estudio Etnopsicológico del Movimiento de la Mexicanidad.* Mexico City: INAH.

del Castillo, Cristóbal. (1606) 1991. *Historia de la Venida de los Mexicanos y Otros Pueblos e Historia de la Conquista.* Trans. Federico Navarette Linares. Mexico City: Instituto Nacional de Antropología e Historia.

De León, Arnoldo. 2002. *Racial Frontiers: Africans, Chinese, and Mexicans in Western America, 1848–1890.* Albuquerque, NM: University of New Mexico Press.

Delgado, Richard, and Jean Stefancic. 1998. "Racial Depiction in American Law and Culture." In *The Latino/a Condition: A Critical Reader,* ed. Richard Delgado and Jean Stefancic: 209–14. New York: New York University Press.

Delgado, Vivian. 2007. *You're Not Indian, You're Mexican.* Philadelphia: Turtle Island Press.

Deloria, Vine, Jr. 1973. *God Is Red.* New York: Grossett & Dunlap.

———. 2002. *Evolution, Creationism, and Other Modern Myths: A Critical Inquiry.* Golden, CO: Fulcrum.

DeMeo, James. 2005. "Peaceful Versus Warlike Societies in Pre-Columbian America: What Do Archaeology and Anthropology Tell Us?" In *Unlearning the Language of Conquest,* ed. W. Topa: 134–52. Austin, TX: University of Texas Press.

Díaz Balsera, Viviana. 2005. *The Pyramid Under the Cross: Franciscan Discourses of Evangelization and the Nahua Christian Subject in Sixteenth-Century Mexico.* Tucson, AZ: University of Arizona Press.

Domke, David, Kelley McCoy, and Marcos Torres. 2003. "News Media, Immigration, and the Priming of Racial Perspectives." In *Brown and Black Communication,* ed. Diana Rios and A. N. Mohamed: 123–42. Westport, CT: Praeger.

Dresden Codex. (Pre-Columbian) 1972. *A Commentary on the Dresden Codex: A Maya Hieroglyphic Book.* Ed. Eric S. Thompson. Philadelphia: American Philosophical Society.

Durán, Diego. (1581) 1967. *Historia de las Indias de Nueva España.* Ed. Ángel Garibay. Mexico City: Editorial Porrúa.

Duran, Eduardo, and Bonnie Duran. 1995. *Native American Postcolonial Psychology.* New York: SUNY Press.

Dussel, Enrique D. 1995. *The Invention of the Americas: Eclipse of "the Other" and the Myth of Modernity.* New York: Continuum.

Elizondo, Virgilio. 1988. *The Future Is Mestizo.* New York: Crossroad.

Entman, Robert M., and Andrew Rojecki. 2000. *The Black Image in the White Mind: Media and Race in America.* Chicago: University of Chicago Press.

Esteva, Gustavo. 2003a. "Los Árboles de las Culturas Mexicanas." In Esteva and Marielle 2003: 17–28.

———. 2003b. "Las Figuraciones Actuales de Nuestras Culturas." In Esteva and Marielle 2003: 56–58.

———, and Catherine Marielle. 2003. *Sin Maíz No Hay País.* Mexico City: Culturas Populares de México.

Farmer, Gary, dir. 1998. *The Gift.* Montreal: National Board of Canada.

Ferrero, Pat, Mollie Gregory, Ronnie Gilbert, and Emory Sekaquaptewa. 2008. *Hopi: Songs of the Fourth World.* Harriman, NY: New Day Films.

Fields, Virginia M., and Victor Zamudio-Taylor. 2001. *The Road to Aztlan: Art from a Mythic Homeland.* Los Angeles: Los Angeles County Museum.

Figueroa, Alfredo. 2002. *Ancient Footprints of the Colorado River: La Cuna de Aztlan.* National City, CA: Aztec.

Fixico, Donald. 2003. *The American Indian Mind in a Linear World: American Indian Studies and Traditional Knowledge.* New York: Routledge.

Florentine Codex. (1577) 1961, 1976. Bernardino de Sahagún. *General History of the Things of New Spain,* bk. 2, *Earthly Things* (1976), and bk. 10, *The People* (1961). Ed. Charles Dibble and Arthur Anderson. Mexico City: University of Utah.

Florescano, Enrique. 1994. *Memory, Myth, and Time in Mexico: From the Aztecs to Independence.* Austin, TX: University of Texas Press.

———. 1999. *Memoria Indígena.* Mexico City: Taurus.

———. 2002. *Historia de las Historias de la Nación Mexicana.* Mexico City: Taurus.

———. 2003. "Imágenes y Significado del Dios del Maíz." In Esteva and Marielle 2003: 36–55.

———. 2004. *La Bandera Mexicana: Breve Historia de Su Formación y Simbolismo.* Mexico City: Fondo de Cultura Económica USA.

———. 2006. *National Narratives in Mexico: A History.* Norman, OK: University of Oklahoma Press.

Forbes, Jack. 1961–1962. "The Mexican Heritage of Aztlan (The Southwest)." Mimeograph, Native American Movement.

———. 1973. *Aztecas del Norte: The Chicanos of Aztlan.* Greenwich, CT: Fawcett.

———. 2007. *The American Discovery of Europe.* Urbana, IL: University of Illinois Press.

———. 2011. *Columbus and Other Cannibals: The Wetiko Disease of Exploitation, Imperialism, and Terrorism.* New York: Seven Stories Press.

Freire, Paulo. 1970. *Pedagogy of the Oppressed.* Trans. Myra Bergman Ramos. New York: Continuum.

Fussell, Betty Harper. 1992. *The Story of Corn.* Albuquerque, NM: University of New Mexico Press.

Galarza, Joaquín. 1986. *Tlacuilo.* Mexico City: Azteca Films.

———. 1992. *In Amoxtli, in Tlacatl: El Libro, el Hombre, Códices y Vivencias.* Mexico City: Tava Editorial.

———, and Krystyna Libura. 2000. *Para Leer la Tira de la Peregrinación.* Ediciones Tecolote.

———, and Aurore Monod-Becquelin. 1992. *Códices Testerianos: Catecísmos Indígenas: El Pater Noster.* Mexico City: Editorial TAVA.

Gante, Pedro de. (1558) 1970. *Catecismo de la Doctrina Cristiana.* Madrid: Ministerio de Educación y Ciencia.

García, Gregorio. (1500s) 1981. *Origen de los Indios de el Nuevo Mundo e Indias Occidentales.* Ed. Franklin Pease. Mexico City: Fondo de Cultura Económica.

García Cook, Ángel. 1997. "Richard Stockton MacNeish y el Origen de la Agricultura." *Arqueología Mexicana* 5.25: 40–43.

Garcilaso de la Vega. (1609) 1976. *Comentarios Reales de los Incas.* Lima: Editores de Cultura Popular.

Gartner, William Gustav. 1998. "Mapmaking in the Central Andes." In *The History of Cartography,* ed. J. B. Harley and David Woodward, vol. 2, bk. 3: 257–326. Chicago: University of Chicago Press.

George-Kanentiio, Doug. 2000. *Iroquois Culture and Commentary*. Santa Fe, NM: Clear Light.

———. 2006. *Iroquois on Fire: A Voice from the Mohawk Nation*. Westport, CT: Praeger.

Girard, Rafael. 1962. *Los Mayas Eternos*. Mexico City: Antigua Librería Robredo.

———. 1966. *Los Mayas: Su Civilización, Su Historia, Sus Vinculaciones Continentales*. Mexico City: Libro Mex.

Glaser, Lynn. 1989. *America on Paper: The First Hundred Years*. Philadelphia: Associated Antiquaries.

Goetz, Delia, and Sylvanus G. Morley, trans. 2003. *Popol Vuh*. Mineola, NY: Courier Dover.

Gómara, Francisco López de. (1500s) 2000. *Crónica de la Nueva España: La Conquista de México*. Ed. José Luis de Rojas. Madrid: Dastin.

Gómez-Quiñones, Juan. 2012. *Indigenous Quotient/Stalking Words: American Indian Heritage as Future*. San Antonio, TX: Aztlan Libre Press.

Gonzales, Patrisia. 2003. *The Mud People: Chronicles, Testimonios, and Remembrances*. San Jose, CA: Chusma House.

———. 2007. "Birth Is a Ceremony: Story and Formulas of Thought in Indigenous Medicine and Indigenous Communications." PhD dissertation, University of Wisconsin, Madison.

———. 2012. *Red Medicine: Traditional Indigenous Rites of Birthing and Healing*. Tucson, AZ: University of Arizona Press.

Gonzales, Rodolfo. 2001. *Message to Aztlán: Selected Writings of Rodolfo "Corky" Gonzales*. Ed. Antonio Esquibel. Houston, TX: Arte Público Press.

Gruzinski, Serge. 1993. *The Conquest of Mexico: The Incorporation of Indian Societies into the Western World, 16th–18th Centuries*. Cambridge: Polity Press.

———. 1994. *El Águila y la Sibila: Frescos Indios de México*. Barcelona: M. Moleiro.

———. 2001. *Images at War: Mexico from Columbus to Blade Runner (1492–2019)*. Durham, NC: Duke University Press Books.

Gutiérrez, Ramón A. 2000. "Chicano History: Paradigm Shifts and Shifting Boundaries." In *Voices of a New Chicana/o History*, ed. Refugio I. Rochín and Dennis N. Valdés: 91–114. East Lansing, MI: Michigan State University Press.

Harding, Sandra G., ed. 1987. *Feminism and Methodology*. Milton Keynes, UK: Open University Press.

Harjo, Suzan Shown. 2005. "Just Good Sports: The Impact of 'Native' References in Sports on Native Youth and What Some Decolonizers Have Done About It." In Wilson and Yellow Bird 2005: 31–52.

Hernández-Ávila, Inés. 2000. "Mediations of the Spirit." In *Native American Spirituality*, ed. Lee Irwin: 11–36. Lincoln, NE: University of Nebraska Press.

Herrejón, Carlos. 1985. *Morelos: Antología Documental*. Mexico City: Secretaría de Educación Pública.

Herrera, Antonio de. (1605–1615) 1945. *Historia General de los Hechos de los Castellanos en las Islas y Tierra del Mar Océano*. 5 vols. Asunción, Paraguay: Editorial Guarania.

Heyden, Doris. 2000. "From Teotihuacan to Tenochtitlan: City Planning, Caves, and Streams of Red and Blue Waters." In *Mesoamerica's Classic Heritage: From*

Teotihuacan to the Aztecs, ed. Davíd Carrasco, Lindsay Jones, and Scott Sessions: 165–84. Boulder, CO: University Press of Colorado.

Hill, Jane H., and Kenneth C. Hill. 1986. *Speaking Mexicano: Dynamics of Syncretic Language in Central Mexico*. Tucson, AZ: University of Arizona Press.

Historia de la Nación Chichimeca. (1610–1640) 2000. Fernando de Alva Ixtlilxochitl. Madrid: Dastin.

Historia de los Mexicanos por Sus Pinturas. (1531) 1965. Ed. Ángel Garibay. Mexico City: Editorial Porrúa.

Historia Tolteca-Chichimeca. (1550) 1989. Ed. Paul Kirchhoff, Lina Odena Güemes, and Luis Reyes García. Mexico City: Fondo de Cultura Económica.

Hobsbawm, Eric, and Terence Ranger, eds. 1984. *The Invention of Tradition*. Cambridge: Cambridge University Press.

Horne, Tom. 2007. "A State Perspective on the Past and Future of No Child Left Behind." Speech given April 24 to the Heritage Foundation. http://www.heritage.org/research/lecture/a-state-perspective-on-the-past-and-future-of-no-child-left-behind.

Iltis, Hugh H. 2000. "Homeotic Sexual Translocations and the Origin of Maize (*Zea mays*, Poaceae): A New Look at an Old Problem." *Economic Botany* 54: 7–42.

Jennings, Francis. 1976. *The Invasion of America*. New York: Norton.

Jensen, Klaus Bruhn. 1995. *The Social Semiotics of Mass Communication*. London: Sage.

Johnson, Jay T., Renee Pualani Louis, and Albertus Hadi Pramono. 2006. "Facing the Future: Encouraging Critical Cartographic Literacies in Indigenous Communities." *ACME: An International E-Journal for Critical Geographies* 4: 80–98.

Johnson, Melissa A., Prabu David, and Dawn Huey-Ohlsson. 2003. "Beauty in Brown: Skin Color in Latina Magazines." In *Brown and Black Communication*, ed. Diana Rios and A. N. Mohamed: 159–74. Westport, CT: Praeger.

Johnson, Tim. 2013. "For Dark-Skinned Mexicans, Taint of Discrimination Lingers." *McClatchy*, August 22. http://www.mcclatchydc.com/2013/08/22/200057/for-dark-skinned-mexicans-taint.html.

Keski-Säntti, Jouko, Ulla Lehtonen, Pauli Sivonen, and Ville Vuolanto. 2003. "The Drum as Map." *Imago Mundi* 55: 120–25.

Klor de Alva, Jorge. 1989. "Aztlán, Borinquen, and Hispanic Nationalism in the United States." In Anaya and Lomelí 1989: 135–71.

———. 1997. "The Invention of Ethnic Origins and the Negotiation of Latino Identity, 1969–1981." In *Challenging Fronteras: Structuring Latina and Latino Lives in the US*, ed. Mary Romero, Pierrette Hondagneu-Sotelo, and Vilma Ortiz: 55–74. New York: Psychology Press.

Kurath, Gertrude Prokosch. 1964. *Dances of Anahuac: The Choreography and Music of Precortesian Dances*. Chicago: Aldine.

Lakoff, George. 2002. *Moral Politics: How Liberals and Conservatives Think*. Chicago: University of Chicago Press.

———. 2004. *Don't Think of an Elephant: Know Your Values and Frame the Debate: The Essential Guide for Progressives*. White River Junction, VT: Chelsea Green.

Landa, Diego de. (1566) 1938. *Relación de las Cosas de Yucatán*. Ed. Héctor Pérez Martínez. Mexico City: Editorial Pearo Robredo.

Las Casas, Bartolomé de. (1552) 1974. *The Devastation of the Indies: A Brief Account.* Trans. Herma Briffault. New York: Seabury Press.

———. (1559) 1993. *Los Indios de México y Nueva España: Antología.* Mexico City: Editorial Porrúa.

———. (1500s) 1985. *Historia de las Indias.* Vol. 1. Caracas: Fundación Biblioteca Ayacucho.

Leal, Luis. 1989. "In Search of Aztlán." In Anaya and Lomelí 1989: 6–13.

Lekson, Stephen H. 1999. *The Chaco Meridian: Centers of Political Power in the Ancient Southwest.* Walnut Creek, CA: Altamira Press.

León, Nicolás. 1924. *Las Castas del México Colonial o Nueva España: Noticias Etno-antropológicas.* Mexico City: Talleres Gráficos del Museo Nacional de Arqueología, Historia y Etnografía.

León-Portilla, Miguel. 1980. *Native Mesoamerican Spirituality: Ancient Myths, Discourses, Stories, Doctrines, Hymns, Poems from the Aztec, Yucatec, Quiche-Maya, and Other Sacred Traditions.* New York: Paulist Press.

———. 1985. *Los Franciscanos Vistos por el Hombre Náhuatl: Testimonios Indígenas del Siglo XVI.* Mexico City: Instituto de Investigaciones Históricas, Universidad Nacional Autónoma.

———. 2003a. *Nuestros Poetas Aztecas/Our Aztec Poets.* Mexico City: Diana/Mexico.

———, ed. 2003b. *Cantos y Crónicas del México Antiguo.* Madrid: Dastin.

———. 2005. *Francisco Tenamaztle: Primer Guerrillero de América, Defensor de los Derechos Humanos.* Mexico City: Editorial Diana.

Lewis, G. Malcolm. 1998. "Maps, Mapmaking, and Map Use by Native North Americans." In *The History of Cartography*, ed. J. B. Harley and David Woodward, vol. 2, bk. 2: 51–182. Chicago: University of Chicago Press.

Long-Solís, Janet. 1998. *Capsicum y Cultura: La Historia del Chilli.* Mexico City: Fondo de Cultura Económica USA.

López, Alma. 2011. "It's Not About the Santa in My *Fe*, but the Santa Fe in My *Santa*." In *Our Lady of Controversy*, ed. Alicia Gaspar de Alba and Alma López, 249–292. Austin, TX: University of Texas Press.

López Austin, Alfredo. 1993. *The Myths of the Opossum: Pathways of Mesoamerican Mythology.* Trans. Bernard R. Ortiz de Montellano and Thelma Ortiz de Montellano. Albuquerque, NM: University of New Mexico Press.

———. 1997. *Tamoanchan, Tlalocan: Places of Mist.* Trans. Bernard R. Ortiz de Montellano and Thelma Ortiz de Montellano. Niwot, CO: University Press of Colorado.

———. 2003. "Cuatro Mitos Mesoamericanos del Maíz." In Esteva and Marielle 2003: 29–35.

López Rosado, Diego G. 1940. *Atlas Histórico-Geográfico de México.* Mexico City: n.p.

Luna, Jennie Marie. 2011. "Danza Mexica: Indigenous Identity, Spirituality, Activism, and Performance." PhD dissertation, University of California, Davis.

Macias, Ysidro. 2007. "Feathered Serpent: A Journey Through Chicano Serpentine Philosophy." Ms., Honolulu.

Maestas, Enrique. 2003. "Culture and History of Native American Peoples of South Texas." PhD dissertation, University of Texas, Austin.

Mann, Charles C. 2005. *1491: New Revelations of the Americas Before Columbus*. New York: Knopf.

Magaloni Duarte, Ignacio. 1969. *Educadores del Mundo: Mayas, Toltecas, Nahuas, Quiches, Quechua, Incas*. Mexico City: Costa Amic.

Mangelsdorf, Paul Christoph. 1974. *Corn: Its Origin, Evolution, and Improvement*. Cambridge, MA: Belknap Press of Harvard University Press.

Mansfield, Portia. 1953. "The Conchero Dancers of Mexico." PhD dissertation, New York University, New York.

Mariscal, George. 2005. *Brown-Eyed Children of the Sun: Lessons from the Chicano Movement, 1965–1975*. Albuquerque, NM: University of New Mexico Press.

Marschall, Wolfgang. 1979. *Influencias Asiáticas en las Culturas de la América Antigua: Estudios de Su Historia*. Mexico City: Ediciones Euroamericanas.

Martinez-Cruz, Paloma. 2011. *Women and Knowledge in Mesoamerica: From East LA to Anahuac*. Tucson, AZ: University of Arizona Press.

Martínez Parédez, Domingo. 1960. *Un Continente y Una Cultura: Unidad Filológica de la América Pre-Hispánica*. Mexico City: Editorial Poesía de América.

———. 1963. *Hunab Ku: Síntesis del Pensamiento Filosófico Maya*. Mexico City: Editorial Orión.

———. 1968. *El Popol Vuh Tiene Razón: Teoría Sobre la Cosmogonía Preamericana*. Mexico City: Orión.

———. 1970. *El Hombre y el Cosmos*. Mexico City: Secretaría de Educación Pública.

———. 1977. *Parapsicología Maya*. Mexico City: Manuel Porrúa.

Melgarejo, V. J. L. 1992. *America Descubre al Viejo Mundo*. Xalapa, Veracruz, Mexico: Gobierno de Estado de Veracruz.

Meltzer, David J. 1999. "North America's Vast Legacy." *Archaeology* 52: 50–59.

Menchaca, Martha. 1998. "Chicano Indianism." In *The Latino/a Condition: A Critical Reader*, ed. Richard Delgado and Jean Stefancic: 387–95. New York: New York University Press.

———. 2000. "History and Anthropology: Conducting Chicano Research." In *Voices of a New Chicana/o History*, ed. Refugio Rochín and Dennis Valdés: 167–82. East Lansing, MI: Michigan State University Press.

———. 2001. *Recovering History, Constructing Race: The Indian, Black, and White Roots of Mexican Americans*. Austin, TX: University of Texas Press.

Mendieta, Jerónimo. (1595–1596) 1997. *Historia Eclesiástica Indiana*. Mexico City: Conaculta.

Mendoza Codex. (1541–1542) 1992. Ed. Frances F. Berdan and Patricia Rieff Anawalt. Berkeley, CA: University of California Press.

Meza Gutiérrez, Arturo. 1993. *Al Otro Lado de las Sombras*. Mexico City: Ediciones Artesanales Malinalli.

Mihesuah, Devon Abbott, and Angela Cavender Wilson, eds. 2004. *Indigenizing the Academy: Transforming Scholarship and Empowering Communities*. Lincoln, NE: University of Nebraska Press.

Mignolo, Walter. 2006. *The Darker Side of the Renaissance: Literacy, Territoriality, and Colonization*. East Lansing, MI: University of Michigan Press.

———. 2012. *Local Histories/Global Designs: Coloniality, Subaltern Knowledges, and Border Thinking.* Princeton, NJ: Princeton University Press.

Montejo, Victor. 2004. "Heart of Heaven, Heart of Earth: The Maya Worldview." In *Native Universe: Voices of Indian America*, ed. Gerald McMaster and Clifford Trafzer: 59–71. Washington, DC: National Museum of the American Indian, Smithsonian Institution, in Association with National Geographic.

Moriarty, Sandra. 2005. "Visual Semiotics Theory." In *Handbook of Visual Communication: Theory, Methods, and Media*, ed. Kenneth L. Smith, Sandra Moriarty, Keith Kenney, and Gretchen Barbatsis: 227–41. Mahwah, NJ: L. Erlbaum.

———, and Lisa Rohe. 2005. "Cultural Palettes in Print Advertising: formative research design method." In *Handbook of Visual Communication: Theory, Methods, and Media*, ed. Kenneth L. Smith, Sandra Moriarty, Keith Kenney, and Gretchen Barbatsis: 117–26. Mahwah, NJ: L. Erlbaum.

———, and Shay Sayre. 2005. "An Intended-Perceived Study Using Visual Semiotics." In *Handbook of Visual Communication: Theory, Methods, and Media*, ed. Kenneth L. Smith, Sandra Moriarty, Keith Kenney, and Gretchen Barbatsis: 243–56. Mahwah, NJ: L. Erlbaum.

Morison, Samuel Eliot. 1971. *The European Discovery of America.* New York: Oxford University Press.

Motolinía, Toribio de Benavente. (1555) 1971. *Memoriales.* Ed. Edmundo O'Gorman. Mexico City: Universidad Nacional Autónoma de México.

Moyers, Bill, and Joseph Campbell. 1991. *The Power of Myth.* New York: Anchor.

Mundy, Barbara. 1996. *The Mapping of New Spain: Indigenous Cartography and the Maps of the Relaciones Gráficas.* Chicago: University of Chicago Press.

Muñoz Camargo, Diego. (1585) 1998. *Historia de Tlaxcala (Ms. 210 de la Biblioteca Nacional de París).* Ed. Luis Reyes García, with Javier Lira Toledo. Tlaxcala, Mexico: Gobierno del Estado de Tlaxcala.

Nabhan, Gary. 2012–2013. "Chapalote Corn—The Oldest Corn in North America Pops Back Up." *Heirloom Gardener*, Winter, 70–71.

Nabokov, Peter. 1998. "Orientations from Their Side: Dimensions of Native American Cartographic Discourse." In *Cartographic Encounters: Perspectives on Native American Mapmaking and Map Use*, ed. G. Malcolm Lewis: 241–69. Chicago: University of Chicago Press.

———. 2002. *A Forest of Time: American Indian Ways of History.* Cambridge: Cambridge University Press.

Nash, June. 1997. "Gendered Deities and the Survival of Culture." *History of Religions* 36: 333–56.

Newcomb, Steven T. 1992. "Five Hundred Years of Injustice: The Legacy of Fifteenth Century Religious Prejudice." *Shaman's Drum*, Fall, 18–20.

———. 2008. *Pagans in the Promised Land.* Golden, CO: Fulcrum.

Nieto-Phillips, John M. 2004. *The Language of Blood: The Making of Spanish-American Identity in New Mexico, 1880s–1930s.* Albuquerque, NM: University of New Mexico Press.

O'Gorman, Edmundo. 1986. *Destierro de Sombras.* Mexico City: Universidad Nacional Autónoma de México.

Olmos, Andrés de. (1547) 1992. *Of the Manners of Speaking that the Old Ones Had.* Ed. Judith Maxwell and Craig Hanson. Salt Lake City, UT: University of Utah Press.

Orozco, Cecilio. 1992. *The Book of the Sun, Tonatiuh.* Fresno, CA: California State University, Fresno.

Orozco y Berra, Manuel, ed. 1944. *Códice Ramírez: Relación del Origen de los Indios que Habitan Esta Nueva Espana, Según Sus Historias.* Mexico City: Editorial Leyenda.

———. (1880) 1954. *Historia Antigua y de las Culturas Aborígenes de México.* Mexico City: Ediciones Fuente Cultural.

Ortiz, Teresa. 2001. *Never Again a World Without Us: Voices of Mayan Women in Chiapas, Mexico.* Washington, DC: Epica Task Force.

Padilla, Genaro. 1989. "Myth and Comparative Cultural Nationalism: The Ideological Uses of Aztlán." In Anaya and Lomelí 1989: 111–34.

Perea, Juan. "Death by English." 1998. In *The Latino/a Condition: A Critical Reader*, ed. Richard Delgado and Jean Stefanic: 359–68. New York: New York University Press.

Pérez, Emma. 1999. *The Decolonial Imaginary: Writing Chicanas into History.* Bloomington, IN: Indiana University Press.

Pérez San Vicente, Guadalupe. 2000. "El Maíz, Nuestra Carne y Sustento." In *Recetario del Maíz*, ed. María Esther Echeverría and Luz Elena Arroyo: 11–20. Mexico City: Conaculta.

Pérez Suárez, Tomás. 1997. "El Dios del Maíz en Mesoamérica." *Arqueología Mexicana* 25: 44–55.

Pérez-Torres, Rafael. 2001. "Refiguring Aztlan." In *The Chicano Studies Reader, 1970–2000: An Anthology of Aztlan*, ed. Chon A. Noriega, Eric Avila, Karen Mary Davalos, Chela Sandoval, and Rafael Pérez-Torres: 213–42. Los Angeles: UCLA Chicano Studies Research Center.

Peterson, Jeanette Favrot. 2005. "Creating the Virgin of Guadalupe: The Cloth, the Artist, and Sources in Sixteenth-Century New Spain." *The Americas* 61: 571–610.

Pewewardy, Cornel. 2005. "Ideology, Power, and the Miseducation of Indigenous Peoples in the United States." In Wilson and Yellow Bird 2005: 135–156.

Pierce, Charles Sanders. 1931. *Collected Papers.* 8 vols. Ed. Charles Hartshorne and Paul Weiss. Cambridge, MA: Harvard University Press.

Pilcher, Jeffrey M. 1998. *Que Vivan los Tamales: Food and the Making of Mexican Identity.* Albuquerque, NM: University of New Mexico Press.

Quiroga, Vasco de. (1535) 1974. *Información en Derecho.* Madrid: Ediciones J. Porrúa Turanzas.

Ramírez Codex. (1500s) 1944. Indigenous Mexican author. *Relación del Origen de los Indios que Habitan Esta Nueva Espana, Según Sus Historias.* Ed. Manuel Orozco y Berra. Mexico City: Editorial Leyenda.

Reissner, Raúl Alcides. 1983. *El Indio en los Diccionarios: Exégesis Léxica de un Estereotipo.* Mexico City: Instituto Nacional Indigenista.

Relación de Tezcoco. (1500s) 1941. Juan Bautista Pomar. *Breve Relación de los Señores de Nueva España; Varias Relaciones Antiguas Siglo XVI.* Mexico City: Editorial Salvador Chávez Hayhoe. (Alonso de Zurita's Relación.)

Rendón, Armando. 1971. *Chicano Manifesto.* New York: Macmillan.

Restall, Matthew. 2003. *Seven Myths of the Spanish Conquest.* New York: Oxford University Press.

Rivas Salmón, Alfonso, and Cecilio Orozco. 1997. *Las Letras del Licenciado Alfonso Rivas Salmón.* San Diego, CA: Marin.

Rodriguez, Jeanette. 1994. *Our Lady of Guadalupe: Faith and Empowerment Among Mexican-American Women.* Albuquerque, NM: University of Texas Press.

Rodríguez, Roberto. 1997. *The X in La Raza II.* Albuquerque: self-published.

———. 2004. "Teo Cintli: Story of the Continent." Video, University of Wisconsin, Madison.

———. 2012a. "Corriendo Educando or Teaching/Learning While Running." *International Journal of Critical Indigenous Studies* 5.1: 79–92.

———. 2012b. "Raza Studies: Inside or Outside of Western Civilization?" *Truthout,* May 6. http://truth-out.org/news/item/8943-raza-studies-inside-or-outside-of-western -civilization.

———, and Patrisia Gonzales. 2002. *Going Back to Where We Came From.* Film. San Antonio, TX: Ozuna Productions.

———, and Patrisia Gonzales. 2004. "The Aztlanahuac Interviews." Contribution to exhibit Aztlanahuac: Mesoamerica in North America, University of California, Los Angeles.

———, and Patrisia Gonzales. 2005. *Amoxtli San Ce Tojuan—We Are One.* Film. Los Angeles: Xicano Records and Film.

———, and Norma Gonzalez. 2012. "Banning the 'Aztec Calendar': Indigenous, Maíz-Based Knowledge at the Heart of Tucson's Mexican American Studies Curriculum and Conflict." *Nakum Journal* 3. http://indigenouscultures.org/ nakumjournal/?p=1244.

Rojas Rabiela, Teresa, and William T. Sanders. 1985. *Historia de la Agricultura Época Prehispánica Siglo XVI.* Mexico City: Instituto Nacional de Antropología e Historia.

Ruiz de Alarcón, Hernando. (1629) 1984. *Treatise on the Heathen Superstitions That Today Live Among the Indians Native to This New Spain.* Trans. and ed. J. Richard Andrews and Ross Hassig. Norman, OK: University of Oklahoma Press.

Sahagún, Bernardino de, ed. (1564) 1944. *Coloquios y Doctrina Christiana.* Mexico City: Editorial Vargas Rea.

———. (1590) 1997. *Primeros Memoriales.* Ed. and trans. Thelma D. Sullivan. Norman, OK: University of Oklahoma Press.

———. (1577) 2010. *Historia General de las Cosas de la Nueva España.* Vol. 1. Barcelona: Linkgua Digital.

Sánchez, Joseph. 1997. *Explorers, Traders, and Slavers: Forging the Old Spanish Trail, 1678–1850.* Salt Lake City, UT: University of Utah Press.

Sánchez Lamego, Miguel A. 1955. *El Primer Mapa General de México Elaborado por un Mexicano.* Mexico City: Instituto Panamericano de Geografía e Historia.

Sando, Joe S., and Herman Agoyo. 2005. *Po'Pay: Leader of the First American Revolution.* Santa Fe, NM: Clear Light.

Sandoval, Marcos. 2003. "El Maíz y los Pueblos Indios." In Esteva and Marielle 2003: 59–66.

Santa Ana, Otto. 2002. *Brown Tide Rising: Metaphors of Latinos in Contemporary American Public Discourse*. Austin, TX: University of Texas Press.

Santos, Boaventura de Sousa. 2007. "Beyond Abyssal Thinking: From Global Lines to Ecologies of Knowledges." *Review, a Journal of the Fernand Braudel Center* 30: 45–89.

Sarmiento Donate, A., ed. 1988. *De las Leyes de Indias: Antología de la Recopilación de 1681*. Mexico City: Secretaría de Educación Pública.

Schele, Linda, and David A. Freidel. 1990. *A Forest of Kings: The Untold Story of the Ancient Maya*. New York: William Morrow.

Scott, James C. 1990. *Domination and the Arts of Resistance: Hidden Transcripts*. New Haven, CT: Yale University Press.

Séjourné, Laurette. 1962. *El Universo de Quetzalcóatl*. Mexico City: Fondo de Cultura Económica.

Silva Galeana, Librado. 1991. *Huehuetlahtolli: Testimonios de la Antigua Palabra*. Mexico City: Fondo de Cultura Económica, Secretaría de Educación Pública.

Siméon, Rémi. 2004. *Diccionario de la Lengua Náhuatl o Mexicana*. Mexico City: Siglo Veintiuno.

Smith, Andrea. 2005. *Conquest: Sexual Violence and American Indian Genocide*. Cambridge, MA: South End Press.

Smith, Linda Tuhiwai. 1999. *Decolonizing Methodologies: Research and Indigenous Peoples*. London: Zed Books.

Steele, Jeffrey. 1996. "Reduced to Images: American Indians in Nineteenth-Century Advertising." In *Dressing in Feathers: The Construction of the Indian in American Popular Culture*, ed. S. Elizabeth Bird: 45–64. Boulder, CO: Westview Press.

Stone, Martha. 1975. *At the Sign of Midnight: The Concheros Dance Cult of Mexico*. Tucson, AZ: University of Arizona Press.

Sugiyama, Saburo. 2000. "Teotihuacan as an Origin for Postclassic Feathered Serpent Symbolism." In *Mesoamerica's Classic Heritage: From Teotihuacan to the Aztecs*, ed. Davíd Carrasco, Lindsay Jones, and Scott Sessions: 117–43. Boulder, CO: University Press of Colorado.

Sullivan, Thelma D., trans. 1994. *A Scattering of Jades: Stories, Poems, and Prayers of the Aztecs*. Ed. Timothy J. Knab. Tucson, AZ: University of Arizona Press.

Tapia, Emily McClung de. 1997. "La Domesticación del Maiz." *Arqueología Mexicana* 5.25: 34–39.

Tedlock, Dennis. 1996. *Popol Vuh: The Mayan Book of the Dawn of Life*. New York: Touchstone Books.

Thomas, Alfred Barnaby. 1982. *Alonso de Posada Report, 1686*. Pensacola, FL: Perdido Bay Press.

Thompson, George. 1992. *Lost Treasures on the Old Spanish Trail*. Salt Lake City, UT: Publisher's Press.

Tilley, Virginia. 2005. *Seeing Indians: A Study of Race, Nation, and Power in El Salvador*. Albuquerque: University of New Mexico Press.

Titu Cusi (Diego de Castro Yupangui). (1570) 2005. *Titu Cusi: A 16th Century Account of the Conquest*. Cambridge, MA: Harvard University Press.

Torquemada, Juan de. (1615) 1975. *Monarquía Indiana*. Mexico City: Universidad Nacional Autónoma de México.

Toscano, Salvador. 1953. *Cuauhtémoc.* Mexico City: Fondo de Cultura Económica.

Trejo, Arnulfo D. 1980. "Of Books and Libraries." In *The Chicanos: As We See Ourselves,* ed. Arnulfo D. Trejo: 167–86. Tucson, AZ: University of Arizona Press.

Trouillot, Michel-Rolph. 1995. *Silencing the Past.* Boston: Beacon Press.

Turner, Victor. 1974. *Dramas, Fields, and Metaphors: Symbolic Action in Human Society.* Ithaca, NY: Cornell University Press.

Valadés, Diego. (1579) 1989. *Retórica Cristiana.* Mexico City: Universidad Nacional Autónoma de México.

Valdés, Dennis Nodín. 2000. "Region, Nation, and World-System: Perspectives on Midwestern Chicana/o History." In *Voices of a New Chicana/o History,* ed. Refugio Rochín and Dennis Valdés: 115–40. East Lansing, MI: Michigan State University Press.

———, and Refugio Rochín. 2000. "The Fruitless Search for a Chicana/o Paradigm." In *Voices of a New Chicana/o History,* ed. Refugio Rochín and Dennis Valdés: vii–ix. East Lansing, MI: Michigan State University Press.

Valdez, Luis. 1973. *Pensamiento Serpentino: A Chicano Approach to the Theater of Reality.* N.p.: Cucaracha.

Vasallo, Miguel. 2004. "Gente de Maiz—Maiz de la Gente." *México Desconocido* 28.329: 28–38.

Vasconcelos, José. 1920. *La Raza Cósmica, Misión de la Raza Iberoamericana: Notas de Viajes a la América de Sur.* Paris: Agencia Mundial de Librería.

Vélez-Ibáñez, Carlos G. 1996. *Border Visions: Mexican Cultures of the Southwest United States.* Tucson, AZ: University of Arizona Press.

Venne, Sharon Helen. 1998. *Our Elders Understand Our Rights: Evolving International Law Regarding Indigenous Peoples.* Penticton, BC, Canada: Theytus Books.

Vento, Arnoldo C. 1998. *Mestizo: The History, Culture and Politics of the Mexican and the Chicano—The Emerging Mestizo-Americans.* Lanham, MD: University Press of America.

Vigil, James Diego. 1998. *From Indians to Chicanos: The Dynamics of Mexican American Culture.* 2nd edition. Prospect Heights, IL: Waveland Press.

———. 2012. *From Indians to Chicanos: The Dynamics of Mexican American Culture.* 3rd edition. Prospect Heights, IL: Waveland Press.

Villagrá, Gaspar Pérez de. (1610) 1933. *History of New Mexico.* Trans. Gilberto Espinosa. Ed. F. W. Hodge. Los Angeles: Quivira Society. Reprint, Chicago: Rio Grande Press, 1962. Vitoria, Francisco de. (1500s) 1980. *Concerning the Indians Lately Discovered: The Indian Cause Before the Law of Nations: Colonial Period.* Ed. S. Lyman Tyler. Salt Lake City, UT: American West Center, University of Utah.

Waldman, Carl. 2000. *Atlas of the North American Indian.* New York: Checkmark Books.

Wallace, Henry, and William L. Brown. 1956. *Corn and Its Early Fathers.* East Lansing, MI: Michigan State University Press.

Warhus, Mark. 1997. *Another America: Native American Maps and the History of Our Land.* New York: St. Martin's Press.

Weatherford, J. McIver. 1988. *Indian Givers: How the Indians of the Americas Transformed the World.* New York: Crown.

———. 1991. *Native Roots: How the Indians Enriched America*. New York: Crown.

Whaley, Rick, and Walt Bresette. 1994. *Walleye Warriors*. Philadelphia: New Society.

Wheat, Carl. 1957. *Mapping the Transmississippi West, 1540–1861*. San Francisco: Institute of Historical Cartography.

Wilson, Clint C., and Félix Gutiérrez. 1995. *Race, Multiculturalism, and the Media: From Mass to Class Communication*. Thousand Oaks, CA: Sage.

Wilson, Waziyatawin Angela, and Michael Yellow Bird, eds. 2005. *For Indigenous Eyes Only: A Decolonization Handbook*. Santa Fe, NM: School of American Research Press.

Wright, Ronald. 2005. *Stolen Continents: 500 Years of Conquest and Resistance in the Americas*. New York: Mariner Books.

Yellow Bird, Michael. 2005. "Tribal Critical Thinking Centers." In Wilson and Yellow Bird 2005: 9–29.

Zamudio-Taylor, Victor. 2001. "Inventing Tradition, Negotiating Modernism: Chicano/a Art and the Pre-Columbian Past." In Fields and Zamudio-Taylor 2001: 342–57.

Zárate Salmerón, Jerónimo de. (1626–1627?) 1966. *Relaciones: An Account of Things Seen and Learned by Father Jerónimo de Zárate Salmerón from the Year 1538 to Year 1626*. Trans. Alicia Ronstadt Milich. Albuquerque, NM: Horn & Wallace.

Zumárraga, Juan de. (1544) 1928. *The Doctrina Breve in Fac-simile*. New York: United States Catholic Historical Society.

Zurita, Alonso de. (1500s) 1909. *Historia de la Nueva España*. Madrid: Librería General de V. Suárez.

Index

Illustrations and figures are indicated by page numbers in *italics*.

abductive reasoning theory, 125

Alurista (Alberto Urrea), 85, 86, 192–93, 214n12, 215n30

Alvarado Peralta, Felipe, xviii, xix, 59, 193, 199n7

Alvarez, Tanya, *Untitled*, xiv

Alzate map, 94, 190

amaranth, 65, 113, 217n1, 218n18

American Indians: American Indian studies, 178; American Indian–white binary, 112; dynamic of exclusion, 74; on food packages, 116–17; stereotypes, 35, 218n24; views of myth, history, and memory, 46–48

Americas: foods indigenous to, 219n30; Indigenous peoples' uniqueness, 210n9; inventing, 202n12; violence among peoples, 211n15. *See also* Turtle Island (the Americas)

Amoxtli San Ce Tojuan (documentary), xvii, 75, 132, 192, 200n17, 204n39

amoxtlis (codices): Aztec/Mexica migration narrative, 88–89; as communications technology, 29; with corn symbology, 101–2; described, 203n27; maíz narratives, xvii; migration codices, 40–41; mistranslations, 52; modern, 75; people of maíz concept, 51; pre-Columbian migrations from north, 95; surviving, 28–29; types of knowledge in, 28

Anasazi migration, 91

Anishinaabe, 44, 47, 208n37

anti-Mexican messages: framing issues, 82–83; reidentification and, 149

ants, incantation to, 59–60

Ants of Quetzalcoatl, xvii–xviii, 59, 60; narrative, xviii; play, 59; *Quetzalcoatl and the ants*, 163; Quetzalcoatl, the Ants, and the Gift of Maíz, 162–68

Argo corn starch, 116–17

Arizona: American Indian studies, 178; anti-immigrant hysteria, 177–78, 213n6, 213n10; ethnic studies controversy, 170, 173–77, 178

axis mundi: from Aztlan to maíz, 159–68; Bible as, 61; Chicana/Chicano shift, 139; Maíz tree as, 61, *158*; radical shift to Christian cross, 7, 159–60; schools imposed, 150

Aztatlan, 87–88, 95

Aztec Calendar: awareness of narrative, 217n9; described, 10, 202n16; prohibition on teaching, 174; revising view of, 29; technology based on maíz, 11

Aztec/Mexica culture: Black Legend of, 211n17; Chicano movement emphasis on, 137; as part of invented traditions, 51, 220n4; predominant in U.S. communities, 131

Aztec/Mexica migration narratives, 87–91; ancient roots, 50; basic storyline, 89–90; childhood stories, 200n21; as European fiction, 91; father's stories, xxv; Great Salt Lake, 48, 49, 94; map literature, 48–49; maps, 94; nationalization of, 100; "native informants," 215n22; New Mexico, 48; non-Indigenous writers, 90; taught as legend or fable, 92; Tenochtitlan map, 100; *Tira de la Peregrinación* (Boturini Codex), 88, *88*. *See also* Aztlanahuac maps

243

70–71, 73; insurgent narratives versus, 45–46; justification of violence, 67, 68; maíz narratives related, 73; Manifest Destiny, 45; Mexicans as unwanted, 82–84; as "official history," 65–66, 68, 72; oppositional views, 72; ownership of history, 212n24; rejection by Chicano Movement, 139. *See also* European chronicles; Western frameworks/scholarship

Maya: authenticity of stories, 203n23; contemporary, 201n2; as grandparents of other peoples, 97; "Maíz sagrado," 25–27; Nahua-Maya expressions, 187–88; oral traditions, 13; zero as germination, 63

Maya Calendar, 13

media: anti-Indigenous bias, 122; colonial-era, 20; Indigenous-style communications, 35–36; textual metaphors, 44–45

media framing, 73

memorialization, 12, 47, 202n21

Men concept, 176

Mendoza Codex (map), 99, 100

mercaditos, 115–16

Mesoamerica: agriculture as key, 69, 211n10; Aztec/Mexica culture as Mesoamerican culture, 51, 52; concept of, 4; continuity, 110, 132; historical unity, 60; Indigenous peoples as living presence, 39; linked societies, 206n22; in North America, 94–96; periodization, 10; rulers' legitimation, 12; urbanization, 127, 221n8

mestizaje, 217n10; children of La Llorona, 183–86

mestizos: cosmic race concept, 43, 207n34; as de-Indigenized Indigenous peoples, 209n55; genetic component, 202n10; Indigenized mestizaje notions, 43; maíz culture and narratives, 50

metate, 110, 119, 217n4; Women using a metate (Borgia Codex), *108*

Mexican American identity, 42, 121

Mexican Americans: Aztlan as theme, 83; as Indigenous, 44; tamaladas, 142; university-trained scholars, 207n30

mexicanidad, la, 51

Mexican Revolution of 1910, 30; Adelita imagery, 121; communal lands, 171; mural art, 135; primary process and principio, 160

Mexicans: caloric intake from maíz, 141; as immigrants, 35; as indigenous to the

continent, 44; mainstream U.S. view, 112–13; nationalized Aztec/Mexica culture, 75; not of Aztec/Mexica heritage, 135, 137; stereotypes, origins of, 34; use of term, 213n5; as wetbacks, 213n5

Mexicans and Central Americans in U.S.: as Indigenous peoples, 53; viewed in master narrative, 15

Mexicans in the U.S., maíz civilization and, 111

Mexican-U.S. war, 10, 207n31

Mexican War of Independence, 30, 100, 101; primary process and principio, 160; turn to pre-Columbian imagery, 135–36, 148

Mexico: Africans in, 113, 207n33, 211n9; associations with, 113; iconic symbols, 18; images that connote Mexicanness, 120; Indigeneity rejected, 148–49; Indigenous images and icons, 111; Mesoamerica as root, 53; Mexicans as Indigenous peoples, 30; *México profundo*, 40, 118, 127; post-Revolutionary nationalism, 207n35; skin color issues, 122, 213n4; student movement, 171; tortillas associated with, 110. *See also* Mexican Revolution of 1910; Mexican War of Independence

Mictlan (place of the dead), 134

Miera y Pacheco map, 94, 191

migration narratives: emergence from Seven Caves, 88, 89, 90–91; migration of maíz, 110

Movimiento Nativo Americano, 85–86

mural art, 134–35; Chicana/Chicano movement, 137–40; *We are Not a Minority*, 138

myth: foundational knowledge contained, 48; ritual and, 47–48; story related, 47

Nahua cultures: oral traditions, 12; types of knowledge, 12

Nahua-Maya expressions, 187–88

Nahuatl: language, 98, 199n1; migrations, 96; origins of word, 91; Our Father prayer, 217n5

naming, ceremony of, 9

narrative exclusion, 74

narratives: common stories and common origins, 97; concept challenged, 15; concerned with morality and the future, 47; conflicting, 16–17; counternarratives, 15, 60; hidden narratives, 96–98; insurgent,

45–46, 52; as metaphoric, 73; satanic,
32; stories as resistance, 45, 60; stories as
science, 47; three sets of, 13–15
nations/nation states, preconquest, 69
Nde/Apache (Athabascan) roots, 207n29
New Mexico, 121, 223n17
New Spain, name imposed, 101
non-Western cultures: academic views of, 61;
aversion to researchers, xxiii
North American Free Trade Agreement
(NAFTA), 170, 171–72, 200n16
nourishment and sustenance, xxv–xxvi. *See
also* diet and food
Nuremberg map, 99

Ohoyo Osh Chisba (Unknown Woman),
180–81
Olmecs, 63, 96, 210n5, 211n9
Olmos, Andrés de, 32, 133–34
Oneida people, 63–64
oppositional narratives, syncretism, 38
oral traditions: Christian syncretism, 133;
collective memory, 47, 48, 221n6; common origins idea, 98; consistency
and reliability, 134; during colonial
repression, 206n21; Indigenous forms of
writing destroyed, 47; maíz narratives,
xxiv, 65; Maya, 13; Nahua, 12–13;
origins of maíz, xxiv; public square, 37;
Quetzalcoatl/Kukulkan, xix; types of
knowledge, 20; Western versus Indigenous views, 202n21; Western view of, 63,
206n24; written records vis-à-vis, 13, 66,
221n6
Oronce Fine map, 92
Otomi migration, 96
Otra Conquista, la (the Other Conquest):
Indigenous sacred songs, 149; as reframing
project, 205n11; as spiritual conquest, 6,
159–60; syncretism, 38–39

Pacha Mama, 161
Palenque, 29
Panche Be, 170, 175–77
Pastorela, 152
PBS series on Latinos, 212n28
Peace and Dignity Journeys, 98, 172
people of maíz concept, 51, 103, 221n9
"El Plan Espiritual de Aztlan," 85, 102–3,
214n12

poetry, 12; Aztlan, 83; in xochitl, in cuicatl,
152; metaphoric language, 20–21
Popol Vuh: ants and hero twins, 59; bundles,
12; creation stories, 3; described, 3;
humans made from maíz, xvii; migration story, 90; mural form, 13; Tollan/
Teotihuacan origins, 41; transcripts
found, 201n1
postcolonial studies, 69
postmodern scholarship, 69, 207n32
primary process, 30, 51–52, 160–61
primary sources, 21, 64
principio, 160–61; after Mexican War of Independence, 136; return to authenticity, 30
Prophecy of the Unity of the Eagle and
Condor, 98, 172
pyramids: as cultural root paradigm, 111; in
Chicana/Chicano art, 135, 138, 140

Quetzalcoatl: attributes, 199n3, 199n11; as
bearded white man, 19; birthplace, xviii; as
bringer of maíz, 147; Christian attributes,
19; in form of eagle, xix; hidden narrative
of, 96–97; as Saint Thomas, 146, 203n30;
syncretism, 39; Tlayölli-Quetzalcoatl
narrative, 156–57; Zapata association, xix.
See also Ants of Quetzalcoatl
Quetzalcoatl, the Ants, and the Gift of Maíz,
162–68
Quetzalcoatl and the ants, *163*
quinceañera, 51, 144

rain, songs to, 149–50, 151
Ramirez, Grecia, *In Lak-ech, 169*
Ramírez, Martha, 197–98
Raza studies, 10, 74
Raza Unida Party, 85
reducciones, 7, 18–19, 203n29
reframing: as centering, 46, 209n46; de-
Indigenization and, 160; master narrative
on equal footing, 212n26; in modern context, 46; reactive by Chicano Movement,
139; Spanish friars as masters of, 46; use of
higher-level frames, 45
Requerimientos, 71–72, 209n43
research protocols, xxiii, 11–15; collaborative
approach, 8; collective copyright, 200n17;
European sources, 11–12; exploitation
issues, xxiii; overview, 22; ownership of
knowledge, xxiii

imagery of maíz, 120; Quetzalcoatl
images, xix; significance, xx
Toltecs, 9, 90, 96, 215n23
Tonantzin (Earth Mother), 38. *See also*
Virgen de Guadalupe/Tonantzin
tortilla: art, 217n12; as civilizational marker,
113–15, 161; as cultural identity, 114;
circular shape, 123; as communion,
109; flour, 217n8; as memory/roots, 114;
memory and place in, 115–16; in Mexican
diet, 110; Mexico associated with, 110;
place and, 114; as racialized identifier,
113; shapes and uses, 219n27; Spanish
culture and, 126; as symbol and metaphor,
110–13; in U.S. culture wars, 111–12;
where consumed (U.S.), 115–16
Tortilla Mapping Project, 116–23, 218n22;
background, 116; circular shape and maíz
imagery, 116–20; Indigenous authenticity,
122–23; Mexican food as Indian food, 123;
Spanish señoritas, 120–21; "who we are,"
121–22
tortilla packaging: effect on consumers,
218n26; Esperanza Tortillas, *125*;
imagery, 117, 118–20; images analyzed,
219nn34–35; Indigenous authenticity,
124–26; Indigenous imagery, 117; locating
Mexicans in the past, 219n31; memory
and place, 115–16; primary images,
124; story of corn on, 219n29; visual-
communication view, 123–27
tradición, 145, 146
Treaty of Guadalupe Hidalgo, *80*, 215n27
Tucson Unified School District, 170, 173–75
Tula, 92–93, 215n23
Turtle Island (the Americas), 4, 210n4
Tzicatl, 164–68

UN Declaration on the Rights of Indigenous
Peoples, 175
United Farm Workers (UFW), 85, 140,
152–53, 214n13
United States: anti-immigrant fervor, 112;
culture wars, 111–12; hypernational-
ism, 112
"Unknown Woman," 180–81

Valdez, Luis, 40, 153
Villegas, Julieta, xxii, xxvi, 154, 198
Virgen de Guadalupe/Tonantzin, 38–39; as
cultural root paradigm, 111; Conchero
danza tradition, 146; *Corn Mother* (Lopez),
54; hidden traditions, 146; role of Indigenous people, 205–6n19
visual-communication theories, 37
Vitoria, Francisco de, 32, 33

Western frameworks/scholarship: abuses,
202n20; compartmentalization and atomization of knowledge, 69; continuity issue,
217n7; larger sociopolitical context and,
214n11; on maps, 49–50; unlearning, xxiii;
Western stories versus Indigenous stories,
203n31. *See also* master narrative of U.S./
Western history
white-nonwhite binary, 111–12
women: attempts to eradicate Indigenous and
maíz cultures, 223n14; centrality of food
and kitchen, 42; danza tradition, 145; maíz
culture, 119; maíz technology, 221n10;
stereotypes, 119; tamaladas, 142–43;
on tortilla wrappers, 119–20; Zapatista
movement, 171
written records: books, 204n36, 240n3;
Christianized Indigenous writers, 29, 33–34;
Christian syncretism, 133; differences as
inferiority/superiority, 55; first Mesoamerican, 29; friars' domination of, 28; hidden
Indigenous narratives, 150–51; Mesoamerican misinterpreted, 41; modern bias, 101;
multilayered Aztec/Mexica, 206n25; oral
tradition vis-à-vis, 13, 66, 221n6; pictorial
as more universal, 204n37; *quipu*, 216n35;
Spanish friars' reliance on, 132; traditions,
131; types of writers, 33; use of European, 21

Xilonen green corn ceremony, 144, 147

Zamora, Pat: *Ce Topiltzin*, 2
Zapata, Emiliano, xix, 85, 214n13
Zapatista revolt (1994), 170, 171
zero, concept of, 4, 63
Zumárraga, Juan de, 32, 64

About the Author

Roberto Rodríguez is an assistant professor in the Department of Mexican American Studies at the University of Arizona. He received his PhD in mass communications from the University of Wisconsin, Madison, in 2008. He has published articles in the peer-reviewed journals the *International Journal of Critical Indigenous Studies*, the *Nakum Journal of the Indigenous Cultures Institute*, the *Revista Canaria de Estudios Ingleses*, the *Journal of Curriculum and Pedagogy*, and the *Urban Review*. He is a board member of the Alianza Indígena sin Fronteras and of Tucson's Mexican American Studies Community Advisory Board. He is the author of *Justice: A Question of Race* (Bilingual Review Press, 1997). Rodríguez was a senior writer for *Black Issues in Higher Education* from 1990 to 2000. He was a nationally syndicated columnist with Chronicle Features and Universal Press Syndicate from 1994 to 2006. In 2013, he received the Ella Baker and Septima Clark Human Rights Award from the American Educational Research Association for his work in defense of ethnic studies.